THE 1999-2000 HOCKEY ANNUAL

THE 1999-2000 HOCKEY ANNUAL

MURRAY TOWNSEND

Warwick Publishing
Toronto Los Angeles
www.warwickgp.com

Published by Warwick Publishing Inc.
162 John Street, Toronto, Ontario M5V 2E5

ISBN: 1-894020-61-8

Front cover photograph: Dan Hamilton, Vantage Point Studios

Printed in Canada.

Contents

Introduction

It's hard to say what made the biggest news last season. Was it Wayne Gretzky's retirement, or the disputed goal to win the Stanley Cup?

It's always about the good and the bad. For example, in the bad category would be my prediction last year that the Toronto Maple Leafs would finish 25th overall and out of the playoffs. I spent the season putting curses on them and cheering for their opponents, all in the interest of trying to make me look less stupid.

I wasn't alone in that prediction and I can tell you that I was as convinced of the dismal prospects of that team as I've been of anything. I did pick the Dallas Stars to go to the Stanley Cup finals, and "possibly win it" so I'm not a complete idiot, thank you very much.

This year there will be no Wayne Gretzky and no disputed in-the-crease goal to win the Stanley Cup. At least not through video replay, which has abolished the procedure for that circumstance. We should see more goals though, with many teams suggesting they're going to the more entertaining offensive style to win games. Defense wins games, but don't tell that to the Toronto Maple Leafs.

Another new wrinkle this year is 4-on-4 overtime, with teams each getting one point at the end of regulation, and fighting it out for an extra point if they win in overtime. This is going to cause trouble, wait and see, although it will be exciting. Shootouts, apparently, were too much

of an abomination. Wait until you see teams laying back in the third period in order to get their one point and an equal chance at two, or throwing four forwards out for overtime. The last ten minutes of a tied hockey game should re-write the definition of boring.

Once again, a special thank you to my father for all his help and support, which could never ever be underestimated or under appreciated. Thanks to my sister, Shirley, as well, for her support this year, and always. The same for lady friend, Janis, and her kids, Laura and Brad.

Thanks to my kids, Holly and Heather, for letting me drive them wherever they want to go, and for getting off the phone on occasion when I needed it for work.

And thanks to the Warwick Publishing staff.

The format of the book has changed slightly, but I'm always looking for improvements. Any comments and suggestions can be emailed to me at mtownsend@mail.interhop.net. And that email address is good for the whole year should you need any help with your hockey pool. I do a weekly pool column for *The Hockey News* which can be found at www.thn.com.

For your convenience I've included the conference standings below. This is exactly how they'll finish in each conference. Pay no attention to last year's Toronto Maple Leafs prediction.

EASTERN CONFERENCE

Atlanta Thrashers

Get used to this headline: Thrashers Get Thrashed.

It's not particularly imaginative, but it's still likely to be very common.

General Manager Don Waddell announced that the the Thrashers are going to play an up-tempo offensive style. This is great news for the NHL, which is suffering from a lack of offense. Mostly, though, it's great news for Thrasher opponents.

It's not how successful expansion teams win. They use a defensive style, much like Nashville did last season.

If you're going to put your firecrackers up against another team's cannons, your best hope is to try and throw water on their fuses. Trying to match their firepower is suicidal.
Waddell says he wants to win games 5-4 instead of 2-1. He's not going to do much of either.

The Thrashers have just one more leak in their arsenal. They don't have any gun powder. The top NHL goal scorer on their roster is Nelson Emerson, who pumped in a grand total of 13. Andrew Brunette had 11 for Nashville, followed closely by well known sniper Terry Yake, who had all of nine. We can't rule out Jody Hull's offensive prowess, either. You don't score three whole goals without being a wizard with a hockey stick.

We have to assume Waddell is serious about the offensive game, so the Thrashers have a chance to be the most futile of expansion teams. Expansion team records in their inaugural season are listed below.

First Season Expansion Records:

	Year	W	L	T	Pts	%
Florida	1993-94	33	34	17	83	.494
Anaheim	1993-94	33	46	5	71	.423
Atlanta (Cgy)	1972-73	25	38	15	65	.417
Buffalo	1970-71	24	39	15	63	.404
Nashville	1998-99	28	47	7	63	.384
Vancouver	1970-71	24	46	8	56	.359
Tampa Bay (NJ)	1992-93	23	54	7	53	.315
Kansas City	1974-75	15	54	11	41	.256
San Jose	1991-92	17	58	5	39	.244
NY Islanders	1972-73	12	60	6	30	.192
Ottawa	1992-93	10	70	4	24	.143
Washington						

STUFF

Damian Rhodes was the first ever Atlanta Thrasher when he was obtained from Ottawa for future considerations.

TEAM PREVIEW

GOAL: Waddell says he wants to build his team around a goaltender. Nothing wrong with having a good goalie, but the notion that it's the key ingredient for an expansion team is way off the mark.

It's not a rookie mistake, it's just a common one. There are only a few goalies in the league capable of determining his team's success night in and night out. In fact, there's only two — Dominik Hasek in Buffalo and Curtis Joseph in Toronto.

Once a goalie makes it to the NHL, he can stop the puck. He can make spectacular saves and he can let in easy goals on occasion. Some nights he will look like a magician and other nights like whatever the opposite of magician is. That's all goalies, we're talking about.

Most goalies are the product of their team. That's not to say a team can't have two goalies, with one superior to the other. It's more likely than not. But, it's rare for one goalie to have considerably better stats than another on the same team.

If you look at teams which have had two goalies play a lot of time, they have remarkably similar stats.

Let's go through the goalie tandems from last year, on teams where two goalies played at least 20 games. On eight teams, they didn't have two goalies play that number of games. That leaves 19 teams. Ten of them had GAA's from two goalies that were amazingly close. All of them in the list below, except one, were within 0.10 of the other goalie on their team.

That's no coincidence because it's the same thing every year. There are some that stand way above their other goalie, but for the most part they're close and there can be no other reason than because it's a team stat.

Dallas	Belfour	1.99
	Turek	2.08
San Jose	Shields	2.22
	Vernon	2.27
St. Louis	McLennan	2.38
	Fuhr	2.44
Washington	Tabaracci	2.51
	Kolzig	2.58
Edmonton	Shtalenkov	2.67
	Essensa	2.75
Florida	Burke	2.66
	McLean	2.74
NY Rangers	Richter	2.63
	Cloutier	2.68
Calgary	Braithwaite	2.45
	Wregget	2.53
Chicago	Thibault	2.71
	Fitzpatrick	2.74
Nashville	Vokoun	2.95
	Dunham	3.08

Interestingly, one of the goalie tandems who were not close to each other was in Ottawa, where Ron Tugnutt was considerably better than Damian Rhodes, at 1.70 to 2.44.

Rhodes, of course, is the goalie the Thrashers plan to build around.

Not taking anything away from the talent of Rhodes, but he's not an impact goalie and isn't going to make any difference whether the Thrashers win or not.

The same is true of probable backup Norm Maracle, and third in line, Corey Schwab.

DEFENSE: The Thrashers did okay in this area in the expansion draft and can actually ice a defense of players who could be fifth or sixth defensemen in a lot of NHL cities. That doesn't sound so great, but it's actually pretty good.

Darryl Shannon, Gord Murphy, and Chris Tamer are experienced NHL defensemen. Brett Clark, Kevin Dean, Maxim Galanov, David Harlock and Yannick Tremblay have some NHL experience.

No NHL team would place them higher than fifth on any of their depth charts, so that's what the Thrashers have to work with in training camp. Some of these guys have to be one through four on this team.

There is no offensive defensemen of note in the bunch, which will make it tough when the power play is on the ice. And it's also strange for a team that professes to want to play an offensive style.

Not to worry, somebody will emerge, because somebody has to.

There is also very little toughness in this group. Tamer would probably be the leader in that regard, but forget about Shannon, Murphy, Dean, Galanov or Clark. In fact, the one thing most of them have in common is a incredibly low penalty totals for defensemen.

	Games	PIM
Clark	61	16
Dean	62	22
Galanaov	51	14
Murphy	51	16
Shannon	71	28
Tremblay	35	16

Petr Buzek, drafted from Dallas, should make the team and may be on the power play.

For an expansion team it's not a bad group of defensemen. The problem is, that still means they're the worst in the league.

FORWARD: It's a known fact that on every hockey team, somebody has to score the goals. What isn't known is who is going to score them on this team.

An up tempo offensive style? Puhleeeze.

Somebody among their group has to score 20 goals, because every team has a 20-goal scorer. Let's put some odds up on who it might be.

Nelson Emerson	10-1
Andrew Brunette	15-1
Patrik Stefan	25-1
Johan Garpenlov	40-1
Tomi Kallio	50-1
Terry Yake	80-1
Randy Robitaille	100-1
Dean Sylvester	200-1
Jody Hull	5,000,000,000-1

Okay, so forget about the 20-goal scorer, let's try to put together a number one line:

LW	C	RW
Brunette	Stefan	Emerson

We're not trying to scare anybody, but that's about it. Top draft pick, Stefan, may be a future star, but he could only manage nine goals last year in the IHL, which isn't known for its defense.

There might be children reading this, so forget about trying to put together a second or third line.

There are some decent character players, however, starting with Kelly Buchberger, Jody Hull and Terry Yake. There's a tough guy in Matt Johnson; an over-the hill floater in Garpenlov; some non-scorers, such as Mike Stapleton and Ed Ward; an underachiever in Jason Botterill; a Russian in Alexei Yegorov, minor league scorers in Dean Sylvester, Randy Robitaille, Herb Vasilyevs and Sylvain Cloutier; a couple Swedes in Andreas Karlsson and Par Svartvadet, and one wild card.

The wild card is Tomi Kallio, who for some reason is expected to make an impact. Not very likely.

Robitaille had 102 points last year for Providence, the Boston affiliate, but the Bruins weren't overly concerned about losing him,

Nothing here that you wouldn't find on a minor league affiliate of a decent NHL team.

To put it into proper perspective, this is pathetic. Nashville looked better at the start of last year, and they couldn't score much, so this group is in trouble.

SPECIAL TEAMS: They don't have any scorers, and they don't have any offensive defensemen. That pretty much spells doom for a power play.

Penalty killing could be decent, though. That's one specific area the team seemed to put some thought into when acquiring their players.

COACHING AND MANAGEMENT: Waddell is a rookie GM and is going to make rookie mistakes. One of them, however, doesn't appear to be not working hard enough.

And while his philosophies are suspect, with regard to goalies, offense and speed, who's to say he couldn't prove to be right? We'll see.

He hasn't pulled off much in the way of pre-season dazzling, like Nashville did last year, but he's still learning the ropes.

He took a long time to hire a coach, however, before finally settling on Curt Fraser. Fraser has no NHL coaching experience, but has had a successful minor league coaching career, which is fitting considering this is a minor league team.

Fraser is a proponent of the wide-open offensive system, but may go into shock on the first day of training camp if he thinks that approach is going to work here.

DRAFT

Player	Pos	Rnd	Sel.	Cntry	Team	Lge	Gms	G	A	P	PIM
Patrick Stefam	C	1	1	Cze	Long Beach	IHL	33	11	24	35	26
Luke Sellars	D	2	30	Can	Ottawa	OHL	56	4	19	23	87
Zdenek Blatny	F	3	68	Cze	Seattle	WHL	44	18	15	33	25
David Kaczowka	LW	4	98	Can	Seattle	WHL	60	3	2	5	247
Rob Zepp	G	4	99	Can	Plymouth	OHL	2.74	897			
Derek MacKenzie	C	5	128	Can	Sudbury	OHL	68	22	65	87	74
Yuri Dopryshkin	W	6	159	Rus	Sovatev	Rus	37	6	4	10	30
Stephan Baby	RW	7	188	USA	Green Bay	USHL					
Garnet Exelby	D	8	217	Can	Saskatoon	WHL	61	5	3	8	91
Tommy Santala	F	9	245	Fin	Jokerit	Fin	30	0	0	0	14
Ray Delauro	D	9	246	USA	St.Lawrence	ECAC	34	17	50	67	18

Patrick Stefan has been playing in the IHL the last two years, without much scoring distinction. Can anyone say Radek Bonk?

In any event, Stefan was considered the most talented player in the draft, but there were some worries about his health after suffering post-concussion syndrome. He was cleared to play, but his agent apparently wasn't releasing his medical documents to just anyone.

Stefan will step right into the Thrashers line-up, and if gets any wingers to set up, he might just do that.

PROGNOSIS: The Thrashers don't have what it takes to even be a good expansion team. They're going to get thrashed, night after night. And it could be very, very ugly.

Boston Bruins

It was the same old story in Boston last year. Actually, remarkably, it was exactly the same. They had a 39-30-13 record last season, which was exactly the same at it was the year before.

It's not such a small deal that the Bruins had exactly the same number of points as the year before. The season before, they were the NHL's most improved team, and whichever team earns that distinction traditionally go for a fall the next year. The second and third most improved, Los Angeles and Washington, both suffered that demise.

So, staying the same was actually quite good.

One other thing remains the same there, as well. Try as they may, they have the absolute worst luck with Europeans. Maybe it's some kind of jinx — maybe The Don Cherry Jinx.

In any event, they've almost all been either absolute disasters or disappointments. You can add Dmitri Khristich to that list, after disappearing for the latter part of last season and the playoffs.

In 1991, the Bruins drafted Mariusz Czercawski and Josef Stumpel. Czercawski was virtually useless, and is currently making his way from team to team around the NHL. Stumpel had one very good season, which may actually qualify him as the best European in team history.

In 1992, Dmitri Kvartalnov was their first round pick at the 16th spot. He played two seasons, and then they couldn't get rid of him fast enough. Sergei Zholtok was a disappointment in the second round and has since moved around the league, actually become a useful defensive player with Montreal.

In 1994, Evgeny Ryabchikov was their first round pick. The Russian goaltender had a tough time even playing for their minor league affiliate.

In the 1997 draft, they picked up Sergei Samsonov with the eighth overall pick. He won the the Calder Trophy as rookie of the year, but tailed off drastically last season. First round draft picks have been terrible as well. We could go back further, but look at the the their first round picks, since 1988.

1988 — Robert Cimetta
1989 — Shayne Stevenson
1990 — Bryan Smolinski
1991 — Glen Murray
1992 — Dmitri Kvartalnov
1993 — Kevyn Adams
1994 — Evegeni Ryabchikov
1995 — Kyle McLaren, Sean Brown
1996 — Johnathan Aitken
1997 — Joe Thornton, Sergei Samsonov

Kyle McLaren has turned out well, and Thornton and Samsonov look as if they will do okay, but most of the other picks were either dogs, or didn't show anything until they had left Boston.

Before them, more horrific first round failures or injuries. In fact, they've gone 20 years without drafting a star first rounder. The last one was in 1979, in the eighth spot, when they picked up a kid by the name of Raymond Bourque.

STUFF: The next time Bourque makes the play-offs it will be his 20th year in the post-season and tie him with Larry Robinson and Gordie Howe for the all-time record.

Ray Bourque became the all-time Bruins leader in games played, when he passed Johnny Bucyk last season. Bourque has 1,453; Bucyk had 1,436.

The Bruins have played the Stanley Cup finalist or winner in each of the last four times they've been in the playoffs: 1999 — Buffalo; 1997 — Washington; 1996 — Florida; 1995 — New Jersey.

Joe Thornton won the Eddie Shore Gallery Gods Award, for the Bruins player who shows the best effort and hustle.

Jay Henderson, who got into four games with the Bruins, was the very last pick in the 1997 draft.

TEAM PREVIEW

GOAL: Byron Dafoe's 10 shutouts were the most by a Bruins goalie since Frank Brimsek, way back in 1938-39. Naturally, shutouts are a product of the style of game being played at a particular time, but Dafoe still led the league, and still earned himself a second-team all-star berth. His save percentage of .926 was second best behind Dominik Hasek, and his goals against average of 1.99 was third, behind Hasek and Ron Tugnutt.

It's easy to get cheap shutouts if your team doesn't give up any shots. So, let's look a little closer to see if that was the case with Dafoe.

Shutouts when outshot: 6
Shutouts on the road: 5
Shutouts vs Over. 500 teams: 5
Shutouts vs Top 10 scoring teams: 5
Shutouts with fewer than 20 shots against: 1

Doesn't look like there's too many cheap shutouts at all. Even more impressive is that he earned shutouts on the road in difficult places, including Colorado, Ottawa, and Pittsburgh.

The Bruins had to do some manouvering to ensure that backup Robbie Tallas returned, which meant giving up Randy Robitaille to Atlanta so they wouldn't pick him in the expansion draft. Good move by the Bruins. Why mess up a good thing.

GOALTENDER	GPI	MINS	AVG	W	L	T	EN	SO	GA	SA	SV %
BYRON DAFOE	68	4,001	1.99	32	23	11	3	10	133	1,800	.926
ROBBIE TALLAS	17	987	2.61	7	7	2	2	1	43	421	.898
BOS TOTALS	82	5,001	2.17	39	30	13	5	11	181	2,226	.919

DEFENSE: Someday Ray Bourque is going to have to retire. But, he's going to have to slow down first. He tied for second in points from defensemen last season, only five behind Al MacInnis, and surprise surprise, earned another all-star berth, this one on the second-team.

Bourque does well on the all-time lists, of course, and since we don't have all day to go into them all, let's look at the all-time offensive leaders among defensemen. With Paul Coffey's career finished, or close to being finished, Bourque could lead all these categories some time this year.

Most Goals Scored by a Defenseman:
Ray Bourque   385
Paul Coffey   385

Most Assists by a Defenseman:
Paul Coffey   1,102
Ray Bourque   1,083

Most Points by a Defenseman:
Paul Coffey   1,487
Ray Bourque   1,468

The Bruins moved out some of their older defensemen to make room for some youth, and so they can attend the Ray Bourque hockey school.

Gone are Dave Ellett and Grant Ledyard. That leaves Hal Gill, Don Sweeney, Kyle McLaren and Darren Van Impe as returning regulars. Mattias Timander has been up and down, but has a good chance of sticking this year.

There are four rookie hopefuls, with one of them virtually guaranteed a spot. Nick Boynton, the pride of Nobleton, Ontario, had an out-standing junior career with the Ottawa 67's, and

this past season earned the MVP trophy in the Memorial Cup. He went back into the draft, after failing to come to terms with Washington, and then when his signing rates were transferred to Chicago. He's a rare breed who brings the whole package with him into the NHL and should step right into the Bruins defense as a regular.

Jonathan Girard, an offensive defenseman from the Quebec League, who made the Bruins last year before being sent back, also has a good shot at sticking this year if there's room. Brandon Smith had an outstanding year at Providence in the AHL, and Boston College grad Bobby Allen could also get a long look.

The Bruins are in great shape at this position, with the ideal scenario of mixing seasoned veter-ans with young up-and-comers.

And of course, they've got Bourque.

FORWARD: The emergence of Joe Thornton means the Bruins can put together two good scoring lines.

Last year, Jason Allison centred Sergei Samsonov and Dmitri Khristich, while Thornton was between Steve Heinze and Anson Carter.

By the playoffs it was difficult to determine which exactly was the top line. Khristich and Allison both were singled out for not living up to expectations in the playoffs. Khristich virtually disappeared in the latter part of the season and received most of Sinden's wrath.

Khristich may be traded, and the Bruins would dearly love to find a taker, but they won't give him away, especially since they don't have somebody to replace him.

Let's look at the top Boston scorers in the first half and second half of the season.

First Half

	GP	G	A	P
Khristich	40	18	26	44
Allison	41	9	27	36
Samsonov	41	15	19	34
Bourque	40	4	22	26
Heinze	40	11	10	21

Second Half

	GP	G	A	P
Allison	41	14	26	40
Bourque	41	6	25	31
Carter	31	18	9	27
Kristich	39	11	16	27
Thornton	40	9	16	25
Heinze	33	11	8	19
Samsonov	38	10	7	17

The numbers show the fall in production from Khristich and Samsonov, the latter dropping his point total a whopping 50 percent. It also shows the rise in prominence of Thornton and Carter.

The Bruins had a great checking line with P.J. Axelsson, Tim Taylor and Rob Dimaio. They were able to contribute offensively, as well, which made them even better. But, Taylor was lost to free agency, and signed with the Rangers, like everybody else. That's a hole they'll need to fill.

Shawn Bates could get full-time duty in that role, and Andre Savage could be ready to move up.

Ken Belanger has taken over the full-time enforcer role, with Ken Baumgartner bought out, so vying for fourth line duty on the wings will be Landon Wilson and Cameron Mann, as well as Eric Niculas. The time has come for Wilson and Mann to show they belong. Both are big power forward types who would give the Bruins another dimension on their wings.

SPECIAL TEAMS: The Bruins led the league in penalty killing, allowing a paltry 33 goals. With Tim Taylor gone, it will be interesting to see if they can still be as good. He and Axelsson were the key penalty-killing forwards.

Interesting correlation between scoring short-handed goals and penalty killing effectiveness. The Bruins were first in penalty killing percentage and dead last in shorthanded goals scored, with just three. Obviously, their effectiveness was the result of not worrying about taking offensive chances, and obviously it worked.

Let's look at the top net power play goals allowed. That's goals allowed less shorthanded goals scored. For example, Boston allowed 33 power play goals and scored three themselves, so their net power play goals allowed were 30.

	PP Goals Allowed	SH Goals Scored	Net
Boston	33	3	30
Detroit	45	14	31
Los Angeles	47	12	35
Montreal	44	8	36

Detroit was second in shorthanded goals scored and Los Angeles was tied for third, so Boston's defense-only approach to penalty killing isn't the only effective way, but it was still the best.

Power Play	G	ATT	PCT
Overall	65	368	17.7% (8th NHL)
Home	31	181	17.1% (11th NHL)
Road	34	187	18.2% (7th NHL)

9 SHORT HANDED GOALS ALLOWED (T-15th NHL)

Penalty Killing	G	TSH	PCT
Overall	33	305	89.2% (1st NHL)
Home	11	145	92.4% (1st NHL)
Road	22	160	86.3% (T-5th NHL)

3 SHORT HANDED GOALS SCORED (27th NHL)

BRUINS SPECIAL TEAMS SCORING

Power play	G	A	PTS
BOURQUE	8	31	39
ALLISON	5	25	30
KHRISTICH	13	7	20
SAMSONOV	6	10	16
THORNTON	7	8	15
HEINZE	9	5	14
VAN IMPE	4	8	12
MCLAREN	3	8	11
CARTER	6	3	9
LEDYARD	1	4	5
ELLETT	0	3	3
FERRARO	1	1	2
DIMAIO	1	1	2
TIMANDER	0	2	2
TAYLOR	0	2	2
SWEENEY	0	2	2
ROBITAILLE	0	2	2
MANN	1	0	1
LAAKSONEN	0	1	1
AXELSSON	0	1	1

Short handed	G	A	PTS
TAYLOR	1	0	1
KHRISTICH	1	0	1
ALLISON	1	0	1
SWEENEY	0	1	1
DIMAIO	0	1	1
BOURQUE	0	1	1
AXELSSON	0	1	1

COACHING AND MANAGEMENT: Harry Sinden is finally going to hand over all the GM duties to Mike O'Connell. Oh, wait. We've been saying that for the last four years, so forget it.

In the meantime, the Bruin tandem appear on the same wave length and they make some outstanding trades.

Pat Burns doesn't seem to get along nearly as well with O'Connell. O'Connell blamed Samsonov's drop in production to a drop in ice-time. While it was actually true, Burns blew up at O'Connell speaking out about it in the press.

Burns has a reputation for preferring veterans, but he also gives ice-time to those who deserve it.

In any event, there's some grumbling starting about Burns in Boston, and this will be his third season there, which is just about the max these days in the NHL.

DRAFT: (see chart) The Bruins went with two re-entries into the draft with their first two picks. Boynton was originally drafted ninth overall by Washington in 1997, and Zultek was the 15th overall selection for Los Angeles in 1997.

Both have used up their junior eligibility and will move right to the pros. Boynton should move right onto the Bruins defense and Zultek will likely go to the farm team.

It's almost like the days of drafting 20-year-olds, where you were drafting for talent, as opposed to potential. Plus, you can get these players higher, because potential always looks better than the finished product. Good move by the Bruins.

PROGNOSIS: No reason to think the Bruins won't be in the playoffs again, but there's also little reason to think they'll advance too far once

DRAFT

Player	Pos	Rnd	Sel.	Cntry	Team	Lge	Gms	G	A	P	PIM
Nick Boynton	C	1	21	Can	Ottawa	OHL	51	11	48	59	83
Matt Zultek	LW	2	56	Can	Ottawa	OHL	56	33	33	66	71
Kyle Wanvig	RW	3	89	Can	Kootenay	WHL	71	12	20	32	119
Jaakko Harikkala	D	4	118	Fin	Lukko	Fin	35	0	0	0	10
Seamus Kotyk	G	5	147	Can	Ottawa	OHL	2.39	.907			
Donald Choukalo	G	6	179	Can	Regina	WHL	3.71	.879			
Greg Barber	RW	7	207	Can	Victoria	BCJHL					
John Cronin	D	8	236	USA	Noble	US-HS	30	8	26	34	24
Mikko Eloranta	W	9	247	Fin	Jokerrit						
Georgijs Pujacs	D	9	264	Lat	Riga						

they get there. But, then again, as we know, anything can happen in the playoffs.

They key may be Thornton finally turning into an impact player. He showed definite signs of it toward the end of last year and in the playoffs.

Their goaltending and defense should be among the best in the league, and the forward lines need to plug a few holes. Not too much to worry about. But, not too much to get overly excited about, either.

STAT SECTION

PLAYER	GP	G	A	PTS	+/-	PIM	PP	SH	GW	GT	S	PCTG
JASON ALLISON	82	23	53	76	5	68	5	1	3	0	158	14.6
DMITRI KHRISTICH	79	29	42	71	11	48	13	1	6	1	144	20.1
RAY BOURQUE	81	10	47	57	7-	34	8	0	3	0	262	3.8
SERGEI SAMSONOV	79	25	26	51	6-	18	6	0	8	1	160	15.6
JOE THORNTON	81	16	25	41	3	69	7	0	1	0	128	12.5
ANSON CARTER	55	24	16	40	7	22	6	0	6	0	123	19.5
STEVE HEINZE	73	22	18	40	7	30	9	0	3	0	146	15.1
KYLE MCLAREN	52	6	18	24	1	48	3	0	0	0	97	6.2
ROB DIMAIO	71	7	14	21	14-	95	1	0	0	0	121	5.8
DARREN VAN IMPE	60	5	15	20	5-	66	4	0	0	0	92	5.4
P.J. AXELSSON	77	7	10	17	14-	18	0	0	2	0	146	4.8
PETER FERRARO	46	6	8	14	10	44	1	0	1	0	61	9.8
GRANT LEDYARD	47	4	8	12	8-	33	1	0	2	0	47	8.5
DON SWEENEY	81	2	10	12	14	64	0	0	0	0	79	2.5
TIM TAYLOR	49	4	7	11	10-	55	0	0	1	0	76	5.3

HAL GILL	80	3	7	10	10-	63	0	0	2	0	102	2.9
SHAWN BATES	33	5	4	9	3	2	0	0	0	0	30	16.7
CHRIS TAYLOR	37	3	5	8	3-	12	0	1	0	0	60	5.0
CAMERON MANN	33	5	2	7	0	17	1	0	1	1	42	11.9
KEN BELANGER	54	2	5	7	1-	182	0	0	0	0	19	10.5
LANDON WILSON	22	3	3	6	0	17	0	0	0	0	32	9.4
MATTIAS TIMANDER	22	0	6	6	4	10	0	0	0	0	22	.0
DAVE ELLETT	54	0	6	6	11	25	0	0	0	0	45	.0
KEN BAUMGARTNER	69	1	3	4	6-	119	0	0	0	1	15	6.7
ANTTI LAAKSONEN	11	1	2	3	1-	2	0	0	0	0	8	12.5
RANDY ROBITAILLE	4	0	2	2	1-	0	0	0	0	0	5	.0
BYRON DAFOE	68	0	2	2	0	25	0	0	0	0	0	.0
ANDRE SAVAGE	6	1	0	1	2	0	0	0	0	0	8	12.5
ERIC NICKULAS	2	0	0	0	0	0	0	0	0	0	0	.0
PETER NORDSTROM	2	0	0	0	1-	0	0	0	0	0	0	.0
DENNIS VASKE	3	0	0	0	3-	6	0	0	0	0	0	.0
JONATHAN GIRARD	3	0	0	0	1	0	0	0	0	0	3	.0
TERRY VIRTUE	4	0	0	0	2	0	0	0	0	0	2	.0
JAY HENDERSON	4	0	0	0	1-	2	0	0	0	0	4	.0
BRANDON SMITH	5	0	0	0	2	0	0	0	0	0	2	.0
MARQUIS MATHIEU	9	0	0	0	1-	8	0	0	0	0	4	.0
ROBBIE TALLAS	17	0	0	0	0	0	0	0	0	0	0	.0

TEAM RANKINGS

		Conference Rank	League Rank
Record	39-30-13	5	13
Home	22-10-9	1	3
Away	17-20-4	6	11
Versus Own Conference	29-20-9	4	7
Versus Other Conference	10-10-4	8	14
Team Plus\Minus	+1	8	16
Goals For	214	7	13
Goals Against	181	3	4
Average Shots For	27.5	7	16
Average Shots Against	27.1	7	12
Overtime	2-2-13	6	12
One Goal Games	14-8	3	4
Times outshooting opponent	38	6	13
Versus Teams Over .500	17-9-5	6	8
Versus Teams .500 or under	22-11-8	5	9
First Half Record	18-14-7	7	9
Second Half Record	21-16-6	4	8

MISCELLANEOUS STATS LEADERS:
FACE OFFS

	W	L	%
Taylor, T	486	348	58.3
Allison	918	842	52.2
Thornton	523	550	48.8
Taylor, C	275	237	53.7
Bates	91	87	51.1

ICE TIME

Bourque	29:31
McLaren	23:25
Allison	22:23
Gill	20:53

HITS

McLaren	205
Sweeney	205
Bourque	174
Gill	144
Thornton	124
DiMaio	106

PLAYOFFS

Results: Defeated Carolina 4-2 in conference quarter-finals.

Lost to Buffalo 4-2 in conference finals.

Record: 6-6
Home: 4-2
Away: 2-4
Goals For: 18 (1.5/game)
Goals Against: 12 (2.0/game)
Overtime: 2-0
Power play: 15.3%
Penalty Killing: 83.0%

PLAYER	GP	G	A	PTS	+/-	PIM	PP	SH	GW	OT	S	PCTG
JASON ALLISON	12	2	9	11	1	6	1	0	0	0	28	7.1
RAY BOURQUE	12	1	9	10	1	14	0	0	0	0	44	2.3
JOE THORNTON	11	3	6	9	1	4	2	0	2	0	15	20.0
STEVE HEINZE	12	4	3	7	1-	0	2	0	0	0	23	17.4
ANSON CARTER	12	4	3	7	3-	0	1	0	1	1	27	14.8
DMITRI KHRISTICH	12	3	4	7	1	6	0	0	1	0	19	15.8
SERGEI SAMSONOV	11	3	1	4	3	0	0	0	0	0	21	14.3
DON SWEENEY	11	3	0	3	2	6	1	0	0	0	16	18.8
DARREN VAN IMPE	11	1	2	3	3-	4	1	0	0	0	18	5.6
TIM TAYLOR	12	0	3	3	1	8	0	0	0	0	11	.0
KYLE MCLAREN	12	0	3	3	4	10	0	0	0	0	21	.0
ROB DIMAIO	12	2	0	2	2	8	0	0	1	0	21	9.5
MATTIAS TIMANDER	4	1	1	2	3	2	0	0	0	0	3	33.3
LANDON WILSON	8	1	1	2	2-	8	1	0	1	0	14	7.1
P.J. AXELSSON	12	1	1	2	1-	4	0	0	0	0	20	5.0
KEN BELANGER	12	1	0	1	2	16	0	0	0	0	7	14.3
ERIC NICKULAS	1	0	0	0	0	2	0	0	0	0	0	.0
CAMERON MANN	1	0	0	0	0	0	0	0	0	0	0	.0
RANDY ROBITAILLE	1	0	0	0	0	0	0	0	0	0	0	.0
GRANT LEDYARD	2	0	0	0	1-	2	0	0	0	0	4	.0
KEN BAUMGARTNER	3	0	0	0	0	0	0	0	0	0	0	.0
DAVE ELLETT	8	0	0	0	0	4	0	0	0	0	4	.0
BYRON DAFOE	12	0	0	0	0	2	0	0	0	0	0	.0
SHAWN BATES	12	0	0	0	1-	4	0	0	0	0	11	.0
HAL GILL	12	0	0	0	1-	14	0	0	0	0	10	.0

GOALTENDER	GPI	MINS	AVG	W	L	T	EN	SO	GA	SA	SV %
BYRON DAFOE	12	768	2.03	6	6		1	2	26	330	.921
BOS TOTALS	12	772	2.10	6	6		1	2	27	331	.918

Buffalo Sabres

Just when Buffalo Sabres fans thought it couldn't get worse, history tells us it will.

More on that in a minute.

So, was it a goal?

The NHL's worst possible nightmare came true in the third overtime of the sixth game of the Stanley Cup finals when Brett Hull scored the winning goal while in the crease.

In 100 percent of those situations throughout the season, the goal would be announced as being under review. Not this time, as the media flooded out onto the ice and the Dallas Stars went wild.

It was a joke. A bad one. In fact, the rule was a joke, although nobody in the league office was laughing. The NHL abolished video review for crease violations almost immediately after the season ended.

The league did its best to alleviate any doubts that it was in fact a goal, citing a little known proverb about he who has possession being ten/tenths of the law. They put up a convincing enough argument, but they still botched the whole procedure, which will now become a memory. A bad one, especially for Buffalo fans. Now for the worse news. History suggests this will not be a very good season for the Sabres.

Consider what has happened to the Stanley Cup finalist losers in the chart below.

Stanley Cup Finalist Loser the following year (since conference setup in 1982)

Final	Loser	Next Year
1999	Buffalo	?
1998	Washington	Missed Playoffs
1997	Philadelphia	Lost First Round
1996	Florida	Lost First Round
1995	Detroit	Lost Conference Finals
1994	Vancouver	Lost Conference Semi-Finals
1993	Los Angeles	Missed Playoffs
1992	Chicago	Lost first round
1991	Minnesota	Lost first round
1990	Boston	Lost Conference Finals
1989	Montreal	Lost Division Finals
1988	Boston	Lost Division Finals
1987	Philadelphia	Lost First Round
1986	Calgary	Lost First Round
1985	Philadelphia	Lost First Round
1984	NY Islanders	Lost Division Finals
1983	Edmonton	WON STANLEY CUP
1982	Vancouver	Lost first round

SUMMARY

• of the 17 finalist losers since the conference setup in 1982, eight of them were knocked out in the first round the next year, and two of them didn't even make the playoffs.

• only three of the 17 made it as far as the conference finals the next year, and only one won the Stanley Cup (Edmonton in 1983).

• only one team has made it back to the finals (Edmonton) and nobody has done it in the last 15 years.

STUFF: The Sabres didn't lose a game in the playoffs when they were leading after the first period or second period.

In their last 13 games of the regular season, the Sabres scored exactly one goal in eight of them.

TEAM PREVIEW

GOAL: Could the Sabres be any better off in net? Not only do they have the top goalie in the NHL, but they may also have the top goalie who's not in the NHL.

Enough has been said about Hasek, who probably has to be considered among the best goalies ever.

But, what are the Sabres going to do about Martin Biron? He tore up the AHL with Rochester, posting a league leading 2.07 goals against average during the regular season, and a league leading 2.16 GAA in the playoffs. They just don't have room for him right now and have no intentions of trading him.

It won't do Biron much good to sit on the bench and watch Hasek, so he'll probably play another season in the AHL, while Dwayne Roloson gets the better view.

But, soon, they're going to have to do something. Biron, who was selected the top NHL prospect by *The Hockey News,* could be playing in the NHL this year for a lot of teams.

DEFENSE: Any team defense would look better when they have Dominik Hasek behind them, but as a unit the Sabres defense is among the best mixes in the league.

Gone is Darryl Shannon, who was picked up by Atlanta in the expansion draft. Shannon led the team with a +28, but fell out of favor with the team as the season went on and hardly played in the playoffs. Veteran fill-in James Patrick became an unrestricted free agent, although it's possible the Sabres could recognize his value for what it is and re-sign him.

The offensive specialist is Jason Wooley, who had a tremendous season after it appeared he was headed to the scrapheap of offensive defensemen who can't play defense. Buffalo, his fourth NHL team, picked him up from Florida two years ago for a fifth round draft pick, and couldn't be happier.

Wooley tied Alexei Zhitnik for the team scor-

GOALTENDER	GPI	MINS	AVG	W	L	T	EN	SO	GA	SA	SV %
DOMINIK HASEK	64	3,817	1.87	30	18	14	2	9	119	1,877	.937
MARTIN BIRON	6	281	2.14	1	2	1	1	0	10	120	.917
D. ROLOSON	18	911	2.77	6	8	2	1	1	42	460	.909
BUF TOTALS	82	5,020	2.09	37	28	17	4	10	175	2,461	.929

ing lead in the playoffs, and while he can be inconsistent, he's still an offensive force and had the most minutes per game of any Sabre in the playoffs and the regular season.

Jay McKee was supposed to be an offensive threat when he first came to the NHL, but has instead turned himself into a solid defensive type. The same is true of Richard Smehlik, who showed offense in his first couple NHL seasons, but not so much since missing time with so many injuries.

Rhett Warriner, an outstanding in-season pick-up from Florida, rounded out the defense perfectly.

Best of all, the Sabres have some excellent prospects on the way up. Cory Sarich played some with Buffalo last year and looks like he will be in the lineup, and Jean-Luc Grand-Pierre, hyphens and all, should get plenty of playing time as well.

Overall, opposing forwards don't particularly enjoy chasing the puck in Buffalo's end. They know they're going to get hit if they have the puck, they're not likely to stand close enough to Hasek to get his autograph, and they know the Sabres defense can turn the puck up ice quickly.

FORWARD: The Sabres need more scoring. They said before, during and after their trek to the Stanley Cup finals. They'd even be saying it if Buffalo had managed to win the whole thing.

They had a losing record against the Western Conference, which generally has a more wide-open offensive style, so that's maybe where it hurts them. Just to put it to the test, let's see how they performed against the top six scoring teams.

Versus:	W	L	T	GF	GA
Toronto	3	2	0	17	10
New Jersey	1	2	1	8	10
Detroit	0	1	1	5	6
Pittsburgh	2	1	1	11	10
Colorado	1	1	0	6	5
Ottawa	0	1	4	7	8
Total	7	8	7	54	49

Considering five of those teams were in the top six in league standings, Buffalo did pretty well, actually outscoring them in total over the 22 games.

It seems as if those other teams need more scoring, at least when they play Buffalo. All of them scored less than their overall average, and versus half of them, the Sabres scored higher than their average.

It appears that the Sabres are able to adjust their game to fit their opponent, but that their opponents have a difficult time.

So, where is it that they need more scoring, exactly? And when you get more scoring, there's usually a trade-off, meaning defense suffers. In theory, more scoring makes perfect sense, just as more everything does. But, would it help them win more often if they gave up more goals at the same time?

The Sabres did manage 40 goals out of Miroslav Satan, 27 from Mike Peca, and 20 each from Dixon Ward and Michal Grosek. Neither Grosek or Satan was a factor in the playoffs, so we'd have to question their consistency and ability to put up the same numbers again this year. Peca is one of the best all-round players in the league, and Ward has to be near the top of the list in the under-rated category.

Curtis Brown had his coming out season and

looks as if he's only going to get better as a two-way hockey player. Rob Ray is still an intimidating presence on the ice, although he hardly played at all in the playoffs.

Funny that there's so many question marks on a Stanley Cup finalist, however, apart from those about Satan and Grosek's consistency.

Can Geoff Sanderson ever regain his scoring touch?

Who's the real Stu Barnes? The one who scored no goals in 17 regular season games for the Sabres, or the one who scored seven in 21 playoff games.

Is there something more from Brian Holzinger in the scoring department?

Is Eric Rasmussen ready to take a regular shift?

Can Wayne Primeau get enough ice-time to be effective?

What does that mean when Vaclav Varada only scores one goal in the entire second half of the season?

Question marks usually mean trouble. They had a similar amount of them before last season and still did well, so we'll have to see if they can do it again.

SPECIAL TEAMS: Only four teams had more man-advantage penalties called against them than Buffalo, last season. Their penalty killing was good, but they suffered overall on special teams because their power play wasn't. They scored 49 power play goals, and allowed 55 against.

In the playoffs, their power play caught on fire, and they scored 19 goals in their 21 games. Zhitnik and Woolley were great on the points, and Barnes, Brown and Peca were the best forwards. Satan and Grosek, who were both instumental in the power play during the regular sea-

son, saw considerably less time with the extra man and the team appeared to benefit from it.

Power Play	G	ATT	PCT
Overall	49	363	13.5% (21st NHL)
Home	24	181	13.3% (22nd NHL)
Road	25	182	13.7% (18th NHL)

7 SHORT HANDED GOALS ALLOWED (T-9th NHL)

Penalty Killing	G	TSH	PCT
Overall	55	399	86.2% (7th NHL)
Home	28	195	85.6% (15th NHL)
Road	27	204	86.8% (4th NHL)

6 SHORT HANDED GOALS SCORED (T-21st NHL)

Penalties	GP	MIN	AVG
SABRES	82	1561	19.0 (24th NHL)

SABRES SPECIAL TEAMS SCORING

Power play	G	A	PTS
SATAN	13	8	21
WOOLLEY	4	16	20
PECA	10	9	19
BARNES	13	4	17
ZHITNIK	3	13	16
JUNEAU	2	12	14
GROSEK	4	8	12
HOLZINGER	5	5	10
BROWN	5	5	10
WARD	2	6	8
SANDERSON	1	5	6
VARADA	1	3	4
SHANNON	1	2	3
WARRENER	0	3	3
SMEHLIK	0	1	1
PRIMEAU	0	1	1

Short handed	G	A	PTS
SATAN	3	0	3
BROWN	1	1	2
ZHITNIK	1	0	1
WARD	1	0	1
JUNEAU	1	0	1
PECA	0	1	1
MCKEE	0	1	1
HOLZINGER	0	1	1

COACHING AND MANAGEMENT: The Sabres didn't have a great regular season, but it's the playoffs that count and that's generally where you judge a coach's effectiveness. Lindy Ruff pulled all the right strings and got the most out of his players.

While everyone things they should have generated more offense, turning that on and off is a lot easier said than done.

The same thing goes for GM Darcy Regier. He got the playoff-type players that Ruff needed, and made valiant attempts to add offense with Sanderson, Barnes and Joe Juneau, who was lost to free agency after the season. He also improved the defense with the acquisition of Warrener.

DRAFT: (see chart) Barrett Heisten is from Alaska, but played his hockey with Black Bears, instead of polar bears, at the University of Maine. He's projected as a grinding type winger without much of a scoring touch.

Second round selection Michael Zigomanis was once rated in the top 10 among North Americans by the Central Scouting Bureau. The main concern about him is his skating.

PROGNOSIS: It's tough not to think about that Stanley Cup finalist jinx. The Sabres are a young team and should be an improving team, but you never know. And if Hasek is ever injured for any length of time, that could spell further trouble.

Remember the Sabres only finished seventh in the Eastern Conference last year and with teams such as the Rangers and Panthers expected to improve, they're going to have to battle to make the playoffs.

DRAFT

Player	Pos	Rnd	Sel.	Cntry	Team	Lge	Gms	G	A	P	PIM
Barrett Heisten	LW	1	20	USA	Maine	H.E	34	12	16	28	72
Milan Bartovic	RW	2	30	Slo	Trencin, Jr	Slo	44	35	24	59	52
Doug Janik	D	2	55	USA	Maine	H.E.	29	3	12	15	40
M. Zigomanis	C	2	64	Can	Kingston	OHL	67	29	56	85	36
Tim Preston	LW	3	73	Can	Seattle	WHL	60	12	15	27	98
Karel Mosovsky	LW	4	117	Cze	Regina	WHL	68	26	25	51	58
Ryan Miller	G	5	138	USA	Soo	NAHL	2.25	.926			
Matthew Kinch	D	5	146	Can	Calgary	WHL					
S. Hyacinthe	LW	6	178	Can	Val D'or	QMJHL	63	24	33	57	106
Bret Dececco	RW	7	206	Can	Seattle	WHL	72	57	43	100	81
Brad Self	C	8	235	Can	Peterborough	OHL	48	17	12	298	
Craig Brunel	RW	9	263	Can	Prince Albert	WHL	50	10	8	18	173

STAT SECTION

PLAYER	GP	G	A	PTS	+/-	PIM	PP	SH	GW	GT	S	PCTG
MIROSLAV SATAN	81	40	26	66	24	44 1	3	3	6	1	208	19.2
MICHAEL PECA	82	27	29	56	7	81	10	0	8	1	199	13.6
MICHAL GROSEK	76	20	30	50	21	102	4	0	3	1	140	14.3
CURTIS BROWN	78	16	31	47	23	56	5	1	3	3	128	12.5
DIXON WARD	78	20	24	44	10	44	2	1	4	1	101	19.8
JOE JUNEAU	72	15	28	43	4-	22	2	1	3	0	150	10.0
JASON WOOLLEY	80	10	33	43	16	62	4	0	2	1	154	6.5
STU BARNES	81	20	16	36	11-	30	13	0	3	0	180	11.1
BRIAN HOLZINGER	81	17	17	34	2	45	5	0	2	0	143	11.9
ALEXEI ZHITNIK	81	7	26	33	6-	96	3	1	2	0	185	3.8
VACLAV VARADA	72	7	24	31	11	61	1	0	1	0	123	5.7
GEOFF SANDERSON	75	12	18	30	8	22	1	0	1	0	155	7.7
DARRYL SHANNON	71	3	12	15	28	52	1	0	0	1	80	3.8
RICHARD SMEHLIK	72	3	11	14	9-	44	0	0	0	0	61	4.9
WAYNE PRIMEAU	67	5	8	13	6-	38	0	0	0	1	55	9.1
ERIK RASMUSSEN	42	3	7	10	6	37	0	0	0	0	40	7.5
JAMES PATRICK	45	1	7	8	12	16	0	0	0	0	31	3.2
RHETT WARRENER	61	1	7	8	2	84	0	0	0	0	44	2.3
JAY MCKEE	72	0	6	6	20	75	0	0	0	0	57	.0
R. CUNNEYWORTH	14	2	2	4	1	0	0	0	1	0	12	16.7
ROB RAY	76	0	4	4	2-	261	0	0	0	0	23	.0
PAUL KRUSE	43	3	0	3	0	114	0	0	0	0	33	9.1
J-L. GRAND-PIERRE	16	0	1	1	0	17	0	0	0	0	11	.0
MIKE HURLBUT	1	0	0	0	2	0	0	0	0	0	2	.0
DEAN SYLVESTER	1	0	0	0	1-	0	0	0	0	0	1	.0
DOMENIC PITTIS	3	0	0	0	0	2	0	0	0	0	1	.0
JASON HOLLAND	3	0	0	0	1-	8	0	0	0	0	2	.0
CORY SARICH	4	0	0	0	3	0	0	0	0	0	2	.0
MARTIN BIRON	6	0	0	0	0	0	0	0	0	0	0	.0
DWAYNE ROLOSON	18	0	0	0	0	4	0	0	0	0	0	.0
DOMINIK HASEK	64	0	0	0	0	14	0	0	0	0	0	.0

TEAM RANKINGS

		Conference Rank	League Rank
Record	37-28-17	6	9
Home	23-12-6	3	5
Away	14-16-11	5	10
Versus Own Conference	28-17-12	3	4
Versus Other Conference	9-11-5	10	20
Team Plus\Minus	+38	4	4
Goals For	207	10	17
Goals Against	175	1	2
Average Shots For	26.2	9	19
Average Shots Against	30.2	12	22
Overtime	3-3-17	5	11
One Goal Games	10-14	11	21
Times outshooting opponent	29	11	22
Versus Teams Over .500	16-15-12	5	7
Versus Teams .500 or under	21-13-5	9	15
First Half Record	22-12-7	4	6
Second Half Record	15-16-10	7	16

MISCELLANEOUS STATS
FACEOFFS

	W	L	%
Barnes	121	115	51.7
Holzinger	429	423	50.4
Peca	917	938	49.4
Brown	539	659	45.0

ICE-TIME LEADERS

Zhitnik	25:39
Smehlik	21:50
Satan	20:49
Peca	20:44
McKee	20:28
Juneau	19:11
Woolley	18:43

HIT LEADERS

McKee	204
Varada	185
Peca	181
Zhitnik	122
Smehlik	107
Rasmussen	104
Warrener	103

PLAYOFFS

Results:

Defeated Ottawa 4-0 in conference quarter-finals

Defeated Boston 4-2 in conference semi-finals

Defeated Toronto 4-2 in conference finals

Lost to Dallas 4-2 in finals

Record: 14-7

Home: 8-2

Away: 6-5

Goals For: 59 (2.8/game)

Goals Against: 49 (2.3/game)

Overtime: 2-1

Power play: 20.0% (3rd)

Penalty Killing: 85.6% (5th)

PLAYER	GP	G	A	PTS	+/-	PIM	PP	SH	GW	OT	S	PCTG
JASON WOOLLEY	21	4	11	15	0	10	2	0	1	1	43	9.3
ALEXEI ZHITNIK	21	4	11	15	6-	52	4	0	2	0	58	6.9
CURTIS BROWN	21	7	6	13	3	10	3	0	3	0	34	20.6
MICHAEL PECA	21	5	8	13	1	18	2	1	0	0	37	13.5
DIXON WARD	21	7	5	12	6	32	0	2	3	0	38	18.4
JOE JUNEAU	20	3	8	11	2-	10	0	1	0	0	29	10.3
STU BARNES	21	7	3	10	1-	6	4	0	1	0	30	23.3
GEOFF SANDERSON	19	4	6	10	5	14	0	0	1	0	53	7.5
VACLAV VARADA	21	5	4	9	2	14	1	0	0	0	38	13.2
MIROSLAV SATAN	12	3	5	8	3	2	1	0	1	1	25	12.0
BRIAN HOLZINGER	21	3	5	8	1	33	1	0	0	0	32	9.4
WAYNE PRIMEAU	19	3	4	7	0	6	1	0	0	0	22	13.6
ERIK RASMUSSEN	21	2	4	6	2	18	0	0	1	0	23	8.7
RHETT WARRENER	20	1	3	4	12	32	0	0	0	0	21	4.8
MICHAL GROSEK	13	0	4	4	1	28	0	0	0	0	20	0
RICHARD SMEHLIK	21	0	3	3	4-	10	0	0	0	0	20	.0
JAY MCKEE	21	0	3	3	13	24	0	0	0	0	13	0
ROB RAY	5	1	0	1	1	0	0	0	1	0	1	100.0
DOMINIK HASEK	19	0	1	1	0	8	0	0	0	0	0	0
JAMES PATRICK	20	0	1	1	6	12	0	0	0	0	11	0
DARRYL SHANNON	2	0	0	0	1-	0	0	0	0	0	7	.0
R. CUNNEYWORTH	3	0	0	0	1-	0	0	0	0	0	2	.0
DEAN SYLVESTER	4	0	0	0	1-	2	0	0	0	0	2	.0
DWAYNE ROLOSON	4	0	0	0	0	0	0	0	0	0	0	.0
PAUL KRUSE	10	0	0	0	0	4	0	0	0	0	0	.0

GOALTENDER	GPI	MINS	AVG	W	L	T	EN	SO	GA	SA	SV %
DOMINIK HASEK	19	1,217	1.77	13	6	2	2	0	36	587	.939
D. ROLOSON	4	139	4.32	1	1	1	0	0	10	67	.851
BUF TOTALS	21	1,361	2.16	14	7	3	2	0	49	657	.925

Florida Panthers

The Florida Panthers have very quickly made a transition from a gritty, hard-working team to a flashy, offensive outfit.

Never mind that the former method got them to the Stanley Cup finals, and the latter method has shown to be an early ticket out of the playoffs.

The Panthers have to make the playoffs first, and while Pavel Bure may have appeared to be the second coming in his limited exposure last season, that doesn't necessarily translate to winning hockey, as was so obvious in Vancouver.

Bure played 11 games, scoring a remarkable 13 goals and three assists. Despite that outbreak, the team only went 5-4-2 when he was in the lineup. And, it's not unusual, anyway, for holdout players to come back into the game with a bang.

Bure's season was lost after that, to reconstructive knee surgery.

The Panthers are going to be big on European players this year, who are most often defined as "skill players."

Interesting that Jaromir Jagr himself once suggested that too many Europeans on a team isn't good, especially when it comes to the playoffs. His inference was that they did not possess the same drive to excel as a team when it counted.

The Stanley Cup champion, Dallas Stars, had just two Europeans as key components of their team — Jere Lehtinen and Sergei Zubov.

There's little doubt that European players are making a larger impact in the game each year. Let's look at a comparison.

Europeans in the NHL:

	1998-99	1993-94	1988-89	1983-84
Leading Team in Scoring	12	7	5	2
Top 15 in League Scoring	6	3	1	2

You can see the tremendous difference just over the last 10 years. The Europeans are being counted on for their scoring, more and more. What that might mean is that it's no longer a bad decision in some ways to build your team with Europeans. And you can win that way during the regular season, now more than ever, simply because so many other teams are doing the same thing. So, it becomes a matter of who has the most talented offensive players.

Mind you, it remains to be seen if that is an effective way of winning in the playoffs, because so far the answer is no.

STUFF: Ryan Johnson scored a goal in his first NHL game on his first NHL shot on net.

The Panthers have never won a game without Bill Lindsay in the lineup. Their record is 0-12-2 when he's been sidelined.

The Panthers became only the seventh team in NHL history to blow a five-goal lead when they lost 7-5 to Colorado, after leading 5-0.

A four-goal game by rookie Mark Parrish was the most by a player in team history.

TEAM PREVIEW

GOAL: The Panthers either have two number one goalies, or two number two goalies, or two goalies fighting it out for number one.

Both Sean Burke, and Trevor Kidd, obtained from Carolina through Atlanta, have had some problems in recent years. But, they've both been tremendously good at times, as well.

Kidd has the most to prove after losing his starting job to Arturs Irbe in Carolina, just a couple games into last season. He never got a fair opportunity to win it back, mostly because Irbe played so well.

There are going to be some difficult nights in Miami, with the team concentrating less on defense, and both goalies should get plenty of playing time.

DEFENSE: With veterans, Gord Murphy and Terry Carkner, no longer in the picture, the Panthers will feature a speedier, more mobile defense, with some good toughness.

Robert Svehla is supposed to be the quarterback on the point, but he was particurlarly unimpressive in that role after signing a big contract. It may help his offensive stats with a more offensive approach up front, coming from more offensive-type players. If Bure is scoring on the power play, it won't hurt him, either.

Jaroslav Spacek was a bust at first, but seemed to improve after a stint in the minors. But, he needs to provide an offensive presence to be useful.

Bret Hedican has amazing speed, but is not an offensive force unless he's on the power play or makes a conscious effort to play that way.

Lance Pitlick was signed as a free agent and the hard-hitting bruiser will definitely ensure opposing forwards will keep their heads up.

Big Mike Wilson and enforcer Paul Laus are also in the mix, but the surprise last year was the play of Dan Boyle, when the Panthers brought him up from the minors. He was just one year removed from being a finalist for the Hobey Baker Award as the top college player, and could be the offensive force on the blueline that the team needs.

In fact, the Panthers are very strong with defense prospects, possibly as strong as any team in the league. They've got Filip Kuba, who made an impression late in the year; tough- guy Brad Ference, a first round pick of the Canucks, obtained in the Bure deal; Peter Ratchuk, a speedy offensive prospect who was up and down

GOALTENDER	GPI	MINS	AVG	W	L	T	EN	SO	GA	SA	SV %
SEAN BURKE	59	3,402	2.66	21	24	14	3	3	151	1624	.907
KIRK MCLEAN	30	1,597	2.74	9	10	4	1	2	73	727	.900
FLA TOTALS	82	5,017	2.73	30	34	18	4	5	228	2,355	.903

with the team last season; Big John Jakopin, who is a physical force; and Chris Allen, another offensive type with a good shot. They've even got a few others, who may not be far away from being ready.

Defensemen at the NHL level usually need to be brought along slowly, because it's a tough position to learn, but having so much potential quality at this position means at the very least they're in a position to make trades at the trading deadline if they find themselves in contention.

FORWARD: The big question is who will play on Pavel Bure's line. It's a cushy assignment, guaranteed to make a couple guys look especially good with their point totals. At centre, both Viktor Kozlov and Rob Niedermayer had auditions there last year, in the limited time Bure was around. But, the one they want most of all has to be signed.

Jiri Dopita has long been considered a top prospect from the Czech Republic, but so far he has refused to cross the ocean. The Panthers got his rights in a deal with the NY Islanders, who had offered to make him their number one centre. The Panthers were optimistic during the summer that they could get him, too, and he would be a good fit with Bure.

The Panthers also see winger, Ivan Novoseltsev, being in the lineup this year, possibly on Bure's left wing. The 1997 draft pick had 57 goals for Sarnia in the OHL last season, and the Panthers are extremely excited about him.

Florida had three rookie regular forwards in the lineup last season, and in all had 14 rookies suit up. That was the most in the league.

Mark Parrish had a great rookie season, although he did go through periods of inconsis-

tency. Plus, he had the strangest habit of scoring in bunches. He had 24 goals, but 14 of them were scored in multiple-goal games. He also had a habit of not scoring over extended periods, but that was fairly common with everyone on the Panthers.

Big Oleg Kvasha turned in a decent rookie season, as well, and with veterans Dino Ciccarelli, Kirk Muller, and Johan Garpenlov turned out to pasture, a couple more rookies will get playing time again this year, as noted above.

If Dopita and Novoseltsev are with the team, they would actually have the ability to put together four scoring lines. At the very least they have three, with a checking fourth line.

They've got Bure, Novoseltsev, Dopita (maybe), Kvasha, Parrish, Niedermayer, Ray Whitney, Scott Mellanby, Radek Dvorak. That's nine right there. Plus they've got role players Bill Lindsay, Chris Wells, and Alex Hicks, not to mention enforcer Peter Worrell, free agent signee Craig Reichert, and prospect Denis Svidki.

The Panthers could and should shoot the lights out this year, if everything goes well.

SPECIAL TEAMS: The Panthers should be better with the man-advantage, with Bure around all the time, and some incoming scoring prowess. Hard to see how penalty-killing will improve, however, but it can't get much worse.

Power Play	G	ATT	PCT
Overall	51	378	13.5% (21st NHL)
Home	29	183	15.8% (13th NHL)
Road	22	195	11.3% (23rd NHL)
11 SHORT HANDED GOALS ALLOWED (T-23rd NHL)			

Penalty Killing	G	TSH	PCT
Overall	65	365	82.2% (22nd NHL)
Home	31	163	81.0% (23rd NHL)
Road	34	202	83.2% (16th NHL)

10 SHORT HANDED GOALS SCORED (T-6th NHL)

Penalties	GP	MIN	AVG
PANTHERS	81	1502	18.5 (23rd NHL)

PANTHERS SPECIAL TEAMS SCORING

Power play	G	A	PTS
WHITNEY	7	17	24
NIEDERMAYER	6	10	16
SVEHLA	4	12	16
KOZLOV	5	10	15
MELLANBY	4	7	11
PARRISH	5	4	9
KVASHA	4	5	9
CICCARELLI	5	1	6
BURE	5	0	5
SPACEK	2	2	4
BOYLE	1	2	3
HEDICAN	0	3	3
DVORAK	0	3	3
MURPHY	0	2	2
MULLER	0	1	1

Short handed	G	A	PTS
DVORAK	4	0	4
HEDICAN	2	1	3
SVEHLA	0	3	3
SPACEK	1	1	2
KOZLOV	1	1	2
GARPENLOV	1	1	2
BURE	1	1	2
NIEDERMAYER	1	0	1
LINDSAY	1	0	1
HICKS	0	1	1
CARKNER	0	1	1

COACHING AND MANAGEMENT: The Murray brothers are going to look good this year. Bryan for building such a talented outfit. Terry for letting his players play a more offensive style.

It was a mistake to sign old players to long-term contracts, but they were a stop-gap, at least, until the younger players developed, and they have lots of good ones. Getting Pavel Bure was a coup, too. Everybody wanted him, and Bryan Murray got him, so he deserves credit for that.

There was at least one criticism of coach, Terry Murray. Ex-Panther, Rhett Warrener, suggested it was "weird down there." He said that the coach was more in tune to the media than the players.

DRAFT

Player	Pos	Rnd	Sel.	Cntry	Team	Lge	Gms	G	A	P	PIM
Denis Shvidki	RW	1	12	Ukr	Barrie	OHL	61	35	59	94	8
Alexander Auld	G	2	40	Can	North Bay	OHL	3.36	.899			
Niklas Hagman	LW	3	70	Fin	IFK Jr.	Fin	12	2	7	9	4
J-F Laniel	G	3	80	Can	Shawinigan	QMJHL	3.84	.878			
M. McCormick	RW	4	103	Can	Kingston	OHL	34	6	5	11	43
Rod Sarich	D	4	109	Can	Calgary	WHL	65	3	15	18	22
Brad Woods	D	6	169	Can	Brampton	OHL	58	1	5	6	42
Travis Eagles	RW	7	198	Can	Prince George	WHL	48	1	9	10	66
Jonathan Charron	G	8	227	Can	Val D'or	QMJHL	3.98	.875			

DRAFT: (see chart) At one time, Denis Shvidki was being touted as the first overall pick. He slipped in the rankings because he didn't dominate the OHL as he was expected and didn't show his talents consistently. But, he does have plenty of talent, including great playmaking skills, scoring skills, and skating skills. Only eight minutes in penalties in the OHL is almost unheard of, so he appears to be a complete player except for that one area.

PROGNOSIS: Good news, Panther fans. They're going to make the playoffs this year, and should be one of the league's most improved and most surprising teams. If they're not successful this year, then for sure next year. They've built an potential offensive powerhouse.

STAT SECTION

PLAYER	GP	G	A	PTS	+/-	PIM	PP	SH	GW	GT	S	PCTG
RAY WHITNEY	81	26	38	64	3-	18	7	0	6	1	193	13.5
ROB NIEDERMAYER	82	18	33	51	13-	50	6	1	3	2	142	12.7
VIKTOR KOZLOV	65	16	35	51	13	24	5	1	1	0	209	7.7
SCOTT MELLANBY	67	18	27	45	5	85	4	0	3	3	136	13.2
RADEK DVORAK	82	19	24	43	7	29	0	4	0	0	182	10.4
MARK PARRISH	73	24	13	37	6-	25	5	0	5	1	129	18.6
ROBERT SVEHLA	80	8	29	37	13-	83	4	0	0	1	157	5.1
BILL LINDSAY	75	12	15	27	1-	92	0	1	2	0	135	8.9
OLEG KVASHA	68	12	13	25	5	45	4	0	2	1	138	8.7
BRET HEDICAN	67	5	18	23	5	51	0	2	1	1	90	5.6
JOHAN GARPENLOV	64	8	9	17	9-	42	0	1	0	1	71	11.3
PAVEL BURE	11	13	3	16	3	4	5	1	0	1	44	29.5
KIRK MULLER	82	4	11	15	11-	49	0	0	1	0	107	3.7
JAROSLAV SPACEK	63	3	12	15	15	28	2	1	0	0	92	3.3
TERRY CARKNER	62	2	9	11	0	54	0	0	0	0	25	8.0
PAUL LAUS	75	1	9	10	1-	218	0	0	0	0	54	1.9
PETER WORRELL	62	4	5	9	0	258	0	0	2	0	50	8.0
DAN BOYLE	22	3	5	8	0	6	1	0	1	0	31	9.7
DINO CICCARELLI	14	6	1	7	1-	27	5	0	1	0	23	26.1
GORD MURPHY	51	0	7	7	4	16	0	0	0	0	56	.0
ALEX HICKS	55	0	7	7	5-	62	0	0	0	0	51	.0
SEAN BURKE	59	0	4	4	0	27	0	0	0	0	0	.0
MIKE WILSON	34	1	2	3	12	47	0	0	1	0	48	2.1
MARCUS NILSON	8	1	1	2	2	5	0	0	1	0	7	14.3

Player												
PETER RATCHUK	24	1	1	2	1-	10	0	0	0	0	34	2.9
CHRIS WELLS	20	0	2	2	4-	31	0	0	0	0	28	.0
RYAN JOHNSON	1	1	0	1	0	0	0	0	0	0	1	100.0
DAVID NEMIROVSKY	2	0	1	1	1	0	0	0	0	0	2	.0
FILIP KUBA	5	0	1	1	2	0	0	0	0	0	5	.0
JEFF WARE	6	0	1	1	6-	6	0	0	0	0	1	.0
CHRIS ALLEN	1	0	0	0	1	0	0	0	0	0	0	.0
JOHN JAKOPIN	3	0	0	0	1-	0	0	0	0	0	0	.0
HERBERT VASILJEVS	5	0	0	0	1-	2	0	0	0	0	6	.0
DWAYNE HAY	9	0	0	0	1-	0	0	0	0	0	3	.0
KIRK MCLEAN	30	0	0	0	0	2	0	0	0	0	0	.0

TEAM RANKINGS

		Conference Rank	League Rank
Record	30-34-18	9	17
Home	17-17-7	10	18
Away	13-17-11	10	17
Versus Own Conference	22-25-11	9	16
Versus Other Conference	8-9-7	9	16
Team Plus\Minus	-2	9	17
Goals For	210	8	15
Goals Against	228	11	20
Average Shots For	27.7	6	14
Average Shots Against	28.4	9	16
Overtime	1-2-18	8	15
One Goal Games	12-10	7	10
Times outshooting opponent	34	9	17
Versus Teams Over .500	7-20-13	12	23
Versus Teams .500 or under	23-14-12	8	14
First Half Record	16-15-11	9	12
Second Half Record	14-19-7	11	21

MISCELLANEOUS STAT LEADERS:

FACEOFFS

Muller	49.1%
Niedermayer	47.1%
Kozlov	41.2%

ICE TIME

Svehla	24:46
Garpenlov	21:41
Niedermayer	21:17
Hedican	20:04

HITS

Niedermayer	152
Lindsay	149
Hedican	106
Svehla	101
Worrell	100

PLAYOFFS

- Did not make the playoffs

Montreal Canadiens

What a mess.

Consider:

The Canadiens had the largest goal production decrease in the league last year.

Largest Goal Decreases:

	1997-98	1998-99	Difference
Montreal	235	184	-51
Los Angeles	227	189	-38
Vancouver	224	192	-32

They were the only team in the league without a 20-goal scorer. Tampa Bay had one, the Islanders had a couple, and even Nashville had two. The leader on Montreal was 17, by Martin Rucinsky. The worst part is that only Brian Savage would have scored 20, even if you projected their totals over 82 games. It had been 58 years since a Canadiens team failed to have a 20-goal scorer in a full season.

No team in the league was as disappointing as the Canadiens. Almost every single one of their players had a poor season.

Their players are injury-prone. Some of the same guys are missing a quarter of every season.

The prospects are having a tough time making it to the NHL, and they have very little coming up that they can get excited about. Jonas Hoglund was a bust, and released, along with a couple others who didn't make the grade. Their first round draft selections have not worked out recently.

Not one of the Canadiens forwards is a consistent scorer. Not one of them can be relied on to reach a respectable level each year.

Newcomer Trevor Linden can provide leadership, but not much scoring.

They have very little trade material, except maybe Vladimir Malakhov, and everybody knows he's a slacker.

Their best and most reliable players are third or fourth liners.

They have very few French Canadians. Don't know what that has to do with anything, but apparently it's a concern to the French language media in Montreal.

Budget restraints means immediate help isn't likely.

Most of the teams in and around the 19th overall place Montreal occupied in the overall standings have improved. The Canadiens have not.

There is little cause for optimism. No Montreal team has missed the playoffs two years in a row since the 1920-21 and 1921-22 seasons.

There's a good bet it will happen again this year.

STUFF: When Vincent Damphousse was traded he became the sixth consecutive Montreal captain to be traded while still captain. The previous five were Pierre Turgeon, Mike Keane, Kirk Muller, and Guy Carbonneau.

TEAM PREVIEW

GOAL: Jeff Hackett did a good job when acquired by the Canadiens from Chicago. He actually had a winning record. The oddity though is that he was playing terribly for the Blackhawks, and Thibault, who wasn't playing well in Montreal, did a much better job in Chicago.

That means that the initial adreneline that's so common from in-season trades could wear off this season, and Hackett won't be quite so good.

With Chabot lost to free agency, Jose Theodore will get an opportunity to be a full-time backup. He's still young, but he hasn't shown much at all, yet.

Mathieu Garon is supposed to be the goalie of the future, but he hasn't shown much yet, either.

DEFENSE: With Stephane Quintal gone to the New York Rangers through free agency, the Canadiens can look at having one of the weakest defense groups in the league.

They've got one star talent in Vladimir Malakhov, who might be the least desirable star in the league. He has no heart and would sit out a game if his baby toe was sore. Most of the talk about Malakhov is what the team could get for him in a trade.

Patrice Brisebois has a good season every couple years, but the rest of the time he's injured or everybody is wondering what's the matter with him.

Eric Weinrich can provide some offense when needed, but he's hardly a premier player in that regard. Scott Lachance was a decent pickup from the Islanders. Igor Ulanov and Craig Rivet round out the rearguards

They will need some replacement parts and are probably going to bring in a couple older Europeans. Miroslav Guren, another disappointment so far, will get a chance to stick this year.

FORWARD: Where are the goals going to come from? And can anybody stay healthy long enough to score them?

Saku Koivu is a decent playmaker for the 60 or so games he manages to play each season, but the snipers are unreliable. Martin Rucinsky is streaky; Brian Savage is streaky; Shayne Corson is aging, injury-prone, and scores most of his goals on the power play; Trevor Linden is not a big goal-scorer any more; Danius Zubrus could maybe score, but he'd need to be playing on the wing with Eric Lindros and John LeClair; Patrick Poulin hasn't scored since the 1991-92 season,

GOALTENDER	GPI	MINS	AVG	W	L	T	EN	SO	GA	SA	SV %
F. CHABOT	11	430	2.23	1	3	0	0	0	16	188	.915
JEFF HACKETT	53	3,091	2.27	24	20	9	2	5	117	1,360	.914
J. THIBAULT	10	529	2.61	3	4	2	0	1	23	250	.908
JOSE THEODORE	18	913	3.29	4	12	0	1	1	50	406	.877
MTL TOTALS	82	4,988	2.51	32	39	11	3	7	209	2,207	.905

and the Canadiens were worried about losing him in the expansion draft; Benoit Brunet sometimes scores, but that's only during the rare times he's not injured; Jonas Hoglund, Jason Dawe and Eric Houde couldn't score, so they weren't re-signed; Oleg Petrov can score, as long it's in Switzerland and they promise not to hit him; and the prospects can't even score in the minors.

The checking line centre, Scott Thornton, could probably score more if they moved him up to the second line, which tells you where they're at. Thornton is a valuable third or fourth liner, along with Turner Stevenson and Sergei Zholtok. Jim Cummins, obtained in the off-season will apparently handle the enforcer role.

The only hope, and it's not a great one, is that the Montreal forwards can stay healthy for a full season, and inconsist scorers can suddenly change their spots.

Prospects include Matt Higgins, Arron Asham, and Jason Ward. None have shown any indication that they could break into the top 100 in scoring in the NHL.

It's not a good scenario at all and they're going to have to use their limited trade bait to get some goals up front.

SPECIAL TEAMS: The Canadiens should be able to do better on the power play. They have some decent playmakers, such as Koivu, and snipers, such as Corson, when they're not injured. Malakhov is good on the point when he feels like it.

Interesting contrast between home and away last season. They were last on the road on the power play at a horrendous 9.5%, but second in penalty killing on the road.

Power Play	G	ATT	PCT
Overall	49	341	14.4% (18th NHL)
Home	33	172	19.2% (8th NHL)
Road	16	169	9.5% (27th NHL)

10 SHORT HANDED GOALS ALLOWED (T-19th NHL)

Penalty Killing	G	TSH	PCT
Overall	44	338	87.0% (5th NHL)
Home	24	169	85.8% (13th NHL)
Road	20	169	88.2% (2nd NHL)

8 SHORT HANDED GOALS SCORED (T-8th NHL)

Penalties	GP	MIN	AVG
CANADIENS	81	1273	15.7 (T-11th NHL)

Power play	G	A	PTS
KOIVU	4	14	18
MALAKHOV	8	9	17
CORSON	7	8	15
WEINRICH	4	10	14
RUCINSKY	5	6	11
SAVAGE	5	3	8
BRUNET	4	2	6
ZHOLTOK	2	4	6
BRISEBOIS	1	3	4
LACHANCE	1	2	3
QUINTAL	1	1	2
HOGLUND	1	1	2
THORNTON	1	0	1
ZUBRUS	0	1	1
ULANOV	0	1	1
STEVENSON	0	1	1
DAWE	0	1	1

Short handed	G	A	PTS
KOIVU	2	1	3
BRUNET	2	1	3
QUINTAL	1	2	3
ZUBRUS	1	0	1

POULIN	1	0	1
RUCINSKY	0	1	1
MALAKHOV	0	1	1

COACHING AND MANAGEMENT: It's amazing what a difference a year makes. Before last season, coach Alain Vigneault was being heralded as a coaching genius, and GM Rejean Houle was a GM genius.

Now, they're close to being idiots, at least in perception. Vigneault is a prime candidate to be the first coach fired this year. He made a healthy jump in the standings his first year with the team, but coaching and motivational effectiveness tends to wear off quickly. After being traded, former captain Vincent Damphousse, said there were communication problems with Vigneault.

Interesting that Houle traded their first round pick this year for Trevor Linden. That's not a bad deal, but it used to be that Montreal would raid everybody else's first round picks.

There does appear some concern with budget constraints, and now the Canadiens aren't even going to have their own farm team, after shutting down operations in Frederiction.

Not exactly the good old days, is it?

DRAFT: (see chart) The Canadiens traded their first round pick to the Islanders in the Trevor Linden deal. Their first second round pick, Alexander Buturlin, was ranked number four on the European list of prospects, but *The Hockey News* had him ranked 31st overall. He's not very big, and he's not a great skater, but he's good with the puck, both passing and scoring. Hard to tell by the fact that he only had one goal for the Russian team, but he didn't get a lot of ice time.

PROGNOSIS: Montreal will probably miss the playoffs for the second year in a row, which will be the first time since the early 1920's. But, if you believe in the mystique of the Canadiens, it's not out of the realm of possibility that they will somehow turn it around and have a great season.

Doubt it.

DRAFT

Player	Pos	Rnd	Sel.	Cntry	Team	Lge	Gms	G	A	P	PIM
Alexander Buturlin	LW	2	39	Rus	CSKA Jr.	Rus	16	1	0	1	6
Matt Carkner	D	2	58	Can	Peterborough	OHL	60	2	16	18	173
Chris Dyment	D	4	97	USA	Boston U.	H.E.	22	1	4	5	16
Evan Lindsay	G	4	107	Can	Prince Albert	WHL	2.84				
Dustin Jamieson	LW	5	136	Can	Sarnia	OHL	66	16	28	44	10
M-A Thinel	RW	5	145	Can	Victoriaville	QMJHL	66	45	58	103	16
Matt Shasby	D	5	150	USA	Des Moines	USHL	49	4	22	26	34
Sean Dixon	D	6	167	Can	Erie	OHL	55	2	12	14	57
Vadim Tarasov	G	7	196	Rus	Novokuznetsk	Rus	1.43				
Mikko Hyytia	C	8	225	Fin	Jyvaskyla	Fin	12	2	7	9	4
Jerome Marois	LW	9	253	Can	Quebec	QMJHL	52	8	15	23	48

STAT SECTION

PLAYER	GP	G	A	PTS	+/-	PIM	PP	SH	GW	GT	S	PCTG
SAKU KOIVU	65	14	30	44	7-	38	4	2	0	0	145	9.7
MARTIN RUCINSKY	73	17	17	34	25-	50	5	0	1	0	180	9.4
V. MALAKHOV	62	13	21	34	7-	77	8	0	3	0	143	9.1
SHAYNE CORSON	63	12	20	32	10-	147	7	0	4	0	142	8.5
BENOIT BRUNET	60	14	17	31	1-	31	4	2	0	0	115	12.2
T. STEVENSON	69	10	17	27	6	88	0	0	2	1	102	9.8
S. QUINTAL	82	8	19	27	23-	84	1	1	4	0	159	5.0
BRIAN SAVAGE	54	16	10	26	14-	20	5	0	4	1	124	12.9
PATRICK POULIN	81	8	17	25	6	21	0	1	1	0	87	9.2
SERGEI ZHOLTOK	70	7	15	22	12-	6	2	0	3	0	102	6.9
ERIC WEINRICH	80	7	15	22	25-	89	4	0	1	1	119	5.9
JONAS HOGLUND	74	8	10	18	5-	16	1	0	0	1	122	6.6
DAINIUS ZUBRUS	80	6	10	16	8-	29	0	1	1	0	80	7.5
JASON DAWE	59	6	8	14	0	22	1	0	1	0	81	7.4
PATRICE BRISEBOIS	54	3	9	12	8-	28	1	0	1	0	90	3.3
IGOR ULANOV	76	3	9	12	3-	109	0	0	0	0	55	5.5
SCOTT THORNTON	47	7	4	11	2-	87	1	0	1	1	56	12.5
SCOTT LACHANCE	76	2	9	11	21-	41	1	0	0	0	59	3.4
CRAIG RIVET	66	2	8	10	3-	66	0	0	0	0	39	5.1
BRETT CLARK	61	2	2	4	3-	16	0	0	0	0	36	5.6
ERIC HOUDE	8	1	1	2	2-	2	0	0	1	0	4	25.0
MATT HIGGINS	25	1	0	1	2-	0	0	0	0	0	12	8.3
MILOSLAV GUREN	12	0	1	1	1-	4	0	0	0	0	11	.0
JEFF HACKETT	63	0	1	1	0	12	0	0	0	0	0	.0
TERRY RYAN	1	0	0	0	0	5	0	0	0	0	0	.0
JONATHAN DELISLE	1	0	0	0	0	0	0	0	0	0	0	.0
SYLVAIN BLOUIN	5	0	0	0	0	19	0	0	0	0	1	.0
J-FRANCOIS JOMPHE	7	0	0	0	0	2	0	0	0	0	4	.0
ARRON ASHAM	7	0	0	0	4-	0	0	0	0	0	5	.0
DAVE MORISSETTE	10	0	0	0	1	52	0	0	0	0	2	.0
ANDREI BASHKIROV	10	0	0	0	3-	0	0	0	0	0	4	.0
FREDERIC CHABOT	11	0	0	0	0	2	0	0	0	0	0	.0
ALAIN NASREDDINE	15	0	0	0	1-	52	0	0	0	0	3	.0
JOSE THEODORE	18	0	0	0	0	0	0	0	0	0	0	.0
TRENT MCCLEARY	46	0	0	0	1-	29	0	0	0	0	18	.0

TEAM RANKINGS

		Conference Rank	League Rank
Record	32-39-11	11	19
Home	21-15-5	8	13
Away	11-24-6	13	24
Versus Own Conference	21-28-7	12	21
Versus Other Conference	11-11-4	8	14
Team Plus\Minus	-31	11	22
Goals For	184	13	26
Goals Against	209	7	13
Average Shots For	27.5	8	17
Average Shots Against	26.6	6	8
Overtime	0-4-11	13	26
One Goal Games	13-15	9	16
Times outshooting opponent	38	6	12
Versus Teams Over .500	14-27-6	11	20
Versus Teams .500 or under	18-12-5	10	16
First Half Record	15-19-7	11	18
Second Half Record	17-20-4	9	18

MISCELLANEOUS STAT LEADERS

FACEOFFS

Thornton	53.0%
Koivu	52.6%
Zholtok	45.1%
McClearly	45.0%

ICE TIME

Weinrich	23:56
Malakhov	23:29
Brisebois	22:26
Quintal	22:06
Lachance	21:46
Corson	20:43
Koivu	20:02

HITS

Quintal	142
Ulanov	136
Weinrich	127
Zholtok	92

PLAYOFFS

- did not make the playoffs.

New Jersey Devils

Seems there's a panic in New Jersey about their lack of recent playoff success.

They won the Stanley Cup in 1995, in the labour shortened season. The following year they missed the playoffs. In 1997, they lost in the second round. In 1998 and 1999, they lost in the first round.

They weren't the only 100-point team to lose in the first round this year. Ottawa also got knocked off. Ironically, the year before, New Jersey also were a 100-point team and got knocked off by Ottawa.

Four times, since the one versus eight conference setup began in 1994, has the top seed been knocked off by the bottom seed. It's happened to New Jersey each of the last two seasons.

So, let's look at the possible explanations.

They play too defensive a system, so they can't turn it on when they get in trouble. Well, no, that couldn't be it, because new coach Robbie Ftorek opened up the offense, and the Devils were the second highest scoring team during the regular season.

They're a team built for the regular season. That's something they used to say about the Washington Capitals, which had a great regular season followed by a playoff disappointment. The difference is the Capitals never won the Stanley Cup.

No star player to step up and dominate. Sure, it would be good to have that type of player who raises his level of play in the playoffs and carries the team. Oddly enough, Buffalo didn't have one of those types, outside of their net, and they made it to the finals. Balance isn't usually considered a negative trait for a team, so this excuse is a reach.

Lack of leadership. We don't know what goes on in the dressing room, but Scott Stevens is considered a decent leader, despite an incident here or there, including some silly ones, such as being criticized for being the only one to miss an optional skate during the playoffs. And the Devils had Doug Gilmour in 1998, when they also got knocked off early.

Too many Europeans. Four of the forwards on the top two lines were Europeans, but four of top five playoff scorers were European. Sometimes their playoff intensity has been questioned, but hard to see it in this case.

The breaks. Well, the Devils had a 3-2 lead on the Penguins this year, and lost the sixth game in overtime. If they had scored, instead of

Jaromir Jagr, then we'd have to scratch off reasons one through five.

STUFF: The Devils recorded a team record 57 shots in a game against the Islanders, but still lost 4-2.

Ken Sutton's goal last season was his first in the NHL since the 1994-95 season.
The last six times the Devils have been involved in a seventh game playoff series, they've lost five of them.

Brian Rolston set a team record with five short-handed goals and tied him for the league lead.

The Devils have a 14-game unbeaten streak versus the NY Rangers, going back to the 1996-97 season.

TEAM PREVIEW

GOAL: Martin Brodeur had his usual stellar season statistically, and Chris Terreri seems to be a more than capable backup.

No problem at all at this position, although the Devils focus on offense meant less protection for the goalies and some shaky moments.

Brodeur has always had a decent defensive team in front of him. While he has to be considered one of the best in the game, wouldn't it be curious to find out how well he did in Tampa Bay's net.

DEFENSE: Few teams have the perfect balance on the blueline that the Devils can boast. Few teams even keep their defensive unit together as long as the Devils do.

Scott Niedermayer is one of the premier offensive players in the game, and probably under rated defensively, where he puts his speed to good use.

Scott Stevens and Ken Daneyko are getting up in years but are still effective. Any team in the league would like to have them.

Daneyko has played 992 games, and while the list of those who have played 1,000 games in the NHL is fairly extensive now, the list of those who have done it all with one team, is not. Only 17 players have accomplished that feat, with Daneyko set to become number 18 this season.

Alex Delvecchio	Detroit	1,549
Ray Bourque	Boston	1,453 *
Henri Richard	Montreal	1,256
Gilbert Perreault	Buffalo	1,191
George Armstrong	Toronto	1,187
Steve Yzerman	Detroit	1,178 *
Bob Gainey	Montreal	1,160
Bobby Clarke	Philadelphia	1,144
Jean Beliveau	Montreal	1,125
Dave Taylor	Los Angeles	1,111
Craig Ramsay	Buffalo	1,070
Rod Gilbert	NY Rangers	1,065
Denis Potvin	NY Islanders	1,060
Ron Ellis	Toronto	1,034
Wayne Cashman	Boston	1.027
Bob Murray	Chicago	1,008
Claude Provost	Montreal	1,005
* still active		

GOALTENDER	GPI	MINS	AVG	W	L	T	EN	SO	GA	SA	SV %
M. BRODEUR	70	4,239	2.29	39	21	10	4	4	162	1,728	.906
CHRIS TERRERI	12	726	2.48	8	3	1	0	1	30	294	.898
N.J TOTALS	82	4,986	2.36	47	24	11	4	5	196	2,026	.903

One interesting thing about that list is that four of the 17 are currently General Managers in the NHL. Bob Gainey is GM in Dallas, but Bob Clarke, Bob Murray and Dave Taylor are with their same teams.

Also on the blueline for the Devils will be Lyle Odelein, Sheldon Souray, and Brad Bombadir. Ken Sutton is insurance for injuries and Colin White looks as if he's ready to step into the lineup. He's a big stay-at-home tough guy who had 265 penalty minutes with Albany last year.

FORWARD: It's doubtful that there's any team in the league that has the balance of the Devils forward lines. The argument against that is that they don't have one dominating type ìgo-toî player. It is, however, easier for opponents to shut down one player than six.

In fact, no team could even possibly do what the Devils did, which was make their second line their first line and their first line their second.

Jason Arnott made a comeback last year and finished the season centring the Devils number one line with Patrik Elias and Petr Sykora.

Bobby Holik, who has a habit of fading each season, was the number one centre earlier in the season, but finished between Sergei Brylin and Randy McKay. Brylin, who did almost nothing all season had a good playoff, which undoubtedly saved his bacon.

With veteran winger Dave Andreychuk and centre Bob Carpenter no longer in the fold, due to free agency and the fact that the Devils didn't want them anymore.

Brendan Morrison got off to a slow start and had a hard time meeting expectations, but came on and finished second in rookie scoring in the league.

Brian Rolston is a streaky scorer, but an excellent penalty killer and particularly adept at scoring shorthanded goals, with five to his credit.

Jay Pandolfo came out of nowhere to be a big contributor early in the season before fading somewhat later.

Denis Pederson should finally get the opportunity to nail down the checking line centre position, rather than moving all over the place. That leaves Vadim Sharifijanov, tough-guy Krzysztof Oliwa, defensive forward Sergei Nemchinov, and reserve tough-guy Sasha Lakovic.

John Madden, a high scoring minor-league scorer, should also find regular duty this year.

SPECIAL TEAMS: For some reason, Devils games have the fewest power plays overall. That's for and against. And it's not just a one-season fluke, because it happened last year, too.

Just what does that mean? That they play a clean game and so do their opponents? That would be quite a coincidence. Part of one team not getting called a lot of penalties is that it makes the referee reluctant to call them on the other team, because lop-sided penalty calls tend to get criticized. Referees aren't as likely to ìeven it upî as they did in previous years, but there still has to be that element.

As far as why there are fewer penalties called in Devils games, the answer is quite simple. Don't know.

Power Play	G	ATT	PCT
Overall	58	300	19.3% (4th NHL)
Home	32	152	21.1% (5th NHL)
Road	26	148	17.6% (7th NHL)

5 SHORT HANDED GOALS ALLOWED (T-4th NHL)

Penalty Killing	G	TSH	PCT
Overall	47	320	85.3% (T-12th NHL)
Home	22	152	85.5% (T-15th NHL)
Road	25	168	85.1% (10th NHL)

6 SHORT HANDED GOALS SCORED (T-19th NHL)

Penalties	GP	MIN	AVG	
DEVILS	81	1335	16.5	(16th NHL)

DEVILS SPECIAL TEAMS SCORING

Power play	G	A	PTS
SYKORA	14	10	24
NIEDERMAYER	1	20	21
ARNOTT	8	11	19
MORRISON	5	13	18
ROLSTON	5	9	14
HOLIK	5	9	14
ELIAS	2	10	12
ODELEIN	1	11	12
ANDREYCHUK	4	4	8
MCKAY	3	4	7
PEDERSON	3	2	5
SHARIFIJANOV	1	4	5
BRYLIN	3	0	3
NEMCHINOV	2	0	2
PANDOLFO	1	1	2
DEAN	1	1	2
MADDEN	0	1	1
CARPENTER	0	1	1
BOMBARDIR	0	1	1

Short handed	G	A	PTS
ROLSTON	4	0	4
STEVENS	0	3	3
SHARIFIJANOV	0	2	2
PANDOLFO	1	0	1
NIEDERMAYER	1	0	1

COACHING AND MANAGEMENT: There was some speculation that Robbie Ftorek was outcoached in the opening round series against Pittsburgh. His player selection was questioned, as well as his inability to match lines.

The good news is that he made good on his pre-season promise to let the Devils play a more offensive game. He managed to do that and still keep the Devils a winner, so he can hardly be criticized.

Lou Lamoriello is maybe the prototypical general manager. Everybody should pattern themselves after him. He has a top team every year, and when players move on he has replacement parts ready because he's allowed them to develop on the farm team. Players within the system know if they work hard they will at least have a chance of making the big club. That's why some of them stay in the organization for years and years.

DRAFT: (see chart) The Devils surprised with their number one pick, goalie Ari Ahonen, partly because he wasn't rated as a first rounder, and partly because they're already loaded with goaltenders in their system, including 1997 first rounder J-F Damphousse. Besides that, Martin Brodeur doesn't appear to be going anywhere soon. As well, there's never been a successful Finnish goalie in the NHL.

PROGNOSIS: You never know what's going to happen in the playoffs so the best you can do is, first, make sure you're in them, and two, make sure you have an opportunity to win.

The Devils do that every year, so as much as anyone they have a chance to go on to win the whole thing.

DRAFT

Player	Pos	Rnd	Sel.	Cntry	Team	Lge	Gms	G	A	P	PIM
Ari Ahonen	G	1	27	Fin	Jyvaskyla	Fin	2.90				
Mike Commodore	D	2	42	Can	N.Dakota	WCHA	32	4	7	11	126
Brett Clouthier	LW	2	50	Can	Kingston	OHL	64	8	14	22	227
Andre Lakos	D	3	95	Can	Barrie	OHL	62	4	23	27	40
Teemu Kesa	D	4	100	Fin	Ilves Jr.	Fin	25	4	4	8	129
Scott Cameron	C	6	185	Can	Barrie	OHL	66	10	32	42	14
Chris Hartsburg	F	7	214	USA	Colorado	WCHA	28	6	3	9	56
Justin Dziama	RW	8	242	USA	Nobles Prep	US HS	27	20	17	37	20

STAT SECTION

PLAYER	GP	G	A	PTS	+/-	PIM	PP	SH	GW	GT	S	PCTG
PETR SYKORA	80	29	43	72	16	22	15	0	7	0	222	13.1
BOBBY HOLIK	78	27	37	64	16	119	5	0	8	0	253	10.7
BRIAN ROLSTON	82	24	33	57	11	14	5	5	3	0	210	11.4
JASON ARNOTT	74	27	27	54	10	79	8	0	3	1	200	13.5
PATRIK ELIAS	74	17	33	50	19	34	3	0	2	0	157	10.8
B. MORRISON	76	13	33	46	4-	18	5	0	2	0	111	11.7
S. NIEDERMAYER	72	11	35	46	16	26	1	1	3	0	161	6.8
RANDY MCKAY	70	17	20	37	10	143	3	0	5	0	136	12.5
LYLE ODELEIN	70	5	26	31	6	114	1	0	0	1	101	5.0
DAVE ANDREYCHUK	52	15	13	28	1	20	4	0	3	1	110	13.6
JAY PANDOLFO	70	14	13	27	3	10	1	1	4	0	100	14.0
V. SHARIFIJANOV	53	11	16	27	11	28	1	0	2	0	71	15.5
SCOTT STEVENS	75	5	22	27	29	64	0	0	1	0	111	4.5
DENIS PEDERSON	76	11	12	23	10-	66	3	0	1	0	145	7.6
S. NEMCHINOV	77	12	8	20	13-	28	2	0	1	0	74	16.2
SERGEI BRYLIN	47	5	10	15	8	28	3	0	1	0	51	9.8
KRZYSZTOF OLIWA	64	5	7	12	4	240	0	0	1	0	59	8.5
KEN DANEYKO	82	2	9	11	27	63	0	0	0	0	63	3.2
KEVIN DEAN	62	1	10	11	4	22	1	0	0	0	51	2.0
BOB CARPENTER	56	2	8	10	3-	36	0	0	0	0	69	2.9
BRAD BOMBARDIR	56	1	7	8	4-	16	0	0	0	0	47	2.1
SHELDON SOURAY	70	1	7	8	5	110	0	0	0	0	101	1.0
MARTIN BRODEUR	70	0	4	4	0	4	0	0	0	0	0	.0
SASHA LAKOVIC	16	0	3	3	0	59	0	0	0	0	10	.0
KEN SUTTON	5	1	0	1	1	0	0	0	0	0	5	20.0

JOHN MADDEN	4	0	1	1	2-	0	0	0	0	0	4	.0
CHRIS TERRERI	12	0	1	1	0	0	0	0	0	0	0	.0
SCOTT DANIELS	1	0	0	0	0	0	0	0	0	0	0	.0

TEAM RANKINGS

		Conference Rank	League Rank
Record	47-24-11	1	2
Home	19-14-8	9	14
Away	28-10-3	1	1
Versus Own Conference	35-15-8	1	2
Versus Other Conference	12-9-3	5	7
Team Plus\Minus	+39	3	3
Goals For	248	2	2
Goals Against	196	4	6
Average Shots For	30.8	1	2
Average Shots Against	24.4	2	4
Overtime	3-1-11	3	5
One Goal Games	17.9	2	3
Times outshooting opponent	61	2	2
Versus Teams Over .500	25-12-5	1	1
Versus Teams .500 or under	22-12-6	6	10
First Half Record	23-13-5	2	4
Second Half Record	24-11-6	1	2

MISCELLEANOUS STAT LEADERS
FACEOFFS

Holik	53.6%
Carpenter	51.4%
Morrison	51.1%
Arnott	49.3%
Pederson	42.8%

ICE TIME

Niedermayer	24:40
Stevens	24:11
Daneyko	20:04
Odelein	19:53
Rolston	18:49

HITS

Holik	217
Arnott	196
Daneyko	182
McKay	124
Oliwa	117
Souray	109
Pederson	105
Pandolfo	103

PLAYOFFS

Results:
Lost 4-3 in conference quarter-finals to Pittsburgh

Record: 3-4
Home: 2-2
Away: 1-2
Goals For: 18 (2.6)
Goals Against: 21 (3.0)
Overtime: 0-1
Power play: 18.5 (4th)
Penalty Killing: 84.6% (7th)

PLAYER	GP	G	A	PTS	+/-	PIM	PP	SH	GW	OT	S	PCTG
BOBBY HOLIK	7	0	7	7	1-	6	0	0	0	0	21	.0
PETR SYKORA	7	3	3	6	3-	4	0	0	1	0	12	25.0
RANDY MCKAY	7	3	2	5	1	2	0	0	1	0	16	18.8
PATRIK ELIAS	7	0	5	5	0	6	0	0	0	0	14	.0
SERGEI BRYLIN	5	3	1	4	2	4	1	0	1	0	12	25.0
JASON ARNOTT	7	2	2	4	3-	4	1	0	0	0	12	16.7
SCOTT NIEDERMAYER	7	1	3	4	5-	18	1	0	0	0	13	7.7
SCOTT STEVENS	7	2	1	3	2-	10	2	0	0	0	14	14.3
LYLE ODELEIN	7	0	3	3	1-	10	0	0	0	0	12	.0
DAVE ANDREYCHUK	4	2	0	2	0	4	0	0	0	0	7	28.6
MARTIN BRODEUR	7	0	2	2	0	2	0	0	0	0	0	.0
BRENDAN MORRISON	7	0	2	2	1-	0	0	0	0	0	10	.0
BRIAN ROLSTON	7	1	0	1	1-	2	0	1	0	0	15	6.7
JAY PANDOLFO	7	1	0	1	5-	0	0	0	0	0	10	10.0
SHELDON SOURAY	2	0	1	1	1	0	0	0	0	0	0	.0
DENIS PEDERSON	3	0	1	1	0	0	0	0	0	0	3	.0
KRZYSZTOF OLIWA	1	0	0	0	0	2	0	0	0	0	0	.0
SERGEI NEMCHINOV	4	0	0	0	2-	0	0	0	0	0	2	.0
VADIM SHARIFIJANOV	4	0	0	0	0	0	0	0	0	0	3	.0
BRAD BOMBARDIR	5	0	0	0	0	0	0	0	0	0	2	.0
BOB CARPENTER	7	0	0	0	1-	2	0	0	0	0	7	.0
KEN DANEYKO	7	0	0	0	3	8	0	0	0	0	5	.0
KEVIN DEAN	7	0	0	0	4-	0	0	0	0	0	7	.0

GOALTENDER	GPI	MINS	AVG	W	L	T	EN	SO	GA	SA	SV %
MARTIN BRODEUR	7	425	2.82	3	4	1	0	0	20	139	.856
N.J TOTALS	7	429	2.94	3	4	1	0	0	21	140	.850

New York Islanders

It could be a record breaking season for the Islanders. For losing records, that is.

Not even in their wildest dreams could they hope to be anything better than perhaps the expansion Atlanta Thrashers. They were one of the worst teams last year, and dumped off their top three scorers, including Ziggy Palffy.

What kind of records are they looking at? All the records below are for a minimum 70-game schedule.

Fewest Wins in a Season:

8	Washington	1974-75
9	Winnipeg	1980-81
10	Ottawa	1992-93

Most Losses in a Season:

71	San Jose	1992-93
70	Ottawa	1992-93
67	Washington	1974-75

Longest Losing Streak:

17	Washington	1974-75
17	San Jose	1992-93

Longest Winless Streak:

30	Winnipeg	1980-81

27	Kansas City	1975-76
25	Washington	1975-76

Fewest Goals

133	Chicago	1953-54
147	Toronto	1954-55
147	Boston	1954-55

Naturally, all this losing business has to do with their financial problems and budget restraints. The one thing you can say in their favor is that they're stockpiling young talent in the hopes that things are better in a few years when that talent has matured.

STUFF: The Islanders became just the second team in NHL history to have four picks in the first round.

TEAM PREVIEW

GOAL: The Islanders must have had second thoughts about getting Felix Potvin last season, after watching him flounder around in most of the games he played. He even made Tommy Salo look good.

There's not much point in paying Potvin's hefty salary, anyway, because Dominik Hasek

GOALTENDER	GPI	MINS	AVG	W	L	.T	EN	SO	GA	SA	SV %
TOMMY SALO	51	3,018	2.62	17	26	7	5	5	132	1,368	.904
M. COUSINEAU	6	293	2.87	0	4	0	0	0	14	119	.882
WADE FLAHERTY	20	1,048	3.03	5	11	2	3	0	53	491	.892
FELIX POTVIN	11	606	3.66	2	7	1	0	0	37	345	.893
NYI TOTALS	82	4,990	2.93	24	48	10	8	5	244	2,331	.895

himself couldn't save this team. They may even trade him, maybe when another team is desperate for a goalie.

The Islanders still have Roberto Luongo, the next goalie superstar, but do they want to throw him to the wolves and ruin any confidence he has. Maybe.

DEFENSE: There's some legitmate NHL defensemen here, if you look hard enough. Well, there's Kenny Jonson, but he's rather fragile and can't be counted on for a full season.

Well, Zdeno Chara figures to be a regular along with Eric Brewer and Richard Pilon, although Pilon is in some trade rumors, because he makes too much money.

Vladimir Chebaturkin is also expected to be a regular, and Jamie Heward was signed as a free agent to help on the power play, despite the fact that the expansion Nashville Predators no longer had any interest in him.

The Islanders think that draft choice Bratislav Mezei also has a chance to make the team.

Eric Cairns, another big guy, should be in the mix somewhere, too. The same with Ray Shultz and Evgeny Korolev.

All in all, it's pitiful and opposing teams should have a field day padding their scoring stats.

FORWARD: The Islanders forwards are so bad that Gino Odjick has a chance to be the leading scorer. That may be stretching things, because he'll probably get traded anyway

The first line is laughable. That's because it's a fourth line. In fact, they're all third or fourth liners.

That's not to say that Olli Jokkinen or Jason Krog doesn't have a future in the NHL, but neither would be vying for the number one centre spot on any other team in the NHL, or even some minor league teams.

Mariusz Czercawski would have to battle for the fourth line on a lot of teams, and Dimitri Nabokov hasn't shown a thing yet, except that he's not worthy of playing in the NHL yet.

Claude Lapointe is actually quite a valuable player for a decent team's third line, but he's wasted in this mess. Odjick can count on being traded. Mark Lawrence wasn't sure if he was restricted or unrestricted agent, but did quite well as a 27-year-old in his first NHL season. Mats Lindgren is a good defensive centre. Steve Webb is a scrapper.

Throw in Vladimir Orsagh, Mike Watt, Josh Green, Brad Isbister, Chris Ferraro, and Jorgen Jonsson, and what you have is not much, unless it was in the IHL.

SPECIAL TEAMS: No reason to think the Islanders shouldn't have the worst power play in the league seeing as how they don't have any scorers. They do have some decent penalty killers, however, and should be better than 18th.

One thing they can count is referees not calling many penalties against them because they feel sorry for them.

Power Play	G	ATT	PCT
Overall	52	338	15.4% (13th NHL)
Home	34	176	19.3% (7th NHL)
Road	18	162	11.1% (T-24th NHL)

7 SHORT HANDED GOALS ALLOWED (T-9th NHL)

Penalty Killing	G	TSH	PCT
Overall	59	357	83.5% (18th NHL)
Home	25	168	85.1% (18th NHL)
Road	34	189	82.0% (20th NHL)

6 SHORT HANDED GOALS SCORED (T-17th NHL)

Penalties	GP	MIN	AVG
ISLANDERS	81	1097	13.5 (7th NHL)

ISLANDERS SPECIAL TEAMS SCORING

Power play	G	A	PTS
LINDEN	8	12	20
JONSSON	6	11	17
SMOLINSKI	7	7	14
PALFFY	4	9	13
JANNEY	2	11	13
CZERKAWSKI	4	5	9
LAWRENCE	4	4	8
RICHTER	0	7	7
BREWER	2	3	5
LAPOINTE	2	2	4
LINDGREN	2	1	3
CROWLEY	1	2	3
ODJICK	1	1	2
WATT	0	1	1

Short handed	G	A	PTS
LAPOINTE	2	2	4
LINDEN	1	2	3
LINDGREN	1	1	2
SACCO	1	0	1
CHARA	1	0	1
JONSSON	0	1	1

COACHING AND MANAGEMENT: Butch Goring is the new coach. Good luck to him.

Mike Milbury is the GM. Good luck to him, too.

DRAFT: (see chart) Quite a draft for the Islanders. Tim Connolly is said to be the complete package. He can skate, shoot, stickhandle and score.

Taylor Pyatt is a terrific skater, and tough, someone the Islanders think could be an excellent power forward. Branislav Mezei is given a good chance to make the team right away. The huge Slovak is mobile, hits, and has a boomer shot.

Kristian Kudroc is yet another big Slovakian defenseman.

PROGNOSIS: There's a possibility the Islanders could finish better than the expansion Thrashers, but it's not a certainty because the Islanders are no better than an expansion team.

In two years the next NHL superstar will be available for the draft. Jason Spezza will play for the Mississauga Ice Dogs in the OHL this year. If the Islanders can manage to stay lousy for two more years it will increase their chances of getting him.

DRAFT

Player	Pos	Rnd	Sel.	Cntry	Team	Lge	Gms	G	A	P	PIM
Tim Connolly	C	1	5	USA	Erie	OHL	46	34	34	68	50
Taylor Pyatt	LW	1	8	Can	Sudbury	OHL	68	37	38	75	95
Branislav Mezei	D	1	10	Slo	Belleville	OHL	60	5	18	23	90
Kristian Kudroc	D	1	28	Slo	Michalovce	Slov	41	11	23	34	68
Mattias Weinhandl	RW	3	78	Swe	Modo	Swe	28	18	15	33	18
Brian Collins	C	3	87	USA	St. John's	US HS	28	38	35	73	30
Juraj Kolnik	RW	4	101	Slo	Rimouski	QMJHL	62	42	42	84	40
Johan Halvardsson	D	4	102	Swe	HV 71	Swe	17	1	2	3	33
Justin Mapletoft	C	5	130	Can	Red Deer	WHL	72	24	22	46	81
Adam Johnson	D	5	140	USA	Greenway	US HS	17	5	13	18	32
Bjorn Melin	RW	6	163	Swe	HV 71	Swe					
Radek Martinek	W	8	228	Cze	Ceske-	Cze	52	12	13	25	50
Brett Henning	C	9	255	USA	Notre Dame	CCHA	35	4	6	10	28
Tyler Scott	D	9	268	Can	Upper Canada Col.						

STAT SECTION

PLAYER	GP	G	A	PTS	+/-	PIM	PP	SH	GW	GT	S	PCTG
ZIGMUND PALFFY	50	22	28	50	6-	34	5	2	1	0	168	13.1
TREVOR LINDEN	82	18	29	47	14-	32	8	1	1	0	167	10.8
BRYAN SMOLINSKI	82	16	24	40	7-	49	7	0	3	0	223	7.2
M. CZERKAWSKI	78	21	17	38	10-	14	4	0	1	2	205	10.2
CLAUDE LAPOINTE	82	14	23	37	19-	62	2	2	1	0	134	10.4
MARK LAWRENCE	60	14	16	30	8-	38	4	0	2	1	88	15.9
CRAIG JANNEY	56	5	22	27	15-	14	2	0	0	1	45	11.1
KENNY JONSSON	63	8	18	26	18-	34	6	0	0	0	91	8.8
MATS LINDGREN	60	10	15	25	6	24	3	1	1	0	83	12.0
MIKE WATT	75	8	17	25	2-	12	0	0	4	0	75	10.7
BARRY RICHTER	72	6	18	24	4-	34	0	0	2	0	111	5.4
ERIC BREWER	63	5	6	11	14-	32	2	0	0	0	63	7.9
ZDENO CHARA	59	2	6	8	8-	83	0	1	0	0	56	3.6
DAVID HARLOCK	70	2	6	8	16-	68	0	0	0	0	35	5.7
GINO ODJICK	23	4	3	7	2-	133	1	0	2	0	28	14.3
KEVIN MILLER	33	1	5	6	5-	13	0	0	0	0	37	2.7
RICHARD PILON	52	0	4	4	8-	88	0	0	0	0	27	.0
JOE SACCO	73	3	0	3	24-	45	0	1	2	0	84	3.6
TED CROWLEY	13	1	2	3	1-	2	1	0	0	0	20	5.0

ERIC CAIRNS	9	0	3	3	1	23	0	0	0	0	2	.0
DMITRI NABOKOV	4	0	2	2	4	2	0	0	0	0	4	.0
VLADIMIR ORSAGH	12	1	0	1	2	6	0	0	0	0	5	20.0
DEAN MALKOC	2	0	1	1	3	7	0	0	0	0	1	.0
MIKE KENNEDY	1	0	0	0	0	2	0	0	0	0	0	.0
RAY SCHULTZ	4	0	0	0	2-	7	0	0	0	0	2	.0
MARCEL COUSINEAU	6	0	0	0	0	0	0	0	0	0	0	.0
VLAD CHEBATURKIN	8	0	0	0	6	12	0	0	0	0	4	.0
MIKE HOUGH	11	0	0	0	2-	2	0	0	0	0	4	.0
WARREN LUHNING	11	0	0	0	4-	8	0	0	0	0	11	.0
FELIX POTVIN	16	0	0	0	0	0	0	0	0	0	0	.0
WADE FLAHERTY	20	0	0	0	0	4	0	0	0	0	0	.0
STEVE WEBB	45	0	0	0	10-	32	0	0	0	0	18	.0

TEAM RANKINGS

		Conference Rank	League Rank
Record	24-48-10	11	25
Home	11-23-7	13	26
Away	13-25-3	12	22
Versus Own Conference	17-37-4	13	26
Versus Other Conference	7-11-6	12	22
Team Plus\Minus	-44	13	25
Goals For	194	12	22
Goals Against	244	13	23
Average Shots For	26.0	10	20
Average Shots Against	28.1	8	14
Overtime	1-6-10	14	27
One Goal Games	8-23	14	27
Times outshooting opponent	32	10	19
Versus Teams Over .500	12-27-6	13	24
Versus Teams .500 or under	12-21-4	13	25
First Half Record	12-26-3	13	26
Second Half Record	12-22-7	13	24

MISCELLANOUS STAT LEADERS

FACEOFFS

Lapointe	56.6%
Linden	50.2%
Janney	49.1%
Miller	49.1%
Lindgren	48.9%

ICE TIME

Jonsson	24:59
Palffy	22:04
Linden	21:19
Richter	21:08

HITS

Chara	214
Harlock	172
Lapointe	168
Pilon	155
Linden	144
Smolinski	105

PLAYOFFS

- did not make the playoffs.

New York Rangers

It appears the Rangers have gone out and bought themselves a shot at the Stanley Cup. But, it's not all Guns 'N Roses.

A team can't miss the playoffs one year and then come right back the next and win it all. Wait on that. Actually, they can. In fact, it's been done five times, the most recent by none other than the NY Rangers.

From Missing Playoffs to Winning Stanley Cup:

NY Rangers	1994
Pittsburgh	1991
Montreal	1971
Toronto	1947
Detroit	1936

It's not as easy to do as when there were just six teams in the league, but with free agency now, it's well within the realm of possibility.

The last time the Rangers did it, there wasn't such a large turnover in personnel from the year before. In fact, they traded away two of their top three goal scorers, including Mike Gartner and Tony Amonte during their Stanley Cup winning season. Mike Richter became the full-time number one with John Vanbiesbrouck traded away.

Oh yes, and they obtained Stephane Matteau, which was the key to their victory. Matteau? Well, yes, you see, he was a favorite of coach Mike Keenan, and usually went where he went. So, in reality, Keenan was why they won. And he was only there for that one season.

But, there are so many new faces on the Rangers that their problem won't be talent, especially during the regular season, but will probably be chemistry. Sometimes, as we've seen with Keenan, that chemistry can be developed through a mutual hate for the coach.

Stanley Cup winners usually are unified in their goal and want to win it not just for themselves, but each other. That kind of togetherness doesn't happen overnight. Plus, what the Rangers have are a bunch of content hockey players armed with great contracts. They may or may not act like fat cats, but that hunger to make the necessary sacrifices to win it all might not be there in the playoffs.

Oh, they can win plenty during the regular season, and foster a lot of hope for their Stanley Cup winning potential, but it's not going to happen.

STUFF: Back-to-back shutouts for Mike Richter were the first by the Rangers since 1977.

TEAM PREVIEW

GOAL: There's nothing wrong with pinning your hopes on Mike Richter. Thirty-three isn't all that old for a goaltender. But, they might miss Dan Cloutier, considered by many to be the best non number one goalie in the league. Cloutier was traded to Tampa Bay along with Niklas Sundstrom and their first and third round picks next year for Tampa Bay's fourth overall pick this year, where they wre able to select Pavel Brendl.

Kirk McLean was signed as the backup and he's been through the ringer in recent years. At this stage of his career, being an occasional starter might work out well for him and the Rangers.

DEFENSE: The Rangers lost Jeff Beukeboom to retirement, and Chris Tamer in the expansion draft. But, they went out and picked up better than average replacements on the free agent market in Stephane Quintal, last of Montreal, and Sylvain Lefebvre, last of Colorado.

Either one would be a good fit with Brian Leetch, allowing the offensive-minded defenseman to concentrate more on offense, while not giving up anything defensively.

The same can be said for the team's other offensive threat, Mathieu Schneider. Two offensive-types paired with two solid defensive types is not a bad way to go.

If they're the top four, then they better make sure they have some big tough guys also on the blueline. Roman Ndur and Jason Doig should fit that scenario fairly well.

Richard Johnsson is considered a good prospect, as is Burke Henry, and offensive-minded tough guy, which is a rarity.

FORWARD: The interesting thing here is trying to figure out the lines. The number one centre won't be difficult, with that Gretzky fella gone, and the number one right winger is easy, too.

There's talk about getting another veteran centre, along the lines of a Doug Gilmour, but with what we have to work with at the moment, they could line up like this.

Number One Line: Petr Nedved at centre and Theoren Fleury on the right side, which means they have to choose from Valeri Kamensky and Adam Graves for the left side. Probably Kemensky would be the best fit, taking into account the law of diminishing returns. Graves is more of a sniper, and they already have enough of those for one line.

Second Line: If they moved Todd Harvey back to centre, he could be between Graves and John MacLean to give them a solid number two scoring line. Graves (38) and MacLean (28) were the two top goal scorers on the Rangers last year.

Third Line: There's some talk of a Kid Line, with Manny Maholtra between rookies Jan Havlat and Pavel Brendl. Havlat is a great prospect acquired from Calgary, while Brendl was the fourth overall selection in the draft. Both are considered

GOALTENDER	GPI	MINS	AVG	W	L	T	EN	SO	GA	SA	SV %
MIKE RICHTER	68	3,878	2.63	27	30	8	6	4	178	898	.910
DAN CLOUTIER	22	1,097	2.68	6	8	3	2	0	49	570	.914
NYR TOTALS	82	4,996	2.73	33	38	11	8	4	227	2,476	.908

NHL ready, and both are expected to fill the net.

Fourth Line: If this is a checking line, then free agent Tim Taylor will centre it. Kevin Stevens, Eric Lacroix and Mark Knuble still have to be fitted in somewhere. And prospect Michael York, from Michigan State will be given a good look during training camp.

This is not going to be a very good defensive forward unit, so they're going to have to score lots of goals. They appear more than capable of doing just that.

SPECIAL TEAMS: The retirement of Wayne Gretzky might affect their ranking, cause who can pass the puck better than he? Adam Graves is the perfect power play sniper, but somebody has to get him the puck. Brian Leetch is one of the best in the business on the point, and Schneider fits there, as well. They may not be the second best in the league, but they should be good.

Power Play	G	ATT	PCT
Overall	71	348	20.4% (2nd NHL)
Home	36	195	18.5% (9th NHL)
Road	35	153	22.9% (1st NHL)
9 SHORT HANDED GOALS ALLOWED (T-15th NHL)			

Penalty Killing	G	TSH	PCT
Overall	48	336	85.7% (10th NHL)
Home	19	180	89.4% (2nd NHL)
Road	29	156	81.4% (21st NHL)
7 SHORT HANDED GOALS SCORED (T-15th NHL)			

Penalties	GP	MIN	AVG
RANGERS	82	1087	13.3 (4th NHL)

RANGERS SPECIAL TEAMS SCORING

Power play	G	A	PTS
GRETZKY	3	27	30
LEETCH	4	25	29
GRAVES	14	6	20
SCHNEIDER	5	15	20
SAVARD	4	15	19
MACLEAN	11	7	18
NEDVED	9	7	16
STEVENS	8	6	14
HARVEY	6	8	14
KNUBLE	3	6	9
SUNDSTROM	1	3	4
BRENNAN	0	3	3
MANELUK	1	1	2
FRASER	1	1	2
MALHOTRA	1	0	1
MERTZIG	0	1	1
LACROIX	0	1	1

Short handed	G	A	PTS
GRAVES	2	1	3
MACLEAN	1	2	3
SUNDSTROM	2	0	2
FEDYK	1	1	2
BEUKEBOOM	0	2	2
NEDVED	1	0	1

COACHING AND MANAGEMENT: GM Neil Smith pulled off some draft day deals to put this team in position to be a contender right away again. Mostly, though, he used his big wallet to sign every decent free agent available. They don't wait around for rebuilding years in New York and he's already rebuilt the team over the summer.

Coach John Muckler is the type who likes to go with his veterans. He's got plenty of them, but he will also have to play some youngsters this year. He's a deciple of the old Emonton Oilers firebrand hockey ways, and that appears to be the way the Rangers are going to play this year.

DRAFT: (see chart) Draft day moves paid off even better than GM Smith could have imagined. They picked up two of the premier players in the draft. Brendl should step right into the lineup after an incredible rookie season in the WHL, the first rookie to win its scoring title. The Rangers were fortunate that Lundmark slipped all the way down the number nine position, an unexpected treat. He will probably stay another year in junior, but with record speed in the Prospects skills competition, scoring and play-making ability, and even some toughness, he's a future star.

PROGNOSIS: Getting back into the playoffs is a given, but being successful in the playoffs isn't. There are a ton of new faces in the lineup, which can be a worry. Meshing them together into a cohesive unit will take time, if it happens at all.

The Rangers are back in the playoffs, but anything after that is up in the air.

DRAFT

Player	Pos	Rnd	Sel.	Cntry	Team	Lge	Gms	G	A	P	PIM
Pavel Brendl	RW	1	4	Cze	Calgary	WHL	68	73	61	134	40
Jamie Lundmark	C	1	9	Can	Moose Jaw	WHL	70	40	51	91	121
David Inman	C	2	59	USA	Notre Dame	CCHA	35	10	10	20	72
Johan Asplund	G	3	79	Swe	Brynas Gavle	Swe	2.90				
Patrick Autiero	C	3	90	USA	Boston U.	H.E.	19	2	1	3	12
Garett Bembridge	RW	5	137	Can	Saskatoon	WHL	68	23	27	50	30
Jay Dardis	C	6	177	USA	Proctor	US HS	26	23	36	59	32
Arto Laatkainen	D	7	197	Fin	Espoo	Fin	48	0	6	6	14
Evgeny Gusakov	LW	8	226	Rus	Togliatti	Rus	0	0	0	0	0
Peter Henning		9	252	Swe	Modo	Swe	1	0	0	0	0
Alexei Bulatov	LW	9	254	Rus	Yekateringburg Rus						

STAT SECTION

PLAYER	GP	G	A	PTS	+/-	PIM	PP	SH	GW	GT	S	PCTG
WAYNE GRETZKY	70	9	53	62	23-	14	3	0	3	1	132	6.8
JOHN MACLEAN	82	28	27	55	5	46	11	1	2	0	231	12.1
BRIAN LEETCH	82	13	42	55	7-	42	4	0	1	0	184	7.1
ADAM GRAVES	82	38	15	53	12-	47	14	2	7	0	239	15.9
PETR NEDVED	56	20	27	47	6-	50	9	1	3	0	153	13.1
MARC SAVARD	70	9	36	45	7-	38	4	0	1	0	116	7.8
KEVIN STEVENS	81	23	20	43	10-	64	8	0	3	0	136	16.9
N. SUNDSTROM	81	13	30	43	2-	20	1	2	3	0	89	14.6
MIKE KNUBLE	82	15	20	35	7-	26	3	0	1	0	113	13.3
M. SCHNEIDER	75	10	24	34	19-	71	5	0	2	0	159	6.3
TODD HARVEY	37	11	17	28	1-	72	6	0	2	1	58	19.0
MANNY MALHOTRA	73	8	8	16	2-	13	1	0	2	0	61	13.1
MIKE MANELUK	45	6	9	15	5	20	1	0	1	0	55	10.9
BRENT FEDYK	67	4	6	10	11-	30	0	1	0	0	47	8.5
JEFF BEUKEBOOM	45	0	9	9	2-	60	0	0	0	0	8	.0
SCOTT FRASER	28	2	4	6	12-	14	1	0	0	0	35	5.7
CHRIS TAMER	63	1	5	6	14-	124	0	0	1	0	48	2.1
PETER POPOVIC	68	1	4	5	12-	40	0	0	0	0	64	1.6
ERIC LACROIX	64	2	2	4	12-	18	0	0	1	0	38	5.3
RICHARD BRENNAN	24	1	3	4	4-	23	0	0	0	0	36	2.8
RUMUN NDUR	39	1	3	4	1-	62	0	0	0	0	22	4.5
ESA TIKKANEN	32	0	3	3	5-	38	0	0	0	0	25	.0
JAN MERTZIG	23	0	2	2	5-	8	0	0	0	0	10	.0
DEREK ARMSTRONG	3	0	0	0	0	0	0	0	0	0	1	.0
GEOFF SMITH	4	0	0	0	5-	2	0	0	0	0	0	.0
JOHAN WITEHALL	4	0	0	0	0	0	0	0	0	0	1	.0
P.J. STOCK	5	0	0	0	1-	6	0	0	0	0	0	.0
CHRISTIAN DUBE	6	0	0	0	0	0	0	0	0	0	0	.0
DAN CLOUTIER	22	0	0	0	0	2	0	0	0	0	0	.0
DARREN LANGDON	44	0	0	0	3-	80	0	0	0	0	8	.0
MIKE RICHTER	68	0	0	0	0	0	0	0	0	0	0	.0

TEAM RANKINGS

		Conference Rank	League Rank
Record	33-38-11	10	18
Home	17-19-5	11	20
Away	16-19-6	8	13
Versus Own Conference	21-28-9	11	20
Versus Other Conference	12-10-2	6	9
Team Plus\Minus	-33	12	23
Goals For	217	6	11
Goals Against	227	10	19
Average Shots For	25.4	14	26
Average Shots Against	30.8	13	23
Overtime	5-3-11	4	8
One Goal Games	16-11	6	8
Times outshooting opponent	24	13	24
Versus Teams Over .500	13-23-9	9	19
Versus Teams .500 or under	20-15-2	11	17
First Half Record	17-17-7	10	13
Second Half Record	16-21-4	10	20

MISCELLANEOUS STAT LEADERS

FACEOFFS

Gretzky	52.0%
Maholtra	43.9%
Nedved	52.5%

ICE TIME

Leetch	29:52
Schneider	24:35
Gretzky	21:04
Graves	20:33
Nedved	20:31
Popovic	20:41

HITS

Schneider	182
Knuble	180
Stevens	176
Leetch	173
Graves	162
Lacroix	145

PLAYOFFS

- did not make the playoffs

Ottawa Senators

Just some bits and pieces from the Ottawa Senators great season and dramatic playoff collapse.

The Senators weren't the only 100-point team to lose in the first round. New Jersey did it for the second year in a row. Ironically, the previous year, the only 100-point upset was pulled off by the Senators over the Devils. Encouraging news is that Dallas was a 100-point team in 1997 and also got beat out in the first round, by Edmonton.

The Senators were the kings of the multi-national team last year, with seven different countries represented on their playoff roster. The top 11 regular season scorers broke down to four Swedes, two Czechs, two Canadians, and a Russian, a Slovak and an American. Of the top 12 Buffalo scorers, seven were Canadian.

Ottawa was the least penalized team in the league, averaging 10.9 minutes per game. That served them well during the regular season. Buffalo was the 24th most penalized team.

Magnus Arvedsson was second in Selke Trophy voting, Marian Hossa second in Calder Trophy voting, and Alexei Yashin second in Hart Trophy voting. Ottawa was also second to Buffalo in first round playoff action.

The Senators were the second most improved team in the regular season, jumping by 20 points, second only to Toronto and their 28 point improvement.

The Senators have improved their winning percentage in each year of their existence:

1992-93	.143
1993-94	.220
1994-95	.240
1995-96	.250
1996-97	.470
1997-98	.506
1998-99	.628

The question is just how much importance should the Senators place on their first round loss to Buffalo. The Sabres, after all, went to the finals, and weren't that far off from winning the Cup. Ottawa did dominate the Sabres in at least the first game, but were held back by Dominik Hasek. The rest of the series they were held back by Mike Peca and a great team effort by the Sabres.

If the Senators should have learned one thing, it's that skill doesn't win out over heart, commitment and dedication over the short term. The Senators don't have enough of that type of thing, and it showed. Team cohesiveness is a necessity during the playoffs, and with so many multi-national factions within the team, you have to wonder if that might have been a problem.

The bottom line is that they're a very talented team, but must do some tinkering in order to be a talented playoff team.

STUFF: Ron Tugnutt's GAA of 1.70 was the best in the NHL since Tony Esposito posted a 1.77 mark in 1971-72 for Chicago.
A win in Pittsburgh near the end of the season was their first ever, breaking off a 17-game winless streak in the Igloo.

TEAM PREVIEW

GOAL: The Ron Tugnutt-Damian Rhodes debate was always interesting, especially at playoff time. Tugnutt clearly shone over Rhodes during the regular season, which was why Rhodes was shipped to Atlanta. The Senators would have lost him anyway, in the expansion draft.

Now, people won't have to reason why teams can't be successful with two number one goalies in the playoffs. Those reasons aren't clear except that other teams don't do it. But, other teams don't have two top goalies, mostly because they don't want to pay twice as much for a job that can be handled by one guy.

In any event, it looks now as if Patrick Lalime will be the backup to Tugnutt. You have to wonder if Tugnutt may not be as effective this year, without Rhodes pushing for his share of the ice-time.

DEFENSE: Most of the Ottawa defensemen can contribute offensively as well as defensively. In other words, they're fairly well rounded. But, none is a wizard with the puck or a quarterback for the power play. But, considering their success, it might be better to have several players who can contribute offensively, as opposed to one dominant force.

Wade Redden, Igor Kravchuk, Jason York, Sammi Salo, Chris Phillips, Janne Laukannen and Patrick Traverse can all make contributions with the puck, which tends to make the forwards that much better, because the puck gets to them.

With the loss of Lance Pitlick they don't have a dominant physical force on the blueline. In fact, their leading penalty minute earner was Redden, who had just 54 minutes.

Redden is moving steadily up among the league's elite, while York's overall game was somewhat of a pleasant surprise. Salo was a pleasant surprise as well, same as Traverse. Kravchuk is a disappointment and doesn't do near what was expected of him offensively. Laukannen had an off-year, and Phillips, who played some at forward, is still finding his roots.

The mobile defense is the thing in today's game, but so is size and toughness. But, Ottawa was successful during the last regular season with their own game, so it makes it difficult to argue.

FORWARD: The lack of aggressiveness by the Ottawa forwards no doubt contributed to their playoff doom. It wasn't a problem for them dur-

GOALTENDER	GPI	MINS	AVG	W	L	T	EN	SO	GA	SA	SV %
RON TUGNUTT	43	2,508	1.79	22	10	8	2	3	75	1,005	.925
DAMIAN RHODES	45	2,480	2.44	22	13	7	1	3	101	1,060	.905
OTT TOTALS	82	4,999	2.15	44	23	15	3	6	179	2,068	.913

ing the regular season, however, and were one of the few teams not to carry an enforcer on their third or fourth line wing.

The addition of Rob Zamuner should help. He was once considered one of the better two-way players in the game. Interestingly, he's the only Canadian projected on the top three lines. He makes an effective replacement for Andreas Johansson, who had a fast start and then flickered out.

Down the middle is Yashin, coming off an outstanding regular season; Radek Bonk, who has been rounding out his game defensively, which is good because he rarely does anything ofrensively; Vaclav Prospal, who had one fluke good year in Philadelphia before being traded to Ottawa; and Shaun Van Allen and Bruce Gardiner, who can help with the defensive chores

On left wing is Shawn McEachern, who put up good numbers playing alongside Yashin; Arvedsson, all of a sudden considered one of the best defensive forwards in the league; Zamuner; and Yves Sarault waiting in the wings.

The right side features Marian Hossa, Andreas Dackell and Daniel Alredsson. The key there is to find the best linemate for Yashin but still allowing for balance. Hossa with Yashin could create a formidable first line. Alfredsson is coming off an injury plagued season and it's easy to forget that he is an outstanding player when not injured. Dackell could find himself moved down to the third line as a checker.

An interesting scenario here is that almost all the Ottawa forwards had career seasons. Players tend to fall off a bit their following year.

SPECIAL TEAMS: They don't have a power play quarterback, but they've got plenty of back-up quarterbacks. With their offensive talent up front, however, they should be among the league leaders. Arvedsson broke through to become one of the best penalty killers in the business.

Alfredsson is a magician on the power power play, so if they can get him playing regularly, the power play will improve tremendously.

Power Play	G	ATT	PCT
Overall	57	387	14.7% (T-15th NHL)
Home	33	217	15.2% (T-16th NHL)
Road	24	170	14.1% (16th NHL)
12 SHORT HANDED GOALS ALLOWED (T-26th NHL)			

Penalty Killing	G	TSH	PCT
Overall	44	311	85.9% (8th NHL)
Home	20	162	87.7% (5th NHL)
Road	24	149	83.9% (13th NHL)
6 SHORT HANDED GOALS SCORED (T-17th NHL)			

Penalties	GP	MIN	AVG
SENATORS	80	874	10.9 (1st NHL)

SENATORS SPECIAL TEAMS SCORING

Power play	G	A	PTS
YASHIN	19	21	40
KRAVTCHOUK	3	13	16
YORK	2	14	16
JOHANSSON	7	8	15
DACKELL	5	10	15
MCEACHERN	7	6	13
REDDEN	3	10	13
ALFREDSSON	3	8	11
PROSPAL	2	8	10
EMERSON	3	6	9
SALO	2	6	8
DONATO	3	4	7
PHILLIPS	2	1	3

TRAVERSE	0	2	2
HOSSA	0	2	2
MARTINS	1	0	1
LAUKKANEN	0	1	1

Short handed	G	A	PTS
ARVEDSON	4	1	5
BONK	1	1	2
VAN ALLEN	1	0	1
YORK	0	1	1
YASHIN	0	1	1
TRAVERSE	0	1	1
REDDEN	0	1	1
GARDINER	0	1	1

COACHING AND MANAGEMENT: Marshall Johnston is the new general manager, not that that means anything. The previous two took off to greener pastures with time still remaining on their contracts. Pierre Gauthier, of course, had personal problems until he signed with Anaheim shortly after leaving. Rick Dudley, and all his great accomplisments (?), was hired as Director of Player Personnel for Tampa Bay.

Johnston has been around a long time and has held virtually every hockey post, except GM.His biggest challenge will be remaining within the budget while still putting out a winning team.

They vote for the Jack Adams Trophy before the playoffs start, which is why Jacques Martin was able to win it. But, a coach's value is probably determined most in the playoffs, and the Senators, of course, were zonked in four straight by Buffalo. Part of that was because Yashin was ineffective against Mike Peca, and Martin didn't do anything about it.

DRAFT: (see chart) Not much of a surprise that the Senators opted for a Czech with their first round pick. The public scouting report on Martin Havlat glows about his offensive prowess and says he's not afraid of the physical game. In other words, he is, or why even mention it? Do you think Chris Pronger's scouting report said he wasn't afraid of the physical game?

The unofficial line on Havlat is that he's a floater and doesn't work hard. If he doesn't do it now, when is he going to do it?

DRAFT

Player	Pos	Rnd	Sel.	Cntry	Team	Lge	Gms	G	A	P	PIM
Martin Havlat	F	1	26	Cze	Trinec	Cze	24	3	2	5	0
Simon Lajeunesse	G	2	48	Can	Moncton	QMJHL	2.95	.891			
Teemu Sainomaa	LW	2	62	Fin	Jokerit Jr	Fin	11	4	5	9	0
Chris Kelly	F	3	94	Can	London	OHL	68	36	41	77	60
Andrw Ianiero	LW	5	154	Can	Kingston	OHL	68	21	26	47	81
Marin Prusek	G	6	164	Cze	Vitkovice	Cze	2.68				
Mikko Ruutu	W	7	201	Fin	IFK Helsinki	Fin	31	3	1	4	12
Layne Ulmer	C	7	209	Can	Swift Current	WHL	72	40	35	75	34
Alexandre Giroux	F	7	213	Can	Hull	QMJHL	67	15	22	37	124
K. Gorovikov	F	9	269	Rus	St. Petersburg	Rus					

PROGNOSIS: The Senators should remain one of the top teams — during the regular season. The playoffs are more of a crapshoot, with some depending on the opponent, and some depending on the type of playoff-ready type players the Sens utilize. Zamuner should be a big help in that regard.

STAT SECTION

PLAYER	GP	G	A	PTS	+/-	PIM	PP	SH	GW	GT	S	PCTG
ALEXEI YASHIN	82	44	50	94	16	54	19	0	5	1	337	13.1
S. MCEACHERN	77	31	25	56	8	46	7	0	4	1	223	13.9
ANDREAS DACKELL	77	15	35	50	9	30	6	0	3	0	107	14.0
M. ARVEDSON	80	21	26	47	33	50	0	4	6	0	136	15.4
A. JOHANSSON	69	21	16	37	1	34	7	0	6	0	144	14.6
NELSON EMERSON	65	13	24	37	8	51	3	0	1	2	188	6.9
VACLAV PROSPAL	79	10	26	36	8	58	2	0	3	0	114	8.8
JASON YORK	79	4	31	35	17	48	2	0	0	1	177	2.3
D. ALFREDSSON	58	11	22	33	8	14	3	0	5	0	163	6.7
RADEK BONK	81	16	16	32	15	48	0	1	6	0	110	14.5
MARIAN HOSSA	60	15	15	30	18	37	1	0	2	2	124	12.1
WADE REDDEN	72	8	21	29	7	54	3	0	1	1	127	6.3
TED DONATO	82	11	16	27	8-	41	3	0	0	0	106	10.4
IGOR KRAVCHUK	79	4	21	25	14	32	3	0	0	0	171	2.3
SAMI SALO	61	7	12	19	20	24	2	0	1	0	106	6.6
SHAUN VAN ALLEN	79	6	11	17	3	30	0	1	0	0	47	12.8
BRUCE GARDINER	59	4	8	12	6	43	0	0	1	0	70	5.7
JANNE LAUKKANEN	50	1	11	12	18	40	0	0	0	0	46	2.2
PATRICK TRAVERSE	46	1	9	10	12	22	0	0	0	0	35	2.9
LANCE PITLICK	50	3	6	9	7	33	0	0	0	0	34	8.8
STEVE MARTINS	36	4	3	7	4	10	1	0	1	0	27	14.8
DAVID OLIVER	17	2	5	7	1	4	0	0	0	0	18	11.1
CHRIS PHILLIPS	34	3	3	6	5-	32	2	0	0	0	51	5.9
BILL BERG	44	2	2	4	4	28	0	0	0	1	40	5.0
DAMIAN RHODES	45	1	1	2	0	4	0	0	0	0	1	100.0
V. BUTSAYEV	3	0	1	1	1-	4	0	0	0	0	5	.0
PHILIP CROWE	8	0	1	1	1	4	0	0	0	0	2	.0
YVES SARAULT	11	0	1	1	1	4	0	0	0	0	7	.0
JOHN GRUDEN	13	0	1	1	0	8	0	0	0	0	10	.0
RON TUGNUTT	43	0	0	0	0	0	0	0	0	0	0	.0

TEAM RANKINGS

		Conference Rank	League Rank
Record	44-23-15	2	3
Home	22-11-8	4	6
Away	22-12-7	2	3
Versus Own Conference	30-18-9	2	3
Versus Other Conference	14-5-6	2	3
Team Plus\Minus	+45	2	2
Goals For	239	4	5
Goals Against	179	2	3
Average Shots For	29.7	3	5
Average Shots Against	24.6	3	5
Overtime	1-2-15	9	17
One Goal Games	12-8	5	6
Times outshooting opponent	55	3	4
Versus Teams Over .500	20-14-8	2	3
Versus Teams .500 or under	24-9-7	1	3
First Half Record	23-13-5	2	4
Second Half Record	21-10-10	2	4

MISCELLANEOUS STAT LEADERS
FACEOFFS

Bonk	50.1%
Van Allen	47.4%
Gardner	45.7%
Yashin	42.0%

ICE TIME

Kravchuk	23:52
York	23:49
Redden	23:26
Yashin	22:05

HITS

Bonk	225
Prospal	202
York	166
Pitlick	120

PLAYOFFS

Results:

Lost 4-0 in conference quarter-finals to Buffalo

Record: 0-4
Home: 0-2
Away: 0-2
Goals For: 6 (1.5/game)
Goals Against: 12 (3.0/game)
Overtime: 0-1
Power play: 11.1% (14th)
Penalty Killing: 77.8% (14th)

PLAYER	GP	G	A	PTS	+/-	PIM	PP	SH	GW	OT	S	PCTG
NELSON EMERSON	4	1	3	4	0	0	0	0	0	0	12	8.3
DANIEL ALFREDSSON	4	1	2	3	1-	4	1	0	0	0	13	7.7
WADE REDDEN	4	1	2	3	1-	2	1	0	0	0	11	9.1
SHAWN MCEACHERN	4	2	0	2	1	6	1	0	0	0	11	18.2
JASON YORK	4	1	1	2	1-	4	0	0	0	0	12	8.3
MARIAN HOSSA	4	0	2	2	1	4	0	0	0	0	11	.0
MAGNUS ARVEDSON	3	0	1	1	1-	2	0	0	0	0	8	.0
ANDREAS DACKELL	4	0	1	1	3-	0	0	0	0	0	3	.0
TED DONATO	1	0	0	0	0	0	0	0	0	0	0	.0
BILL BERG	2	0	0	0	0	0	0	0	0	0	0	.0
RON TUGNUTT	2	0	0	0	0	0	0	0	0	0	0	.0
LANCE PITLICK	2	0	0	0	1-	0	0	0	0	0	2	.0
DAMIAN RHODES	2	0	0	0	0	0	0	0	0	0	0	.0
ANDREAS JOHANSSON	2	0	0	0	3-	0	0	0	0	0	4	.0
BRUCE GARDINER	3	0	0	0	0	4	0	0	0	0	4	.0
CHRIS PHILLIPS	3	0	0	0	1-	0	0	0	0	0	1	.0
SHAUN VAN ALLEN	4	0	0	0	1-	0	0	0	0	0	2	.0
IGOR KRAVCHUK	4	0	0	0	5-	0	0	0	0	0	12	.0
JANNE LAUKKANEN	4	0	0	0	1	4	0	0	0	0	8	.0
ALEXEI YASHIN	4	0	0	0	4-	10	0	0	0	0	24	.0
VACLAV PROSPAL	4	0	0	0	2-	0	0	0	0	0	6	.0
RADEK BONK	4	0	0	0	1-	6	0	0	0	0	8	.0
SAMI SALO	4	0	0	0	3-	0	0	0	0	0	10	.0

GOALTENDER	GPI	MINS	AVG	W	L	T	EN	SO	GA	SA	SV %
DAMIAN RHODES	2	150	2.40	0	2	0	0	0	6	65	.908
RON TUGNUTT	2	118	3.05	0	2	0	0	0	6	41	.854
OTT TOTALS	4	271	2.66	0	4	0	0	0	12	106	.887

Philadelphia Flyers

Punch Imlach, the former Toronto Maple Leafs coach and general manager, once wrote a book titled, Heaven and Hell in the NHL.

If you were to write a book about the Flyers' season you could probably steal the name.

Heaven: The first half of the season when they had a record of 22-9-10, good for first in the Eastern Conference.
Hell: The second half of the season when they had a record of 15-17-9, good for eighth in the Eastern Conference.

Heaven: The goaltending during the season of John Vanbiesbrouck. During one stretch, he and Ron Hextall combined for four consecutive shutouts.
Hell: Goaltending during the playoffs, a familiar problem for the Flyers. Vanbiesbrouck showed a penchant for giving up easy backhand goals. Hell came after the season for Hextall, whose contract was bought out.

Heaven: Eric Lindros was having an outstanding year, was second behind Jaromir Jagr in league scoring and appeared on his way to playing the most games of his career.
Hell: A collapsed lung forced him out of the last nine games of the regular season, and all of the playoffs.

Heaven: Eric Desjardins was on his way to possibly winning a Norris Trophy and leading all defensemen in scoring.
Hell: A knee injury knocked him out of action and then forced him to play hurt for the remainder of the season. He missed 14 games.

Heaven: A 14-game undefeated streak and a stretch of 24 games in late December to early February in which they only lost once in 24 games.
Hell: A 12-game winless streak in February and March, which was a team record.

Heaven: Despite not having Eric Lindros in the lineup, the Flyers jumped out of Toronto in game one of their first round playoff matchup.
Hell: Curtis Joseph

Heaven: For the umpteenth year, the Flyers will go into the season as one of the favorites to win the Stanley Cup.
Hell: Something is bound to go wrong.

STUFF: John LeClair had a consecutive games streak stopped at 317 games when he missed a March game with a sore hip.

John Vanbiesbrouck faced his third playoff penalty shot, stopping Mats Sundin. The only other goaltender to face that many is Andy Moog. Vanbiesbrouck has stopped two and allowed one goal.

The Flyers have lost their last seven playoff overtime games.

TEAM PREVIEW

GOAL: Say goodbye to Ron Hextall. After spending all but two of his 13 NHL seasons in Philadelphia, his contract was bought out and he became a free agent. He leaves a legacy of one Stanley Cup victory, many playoff failures, a few broken bones, and two goals scored.

Vanbiesbrouck had an outstanding regular season and then suffered the Philly Flu in the playoffs, allowing some weak goals. He has another year to prove himself in the post-season.

Meanwhile, the Flyers had to make room for Brian Boucher, one of the Flyers goalie prospects. Jean-Marc Pelletier is another, and should get a full season as number one with the Philadelphia Phantoms in the AHL. Just to be on the safe side, the Flyers used their first round draft choice to take Maxime Oulett.

DEFENSE: If you project Eric Desjardins point totals over 82 games (he missed 14) it gives him 62 points, which would have led all defensemen in the league. Even with the injury, he was voted to the second all-star team and was fifth in Norris Trophy voting.

It seems the Flyers' needs always centre around getting an offensive defenseman for the power play. They even tried it late in the season when they acquired Steve Duchesne, since departed. The question is, what's wrong with Desjardins and McGillis?

The two of them combined for 96 points.

The chart shows the top six defense duos in points. Desjardins and McGillis stack up very well, plus have the added ingredient of not being one-dimensional players. If you can get that kind of point production out of two all-round players, why is it necessary to find something wrong with that?

Lidstrom-Murphy	Det	109
MacInnis-Pronger	StL	108
Zubov-Sydor	Dal	99
Desjardins-McGillis	Phi	96
Leetch-Schneider	NYR	89
Housley-Morris	Cgy	88

Returnees include, Chris Therien, who's often paired with Desjardins: Karl Dykhuis, who had an up and down season; and Adam Burt, a defensive defenseman for the sixth or seventh or eighth spot.

GOALTENDER	GPI	MINS	AVG	W	L	T	EN	SO	GA	SA	SV %
J. VANBIESBROUCK	62	3,712	2.18	27	18	15	4	6	135	1,380	.902
RON HEXTALL	23	1,235	2.53	10	7	4	0	0	52	464	.888
J-M PELLETIER	1	60	5.00	0	1	0	0	0	5	29	.828
PHI TOTALS	82	5,025	2.34	37	26	19	4	7	196	1,877	.896

RON HEXTALL and JOHN VANBIESBROUCK shared a shutout vs CAR on Jan 9, 1999

Tragically, Dmitri Tertyshny was killed in a freak boating accident during the summer while attending a power skating school in British Columbia.

Luke Richardson had a terrible season, doesn't fit into the Flyers scheme, and wasn't even used in the playoffs. He has asked to be traded and the Flyers will do their best to accommodate him.

Rookie hopefuls this season start with Mark Eaton, who is considered to be in the Desjardins mold. Mikail Chernov should also get a look

The Flyers defense is considered their weak link, despite the fact they gave up the second fewest shots in the league. They probably could be a little tougher, but you usually give up something with toughness, as they saw with Richardson. They may not be a spectacular group, but they tend to get the job done.

FORWARD: A first line of John LeClair, Eric Lindros and Mark Recchi, should conceivably be the best in the league. Recchi is coming off a horrendous season, but if he's healthy, he should get back up to the 30 goal range where he's been for most of his career.

Brind'Amour is as good a second line centre as there is in the league, and will probably have Valeri Zelepukin and Mikael Renberg on his wings.

Daymond Langkow could be as good a third line centre as there is in the league. Keith Jones should be on one wing, and maybe Mikael Andersson on the left side, although he should be on the fourth line, with maybe the best fourth line centre in the league in Marc Bureau. Sandy McCarthy, who doesn't mind you calling him racist names as long as you fight him, and Craig Berube, an unrestricted free agent, could line up with him on the left side.

Roman Vopat is still around for some reason,

and it looks as if the Flyers could maybe use a little more scoring on the left side.

The Flyers best prospect is Simon Gagne, but he's a centre and they're already set there for the time being. He was 50-70-120 in the Quebec junior league, and speedy, playmaking, goal scorers don't stay down too long.

SPECIAL TEAMS: The Flyers special teams should have been a lot better. The previous season they were fourth and sixth respectively on the power play and penalty killing.

Power Play	G	ATT	PCT
Overall	65	386	16.8% (10th NHL)
Home	39	189	20.6% (6th NHL)
Road	26	197	13.2% (19th NHL)

7 SHORT HANDED GOALS ALLOWED (T-9th NHL)

Penalty Killing	G	TSH	PCT
Overall	53	333	84.1% (16th NHL)
Home	22	148	85.1% (T-18th NHL)
Road	31	185	83.2% (T-14th NHL)

4 SHORT HANDED GOALS SCORED (26th NHL)

Penalties	GP	MIN	AVG
FLYERS	82	1075	13.1 (3rd NHL)

FLYERS SPECIAL TEAMS SCORING

Power play	G	A	PTS
BRIND'AMOUR	10	22	32
LINDROS	10	17	27
MCGILLIS	6	21	27
LECLAIR	16	9	25
DESJARDINS	6	18	24
RECCHI	3	20	23
DUCHESNE	2	16	18
RENBERG	6	4	10

LANGKOW	4	5	9
JONES	3	4	7
TERTYSHNY	1	3	4
DYKHUIS	1	1	2
ZELEPUKIN	0	2	2
GREIG	0	2	2
THERIEN	1	0	1
MCCARTHY	1	0	1
DELMORE	0	1	1

Short handed	G	A	PTS
LINDROS	1	0	1
LANGKOW	1	0	1
THERIEN	0	1	1
RECCHI	0	1	1
HULL	0	1	1
DYKHUIS	0	1	1
DESJARDINS	0	1	1
BRIND'AMOUR	0	1	1

COACHING AND MANAGEMENT: Bob Clarke will do whatever it takes to make the Flyers a winner. Sometimes he makes mistakes, but he doesn't hesitate to fix them as soon as possible.

There was some whining about the way Hextall found out he was no longer with the team, but Hextall should be grateful to Clarke for sticking with him for so long and giving him so many chances.

Roger Nielson is back as coach. The first round playoff loss can't be considered his fault, because they didn't have Lindros. The late season slide in the standings is curious, though. And with all his knowledge, couldn't he make the special teams more effective?

DRAFT: As if the Flyers don't have enough goalie prospects. It almost seems like an obsession with them to keep drafting them. In three of the last five drafts they've selected a goalie in the first round.

Maxime Ouellet is characterized as a butterfly goalie. All goalies play the butterfly, so figure out what that means.

PROGNOSIS: The Flyers are close, so Clarke will do everything he can to give the Flyers a shot at winning the whole thing. But, they have a solid nucleus, and have a chance to win the whole thing.

DRAFT

Player	Pos	Rnd	Sel.	Cntry	Team	Lge	Gms	G	A	P	PIM
Maxime Ouellet	G	1	22	Can	Quebec	QMJHL	2.70	.909			
Jeff Fenlak	D	4	119	Can	Calgary	WHL	39	1	4	5	81
K. Rudenko	LW	6	160	Kaz	Cheropovec	Rus	0	0	0	0	0
Pavel Kasparik	C	7	200	Cze	Cze		51	20	18	38	0
Vaclav Pletka	LW	7	208	Cze	Trinec	Cze	48	15	11	26	0
David Nystrom	W	8	224	Swe	Frolunda	Swe					

STAT SECTION

PLAYER	GP	G	A	PTS	+/-	PIM	PP	SH	GW	GT	S	PCTG
ERIC LINDROS	71	40	53	93	35	120	10	1	2	3	242	16.5
JOHN LECLAIR	76	43	47	90	36	30	16	0	7	3	246	17.5
ROD BRIND'AMOUR	82	24	50	74	3	47	10	0	3	2	191	12.6
KEITH JONES	78	20	33	53	23	98	3	0	3	0	135	14.8
MARK RECCHI	71	16	37	53	7-	34	3	0	2	0	171	9.4
ERIC DESJARDINS	68	15	36	51	18	38	6	0	2	0	190	7.9
DANIEL MCGILLIS	78	8	37	45	16	61	6	0	4	0	164	4.9
MIKAEL RENBERG	66	15	23	38	5	18	6	0	2	0	154	9.7
D. LANGKOW	78	14	19	33	8-	39	4	1	2	0	149	9.4
STEVE DUCHESNE	71	6	24	30	6-	24	2	0	2	0	118	5.1
VALERI ZELEPUKIN	74	16	9	25	0	48	0	0	5	0	129	12.4
CHRIS THERIEN	74	3	15	18	16	48	1	0	0	0	115	2.6
JODY HULL	72	3	11	14	2-	12	0	0	1	1	73	4.1
SANDY MCCARTHY	80	5	8	13	24-	160	1	0	0	0	107	4.7
MARC BUREAU	71	4	6	10	2-	10	0	0	0	0	52	7.7
DMITRI TERTYSHNY	62	2	8	10	1-	30	1	0	0	0	68	2.9
CRAIG BERUBE	77	5	4	9	10-	194	0	0	0	0	52	9.6
KARL DYKHUIS	78	4	5	9	23-	50	1	0	0	0	88	4.5
M. ANDERSSON	47	2	4	6	7-	4	0	0	0	0	51	3.9
LUKE RICHARDSON	78	0	6	6	3-	106	0	0	0	0	49	.0
MARK GREIG	7	1	3	4	1	2	0	0	0	0	9	11.1
ADAM BURT	68	0	4	4	4	60	0	0	0	0	61	.0
ROMAN VOPAT	54	0	3	3	7-	90	0	0	0	0	27	.0
RON HEXTALL	23	0	2	2	0	2	0	0	0	0	0	.0
ANDY DELMORE	2	0	1	1	1-	0	0	0	0	0	2	.0
RYAN BAST	2	0	1	1	0	0	0	0	0	0	1	.0
J. VANBIESBROUCK	62	0	1	1	0	12	0	0	0	0	0	.0
BRIAN WESENBERG	1	0	0	0	1	5	0	0	0	0	0	.0
J-M PELLETIER	1	0	0	0	0	0	0	0	0	0	0	.0
CHRIS JOSEPH	2	0	0	0	0	2	0	0	0	0	1	.0
DAN KORDIC	2	0	0	0	1-	2	0	0	0	0	0	.0
JASON ZENT	2	0	0	0	0	0	0	0	0	0	1	.0
PETER WHITE	3	0	0	0	0	0	0	0	0	0	0	.0
RICHARD PARK	7	0	0	0	1-	0	0	0	0	0	5	.0

TEAM RANKINGS

		Conference Rank	League Rank
Record	37-26-19	4	6
Home	21-9-11	2	4
Away	16-17-8	4	7
Versus Own Conference	23-21-13	7	12
Versus Other Conference	14-5-6	2	3
Team Plus\Minus	+23	5	7
Goals For	231	5	9
Goals Against	196	4	6
Average Shots For	29.9	2	4
Average Shots Against	22.9	1	2
Overtime	2-3-19	7	14
One Goal Games	12-11	8	12
Times outshooting opponent	62	1	1
Versus Teams Over .500	16-15-11	4	6
Versus Teams .500 or under	21-11-8	6	10
First Half Record	22-9-10	1	3
Second Half Record	15-17-9	8	17

MISCELLANEOUS STAT LEADERS
FACEOFFS

Lindros	50.0%
Brind'Amour	56.5%
Bureau	53.5%
Langkow	48.0%

ICE TIME

Desjardins	25:49
Lindros	22:56
McGillis	21:41
Brind'Amour	21:29
Duchesne	21:23
LeClair	21:03
Therien	20:45
Recchi	20:27

HITS

McGillis	220
Therien	167
McCarthy	144
Lindros	117
Richardson	116

PLAYOFFS

Results:

Lost in conference-quarterfinals 4-2 to Toronto

Record: 2-4
Home: 1-2
Away: 1-2
Goals For: 11 (1.8/game)
Goals Against: 9 (1.5/game)
Overtime: 0-1
Power play: 11.1% (15th)
Penalty Killing: 85.3% (6th)

PLAYER	GP	G	A	PTS	+/-	PIM	PP	SH	GW	OT	S	PCTG
ERIC DESJARDINS	6	2	2	4	1	4	1	0	1	0	21	9.5
ROD BRIND'AMOUR	6	1	3	4	1	0	0	0	0	0	19	5.3
JOHN LECLAIR	6	3	0	3	0	12	2	0	0	0	15	20.0
KEITH JONES	6	2	1	3	4	14	0	0	0	0	11	18.2
MARC BUREAU	6	0	2	2	2	2	0	0	0	0	3	.0
STEVE DUCHESNE	6	0	2	2	2	2	0	0	0	0	10	.0
D. LANGKOW	6	0	2	2	3	2	0	0	0	0	4	.0
VALERI ZELEPUKIN	4	1	0	1	1	4	0	0	1	0	5	20.0
KARL DYKHUIS	5	1	0	1	1	4	0	0	0	0	12	8.3
CRAIG BERUBE	6	1	0	1	1	4	0	0	0	0	7	14.3
MARK GREIG	2	0	1	1	1	0	0	0	0	0	3	.0
MIKAEL ANDERSSON	6	0	1	1	1	2	0	0	0	0	7	.0
MARK RECCHI	6	0	1	1	1-	2	0	0	0	0	18	.0
MIKAEL RENBERG	6	0	1	1	1-	0	0	0	0	0	18	.0
SANDY MCCARTHY	6	0	1	1	1	0	0	0	0	0	7	.0
DANIEL MCGILLIS	6	0	1	1	2	12	0	0	0	0	15	.0
DMITRI TERTYSHNY	1	0	0	0	0	2	0	0	0	0	1	.0
ADAM BURT	6	0	0	0	1	4	0	0	0	0	3	.0
JODY HULL	6	0	0	0	1-	4	0	0	0	0	6	.0
J. VANBIESBROUCK	6	0	0	0	0	2	0	0	0	0	0	.0
CHRIS THERIEN	6	0	0	0	1	6	0	0	0	0	6	.0

GOALTENDER	GPI	MINS	AVG	W	L	T	EN	SO	GA	SA	SV %
J. VANBIESBROUC	6	369	1.46	2	4	0	1	0	9	146	.938
PHI TOTALS	6	372	1.45	2	4	0	1	0	9	146	.938

Pittsburgh Penguins

How do they do it? The Penguins have the longest current season winning streak at nine years, the first two of those Stanley Cup victories. Since then, they haven't done much in the playoffs, but they're always competitive and always perform well during the regular season.

The Penguins may, however, be a team just built for the regular season, which interestingly enough, Jaromir Jagr has noted himself, lamenting that so many Europeans aren't conducive to winning in the playoffs.

The one constant over the nine consecutive winning seasons is GM Craig Patrick. Every year he has to some serious juggling, and every year he comes out smelling like roses. The other constant is having a superstar or two, but that in itself isn't enough to win so consistently.

Most Current Consecutive Winning Seasons:

Pittsburgh	9
Detroit	8
New Jersey	8
Colorado	5
Philadelphia	5

Just to give you an idea of the juggling act

Patrick does, the following are the top three scorers over each of the nine years. Except for one year, when they were identical to the previous season, it shows that they pretty much have the one superstar, while the other scorers change constantly.

1990-91

Mark Recchi	113
John Cullen	94
Paul Coffey	93

1991-92

Mario Lemieux	131
Kevin Stevens	123
Joe Mullen	87

1992-93

Mario Lemieux	160
Kevin Stevens	111
Rick Tocchet	109

1993-94

Jaromir Jagr	99
Ron Francis	93
Kevin Stevens	88

1994-95

Jaromir Jagr	70
Ron Francis	59
Tomas Sandstrom	44

1995-96

Mario Lemieux	161
Jaromir Jagr	149
Ron Francis	119

1996-97

Mario Lemieux	122
Jaromir Jagr	95
Ron Francis	90

1997-98

Jaromir Jagr	102
Ron Francis	87
Stu Barnes	65

1998-99

Jaromir Jagr	127
Martin Straka	83
German Titov	56

TEAM PREVIEW

GOAL: Tom Barrasso is still hanging in there, but on Pittsburgh you have to keep plenty of other NHL ready goalies around, because he's injured so often.

J-Sebastien Aubin has the inside track on the backup job, but that doesn't mean Peter Skudra probably won't play, too.

In fact, the Pens have used tons of goalies over the past few years. Here's a list of them, just over the last six years.

Tom Barrasso
Ken Wregget
Roberto Romano
Rob Dopson
Phillippe DeRouville
Wendel Young
Patrick Lalime
Peter Skudra
J-Sebastien Aubin

DEFENSE: The Penguins should be able to move the puck okay, but they don't scare opposing forwards when they're in the Pittsburgh zone. They don't keep the front of the net clear and they're not very physical anywhere else.

It should help having Darius Kasparaitis for a full season. Apart from that, the Penguins don't look good on paper. Kevin Hatcher is still the main offensive threat, but he's getting older. Plus, his physical play has pretty much been terminated. For much of his career he regularly earned over 100 minutes in penalties. Last year, he had just 24.

Jiri Slegr and Brad Werenka have bounced around in their careers, both from NHL team to NHL team and from the minors to the majors.

GOALTENDER	GPI	MINS	AVG	W	L	T	EN	SO	GA	SA	SV %
J-S. AUBIN	17	756	2.22	4	3	6	0	2	28	304	.908
TOM BARRASSO	43	2,306	2.55	19	16	3	4	4	98	993	.901
PETER SKUDRA	37	1,914	2.79	15	11	5	6	3	89	822	.892
PIT TOTALS	82	5,011	2.69	38	30	14	10	9	225	2,129	.894

They should have regular jobs as should Ian Moran, who has made the transition from forward.

There will probably be changes in the above group anyway before long, but also fighting for jobs will be Sven Butenschon, Victor Ignatjev, Jeff Serowick, and Pavel Skrbek.

What they need is a big, tough, scrappy defenseman, a commodity that suddenly has come into short supply around the league.

FORWARD: The Penguins were among the teams with the fewest shots per game in the league last year. While that may sound worrisome on the surface, it more reflects the European style of working the puck for a good chance on net, rather than just blasting away and hoping somebody will deflect it or pop in the rebound.

The chart shows the best shooting percentages last season.

Best Team Shooting Percentages:
Toronto   11.7%
Pittsburgh   11.6%
Dallas   10.4%
Colorado   10.4%
NY Rangers   10.4%
Lge. Ave.   9.5%

Apart from that, the Penguins forwards, with the exception of Jagr, all have histories of inconsistency.

You can also exclude Kip Miller and Jan Hrdina from that list, both of whom might be playing in the minors if they weren't on the Penguins and especially if the Penguins didn't have Jagr. Miller has played with 13 professional teams, and Hrdina was only a mediocre scorer in two minor pro seasons.

Martin Straka, Alexei Kovalev, German Titov and Robert Lang could write a bestseller about inconsistency. Three of them, Kovelev excluded, had almost non-played themselves right out of the league.

That doesn't inspire a lot of confidence, despite the fact that all of them responded with good seasons in Pittsburgh. Plus the young European prospects are not coming along very well. Alexei Morozov took a step backward, and highly touted Robert Dome wasn't even good in the minors.

Rob Brown plays more of a defensive role now, although he does have a knack on the power play. Matthew Barnaby is the only physical forward on the Penguins, which can be categorized as ridiculous.

A couple bruiser wingers would help here, but apart from Jagr, there's question marks about every single forward being able to repeat last year's season.

SPECIAL TEAMS: Jagr would make every power play good, and with the number of offensive types on the Penguins they should remain up there with the league leaders with the extra man.

A curious statistical note is that the Penguins were second on the road on the power play, but 26th on the road in penalty killing.

Power Play	G	ATT	PCT
Overall	65	363	17.9% (7th NHL)
Home	29	189	15.3% (T-14th NHL)
Road	36	174	20.7% (2nd NHL)
14 SHORT HANDED GOALS ALLOWED (27th NHL)			

Penalty Killing	G	TSH	PCT	
Overall	56	302	81.5%	(23rd NHL)
Home	22	149	85.2%	(17th NHL)
Road	34	153	77.8%	(26th NHL)

10 SHORT HANDED GOALS SCORED (T-6th NHL)

Penalties	GP	MIN	AVG	
PENGUINS	82	977	11.9	(2nd NHL)

PENGUINS SPECIAL TEAMS SCORING

Power play	G	A	PTS
JAGR	10	34	44
STRAKA	5	17	22
TITOV	3	16	19
BROWN	9	6	15
KOVALEV	6	9	15
HATCHER	4	11	15
LANG	7	5	12
HRDINA	3	7	10
MILLER	1	5	6
BARNABY	1	5	6
GALANOV	2	1	3
SEROWIK	0	3	3
WERENKA	1	1	2
KESA	0	2	2
SLEGR	1	0	1
IGNATIEV	0	1	1

Short handed	G	A	PTS
STRAKA	4	2	6
HATCHER	2	0	2
WERENKA	0	2	2
SLEGR	0	2	2
TITOV	1	0	1
MORAN	1	0	1
KOVALEV	1	0	1
JAGR	1	0	1
HRDINA	0	1	1
DOLLAS	0	1	1

COACHING AND MANAGEMENT: Mario Lemieux has already saved Pittsburgh once. Can he do it again?

Craig Patrick saves the Penguins yearly. Can he do it again?

Kevin Constantine keeps winning. Can he do it again?

Maybe, maybe and maybe.

DRAFT

Player	Pos	Rnd	Sel.	Cntry	Team	Lge	Gms	G	A	P	PIM
Konstantin Koltsov	LW	1	18	Bel	Cherepovec	Rus	33	3	0	3	8
Matt Murley	LW	2	51	USA	RPI	ECAC	36	17	32	49	32
Jeremy Van Hoff	D	2	57	Can	Ottawa	OHL	54	0	13	13	46
Sebastien Caron	G	3	86	Can	Rimouski	QMJHL	3.25	.913			
Ryan Malone	LW	4	115	USA	Omaha	USHL	51	14	22	36	81
Tomas Skvardio	F	5	144	Slo	Zvolen Jr	Slov	36	21	13	34	18
V. Malenkykh	D	5	157	Rus	Togliatta	Rus	9	0	0	0	2
Doug Meyer	LW	6	176	USA	Minnesota	WCHA	34	3	3	6	14
Tom Kostopoulos	RW	7	204	Can	London	OHL	66	27	60	87	114
Darcy Robinson	D	8	233	Can	Saskatoon	WHL	48	3	6	9	86
A. McPherson	LW	9	261	Can	RPI	ECAC	29	5	4	9	12

DRAFT: Konstantin Koltsov scored in a couple world junior championship games which makes him ideal for the Penguins, because they love their Europeans. The Penguins also don't draft for character, which is why their much heralded draft selections don't work out very often. Koltsov is considered a great skater, but doesn't have a reputation as the type of player to show up every game. Perfect for the Penguins.

PROGNOSIS: The Penguins could experience their first losing season in 10 years. There are just too many ifs on this team, which didn't even have its ownership settled late in July. There are far too many inconsistent players to depend on them to do it again.

Patrick is a master of pulling rabbits out of his hat, but one of these times he's going to reach in a pull out a skunk instead.

Prediction: Constantine will be the first coach fired, to Jagr's delight, and then the Penguins will catch fire because they'll be happy not to have to answer to him anymore. Then, if they make the playoffs, they'll be bounced in the first round.

STAT SECTION

PLAYER	GP	G	A	PTS	+/-	PIM	PP	SH	GW	GT	S	PCTG
JAROMIR JAGR	81	44	83	127	17	66	10	1	7	2	343	12.8
MARTIN STRAKA	80	35	48	83	12	26	5	4	4	1	177	19.8
GERMAN TITOV	72	11	45	56	18	34	3	1	3	1	113	9.7
ALEXEI KOVALEV	77	23	30	53	2	49	6	1	5	0	191	12.0
ROBERT LANG	72	21	23	44	10-	24	7	0	3	3	137	15.3
KIP MILLER	77	19	23	42	1	22	1	0	4	0	125	15.2
JAN HRDINA	82	13	29	42	2-	40	3	0	2	0	94	13.8
KEVIN HATCHER	66	11	27	38	11	24	4	2	3	0	131	8.4
ROB BROWN	58	13	11	24	15-	16	9	0	1	0	78	16.7
BRAD WERENKA	81	6	18	24	17	93	1	0	4	0	77	7.8
JIRI SLEGR	63	3	20	23	13	86	1	0	0	0	91	3.3
M. BARNABY	62	6	16	22	12-	177	1	0	3	0	79	7.6
ALEXEI MOROZOV	67	9	10	19	5	14	0	0	0	0	75	12.0
DAN KESA	67	2	8	10	9-	27	0	0	0	1	33	6.1
BOBBY DOLLAS	70	2	8	10	3-	60	0	0	0	0	34	5.9
IAN MORAN	62	4	5	9	1	37	0	1	0	0	65	6.2
MAXIM GALANOV	51	4	3	7	8-	14	2	0	0	1	44	9.1
JEFF SEROWIK	26	0	6	6	4-	16	0	0	0	0	26	.0
D. KASPARAITIS	48	1	4	5	12	70	0	0	0	0	32	3.1
TOM BARRASSO	43	0	3	3	0	20	0	0	0	0	0	.0
M. SONNENBERG	44	1	1	2	2-	19	0	0	0	0	12	8.3

PATRICK LEBEAU	8	1	0	1	2-	2	0	0	0	0	4	25.0
GREG ANDRUSAK	7	0	1	1	4	4	0	0	0	0	2	.0
VICTOR IGNATJEV	11	0	1	1	3-	6	0	0	0	0	15	.0
RYAN SAVOIA	3	0	0	0	1-	0	0	0	0	0	0	.0
PAVEL SKRBEK	4	0	0	0	2	2	0	0	0	0	1	.0
BRIAN BONIN	5	0	0	0	2-	0	0	0	0	0	2	.0
SVEN BUTENSCHON	17	0	0	0	7-	6	0	0	0	0	8	.0
J-SEBASTIEN AUBIN	17	0	0	0	0	0	0	0	0	0	0	.0
NEIL WILKINSON	24	0	0	0	2-	22	0	0	0	0	11	.0
PETER SKUDRA	37	0	0	0	0	2	0	0	0	0	0	.0
TYLER WRIGHT	61	0	0	0	2-	90	0	0	0	0	16	.0

TEAM RANKINGS

		Conference Rank	League Rank
Record	38-30-4	7	11
Home	21-10-10	5	7
Away	17-20-4	7	12
Versus Own Conference	26-23-9	6	11
Versus Other Conference	12-7-5	4	6
Team Plus\Minus	+8	7	14
Goals For	242	3	4
Goals Against	225	9	17
Average Shots For	25.5	13	25
Average Shots Against	26.0	4	6
Overtime	7-1-14	2	2
One Goal Games	14-8	3	4
Times outshooting opponent	42	5	9
Versus Teams Over .500	16-19-7	7	9
Versus Teams .500 or under	22-11-7	4	7

First Half Record	20-14-7	6	8
Second Half Record	18-16-7	5	10

MISCELLANEOUS STAT LEADERS

FACEOFFS

Hrdina	56.7%
Lang	44.8%
Straka	43.6%

ICE TIME

Jagr	25:51
Hatcher	24:38
Straka	23:35
Werenka	21:12
Kovalev	20:23

HITS

Kasparaitis	173
Brown	115
Werenka	115
Hrdina	104

PLAYOFFS

Results:

Defeated New Jersey 4-3 in conference quarter-finals

Lost 4-2 to Toronto in conference semi-finals

Record: 6-7

Home: 3-3

Away: 3-4

Goals For: 35 (2.7/game)

Goals Against: 36 (2.8/game)

Overtime: 1-2

Power play: 17.8% (6th)

Penalty Killing: 88.0% (4th)

PLAYER	GP	G	A	PTS	+/-	PIM	PP	SH	GW	OT	S	PCTG
MARTIN STRAKA	13	6	9	15	0	6	1	0	0	0	27	22.2
JAROMIR JAGR	9	5	7	12	1	16	1	0	1	1	32	15.6
ALEXEI KOVALEV	10	5	7	12	0	14	0	0	1	0	24	20.8
KIP MILLER	13	2	7	9	1-	19	1	0	0	0	18	11.1
GERMAN TITOV	11	3	5	8	4	4	0	0	0	0	15	20.0
ROB BROWN	13	2	5	7	2-	8	2	0	0	0	14	14.3
JAN HRDINA	13	4	1	5	1-	12	1	0	1	0	14	28.6
KEVIN HATCHER	13	2	3	5	1	4	1	0	0	0	22	9.1
JIRI SLEGR	13	1	3	4	1	12	0	0	1	0	17	5.9
ALEXEI MOROZOV	10	1	1	2	1	0	0	0	0	0	13	7.7
BRAD WERENKA	13	1	1	2	0	6	0	0	0	0	10	10.0
ROBERT LANG	12	0	2	2	3-	0	0	0	0	0	9	.0
IAN MORAN	13	0	2	2	3-	8	0	0	0	0	12	.0
GREG ANDRUSAK	12	1	0	1	1-	6	0	0	1	0	9	11.1
BOBBY DOLLAS	13	1	0	1	4-	6	0	0	0	0	6	16.7
DAN KESA	13	1	0	1	2-	0	1	0	1	0	5	20.0
VICTOR IGNATJEV	1	0	0	0	0	2	0	0	0	0	0	.0
MAXIM GALANOV	1	0	0	0	0	0	0	0	0	0	0	.0
TODD HLUSHKO	2	0	0	0	0	0	0	0	0	0	1	.0
BRIAN BONIN	3	0	0	0	1-	0	0	0	0	0	4	.0
MARTIN SONNENBERG	7	0	0	0	2-	0	0	0	0	0	0	.0
TOM BARRASSO	13	0	0	0	0	4	0	0	0	0	0	.0
TYLER WRIGHT	13	0	0	0	2-	19	0	0	0	0	3	.0
MATTHEW BARNABY	13	0	0	0	2-	35	0	0	0	0	10	.0

GOALTENDER	GPI	MINS	AVG	W	L	T	EN	SO	GA	SA	SV %
TOM BARRASSO	13	787	2.67	6	7	1	1	0	35	350	.900
PIT TOTALS	13	793	2.72	6	7	1	1	0	36	351	.897

Tampa Bay Lightning

You gotta have hope. At least if you're a Lightning fan, because there's precious little else.

So, here's what hope they have:

An enthusiastic new GM and a creative new coach.

One of the best young goalies in the game.

It can't get any worse?

Many of their players can't possibly be as bad as last year?

Okay, let's go to Plan B, because they can't win playing the way they did last season.

Plan B may be new coach Curt Fraser, but that's only if he's the genius new GM Rick Dudley believes he is, and if anybody should know, it's him, having worked together in the IHL.

Plan C is to get a great goaltender, like Buffalo has, and hope he wins it on his own for them. Dan Cloutier is good, but he may not be quite that good.

Here's what hasn't worked so far.

Getting veterans. Dino Ciccarelli and Stephane Richer come to mind most recently. They didn't work out, although Wendel Clark was dynamite before being traded to Detroit.

Getting underachievers. Alexandre Daigle is the poster child for underachieving. Michael Nylander is close behind, and if Chris Gratton doesn't smarten up, they can put all three of them on it.

Youth movement. Nice idea, but having too many of them around means they all have lousy teachers. Ideally, they should be worked into the lineup.

Jacques Demers. He's gone.

Okay, not much hope, quite yet

But, here's a secret plan that may work.

Anybody on the power play is going to score more than they would otherwise. That's a given, of course, even on the Lightning. Since the team isn't going anywhere this year, what they ought to do is put players on the power play who don't fit into their future plans, and pad their scoring stats. Other teams around the league are always looking for scoring, especially if they have injuries, and especially around the trade deadline. Then they're willing to trade prospects.

Once you deal one guy away, you put another guy who's not in the team's plans and do the same thing. Okay, easier said than done, but that's exactly what happened last year with Wendel Clark and Benoit Hogue. Probably, they could have done the same thing with Dino Ciccarelli, if he hadn't been hurt, and maybe even Petr Svoboda.

The Lightning have a boatload of players they could do that with, including Daigle, Nylander, Richer and Sillinger.

TEAM PREVIEW

GOAL: Dan Cloutier was considered by many to be the best goalie not playing regularly in the NHL. Whether or not that's going to make any difference on the Lightning this year is another question.

But, it should, and at least has to be better than finding injury replacements for Darren Puppa every year. Puppa is supposedly healthy and expected back in a back-up role. Kevin Hodson is third on the depth cchart.

DEFENSE: Not many household names on the Lightning defense, unless you count Petr Svoboda, but he's more like a common doctor's office name. Perhaps the most injured player in the history of sports, nevertheless he's the top defenseman until the second or third game when he becomes injured.

Pavel Kubina was a pleasant surprise, despite being a minus —33. Plus-minus is mostly meaningless, and Kubina had a lot of ice time, was a frequent hitter, and even contributed offensively.

Cory Cross and Jassen Cullimore will be regulars, along with Svoboda, Kubina, and possibly Drew Bannister, Sergey Gusev, Andrei Skopintsev and Paul Mara.

Gusev was obtained from the Stars in the Benoit Hogue deal, and can play the power play. It could be Mara's time, too, to show why he's been such a highly regarded prospect after being selected 7th overall in the 1997 draft. He is an all round player, who contributes at both ends of the rink, which is exactly what they need.

FORWARD: If they all lived up to their promise, the Lightning could put the puck in the net. But, of course they're not going to do that.

Darcy Tucker came out of nowhere to become the team's most valuable forward. He scored 21 goals, after scoring just seven in each of his first two seasons. He can't be considered a number one centre, but he certainly played like one. He led the team with eight power play goals, and had 176 penalty minutes, which puts in a select group of tough guys who can score. The list below shows all the players in the league who had at least 20 goals and 100 penalty minutes. There are just 10 of them.

GOALTENDER	GPI	MINS	AVG	W	L	T	EN	SO	GA	SA	SV %
ZAC BIERK	1	59	2.03	0	1	0	0	0	2	21	.905
KEVIN HODSON	5	238	2.77	2	1	1	0	0	11	118	.907
DAREN PUPPA	13	691	2.87	5	6	1	1	2	33	350	.906
D. WILKINSON	5	253	3.08	1	3	1	0	0	13	128	.898
COREY SCHWAB	40	2,146	3.52	8	25	3	2	0	126	1,153	.891
BILL RANFORD	32	1,568	3.90	3	18	3	2	1	102	858	.881
T.B TOTALS	82	4,974	3.52	19	54	9	5	4	292	2,633	.889

COREY SCHWAB and KEVIN HODSON shared a shutout vs BOS on Apr 8, 1999

Most Penalty Minutes — 20 goals or more:

		Goals	PIM
Eric Lindros	Phi	40	120
Keith Tkachuk	Pho	36	151
Brendan Shanahan	Det	31	123
Bill Guerin	Edm	30	133
Peter Forsberg	Col	30	108
Bobby Holik	NJ	27	119
Rick Tocchet	Pho	26	147
Jeremy Roenick	Pho	24	130
Darcy Tucker	TB	21	176
Michal Grosek	Buf	20	102

Ideally, you want Tucker as the third line centre, which means the Lightning have one of the best third line centres in the league. Hey, that's something, at least.

Vincent LeCavalier should centre the first line, and each year he plays should improve. No, he's not Michael Jordan, just yet.

You could pencil in Michael Nylander on his left side, but make sure the pencil has an eraser. Few players have been able to accomplish so little compared to expectations. Unless you count Alexandre Daigle, who could possibly play on the right side of the top line. More than likely, however, it will Niklas Sundstrom, who was picked up from the Rangers. He's a two-way player, supposedly in the Jere Lehtinen mode.

Chris Gratton will rebound from last year's terrible season. The Lightning will have to try to find a way to get him on the top line, maybe on the left side instead of Nylander, who will either be injured or in the press box not long into the season. Gratton had just eight goals, but at the very least should be back up to 20 this season.

Stephane Richer, if he stays around, has to fit on the top two lines somewhere, although he's definitely on his last legs.

Colin Forbes, obtained from Philadelphia in the Renberg deal, is supposed to develop into a power forward. He's big, and hasn't yet shown a scoring ability or exceptional toughness. A full year with one team could make the difference.

Robert Petrovicky is being counted on to do some scoring as well, although he's been with three other NHL teams and their minor league clubs, and they didn't think so.

Andreas Johansson, obtained from Ottawa along with GM Rick Dudley, for Rob Zamuner, may have gone to Nylander and Petrovicky's hockey school. At the start of the last season, he showed the scoring prowess of Rocket Richard; in the second half, he was about as effective a scorer as Darren Puppa.

Zamuner's loss will be felt, although on a team like this, he's not going to make the difference with his leadership. He might in Ottawa, though.

Mike Sillinger should centre the fourth line, so they have some blanks to fill in. Big blanks.

SPECIAL TEAMS: Coaches can make all the difference in special teams, especially on the power play, where, you know, they outnumber their opponents. We'll see if Curt Fraser can do something about this mess.

Power Play	G	ATT	PCT
Overall	41	305	13.4% (T-22nd NHL)
Home	24	160	15.0% (T-17th NHL)
Road	17	145	11.7% (21st NHL)

10 SHORT HANDED GOALS ALLOWED (T-19th NHL)

Penalty Killing	G	TSH	PCT
Overall	68	385	82.3% (20th NHL)
Home	29	183	84.2% (20th NHL)
Road	39	202	80.7% (T-22nd NHL)

11 SHORT HANDED GOALS SCORED (5th NHL)

Penalties	GP	MIN	AVG
LIGHTNING	81	1292	16.0 (14th NHL)

LIGHTNING SPECIAL TEAMS SCORING

Power play	G	A	PTS
TUCKER	8	7	15
SVOBODA	1	9	10
DAIGLE	4	4	8
GRATTON	1	6	7
LECAVALIER	2	4	6
RICHER	3	2	5
KUBINA	3	2	5
NYLANDER	1	4	5
GUSEV	0	5	5
CROSS	0	5	5
CULLIMORE	1	3	4
WILKIE	0	3	3
SYKORA	0	2	2
BANNISTER	0	2	2

Short handed	G	A	PTS
RICHER	2	1	3
ZAMUNER	1	2	3
TUCKER	2	0	2
SILLINGER	2	0	2
SVOBODA	1	1	2
GRATTON	0	2	2
KUBINA	1	0	1
HELENIUS	1	0	1
FORBES	1	0	1
CULLIMORE	1	0	1
SAMUELSSON	0	1	1
LECAVALIER	0	1	1
GUSEV	0	1	1
CROSS	0	1	1

COACHING AND MANAGEMENT: New GM, Rick Dudley, doesn't have a lot of credentials to back him up, unless you call bailing out on the Ottawa Senators after one year at the helm. But, he can't be any worse than the previous regime, so they're not losing anything.

New coach, Steve Ludzik, is some kind of technical hockey wizard, which is exactly what this team needs — a magician.

The two of them worked together in Detroit in the IHL and were very successful.

Dudley got off to a great start, when he obtained Dan Cloutier, Niklas Sundstrom and draft picks from the Rangers for their top pick last year.

DRAFT: (see chart) The Lightning traded their top draft pick to get Cloutier, which wasn't a bad deal considering what they got in return. Their first pick, Sheldon Keefe, fell way down below where he was predicted to go. He's small, but he's a competitor. There's also some concern about the baggage he carries with him in the form of his advisor agent.

The Lightning think they may have got a steal with their third round pick. He was ranked as the third best goalie in the draft, possibly a first rounder, but was taken seventh. When so many teams pass on a player, there's usually a good reason.

DRAFT

Player	Pos	Rnd	Sel.	Cntry	Team	Lge	Gms	G	A	P	PIM
Sheldon Keefe	RW	2	47	Can	Barrie	OHL	66	51	65	116	140
E. Konstantinov	G	3	67	Rus	Ak-Bars	Rus					
Brett Scheffelmaier	D	3	75	Can	Medicine Hat	WHL	60	3	10	13	252
Jimmie Olvestad	LW	3	88	Swe	Djugarden Jr.	Swe	44	2	4	6	18
Kaspars Astashenko	D	5	127	Lat	Riga	Lat	68	33	58	101	14
Michal Lanicek	G	5	148	Cze	Praha Jr.	Cze	2.16				
Fedor Fedorov	C	6	182	Rus	Port Huron	USL	42	2	5	7	20
Ivan Rachunek	LW	7	187	Cze	Zlin Jr.	Cze	40	37	24	61	70
Erkki Rajamaki	W	8	216	Fin	IFK Helskini	Fin	14	0	0	0	2
Mikko Kuparinen	D	0	244	Fin							

PROGNOSIS: There's not a chance the Lightning can be competitive this season. But, they could start the process and possibly be competitive in a few years. New management teams always come in with such high hopes, but they've also got new ideas, and anything different from what they've been doing can't hurt the Lightning.

The best news for the Lightning is that they've got Atlanta and the NY Islanders in their conference so they won't be the worst team.

STAT SECTION

PLAYER	GP	G	A	PTS	+/-	PIM	PP	SH	GW	GT	S	PCTG
DARCY TUCKER	82	21	22	43	34-	176	8	2	3	0	178	11.8
CHRIS GRATTON	78	8	26	34	28-	143	1	0	1	1	181	4.4
STEPHANE RICHER	64	12	21	33	10-	22	3	2	1	0	139	8.6
V. LECAVALIER	82	13	15	28	19-	23	2	0	2	1	125	10.4
PETR SVOBODA	59	5	18	23	1	81	1	1	1	0	83	6.0
PAVEL KUBINA	68	9	12	21	33-	80	3	1	1	1	119	7.6
COLIN FORBES	80	12	8	20	5-	61	0	1	4	0	117	10.3
ROB ZAMUNER	58	8	11	19	15-	24	1	1	2	0	89	9.0
CORY CROSS	67	2	16	18	25-	92	0	0	0	0	96	2.1
ALEXANDRE DAIGLE	63	9	8	17	13-	4	4	0	1	2	82	11.0
JASSEN CULLIMORE	78	5	12	17	22-	81	1	1	1	0	73	6.8
M. NYLANDER	33	4	10	14	9-	8	1	0	0	0	33	12.1
MIKE SILLINGER	79	8	5	13	29-	36	0	2	0	0	92	8.7
SERGEY GUSEV	36	1	7	8	3-	16	0	0	1	0	46	2.2
DAVID WILKIE	46	1	7	8	19-	69	0	0	0	0	35	2.9
R. PETROVICKY	28	3	4	7	8-	6	0	0	0	0	32	9.4

Player	GP	G	A	PTS	+/-	PIM	PP	SH	GW	GT	S	Pct
MIKE MCBAIN	37	0	6	6	11-	14	0	0	0	0	22	.0
KJELL SAMUELSSON	46	1	4	5	6-	38	0	0	0	0	22	4.5
STEVE KELLY	34	1	3	4	15-	27	0	0	1	0	15	6.7
COREY SCHWAB	40	0	4	4	0	4	0	0	0	0	0	.0
BRENT PETERSON	20	2	1	3	2-	0	0	0	0	0	16	12.5
MICHAL SYKORA	10	1	2	3	7-	0	0	0	1	0	24	4.2
DREW BANNISTER	21	1	2	3	4-	24	0	0	0	0	29	3.4
J. BONSIGNORE	23	0	3	3	4-	8	0	0	0	0	12	.0
PAUL MARA	1	1	1	2	3-	0	1	0	0	0	1	100.0
ANDREI SKOPINTSEV	19	1	1	2	1	10	0	0	0	0	17	5.9
KAREL BETIK	3	0	2	2	3-	2	0	0	0	0	2	.0
SAMI HELENIUS	8	1	0	1	5-	23	0	1	0	0	4	25.0
COREY SPRING	8	0	1	1	0	2	0	0	0	0	6	.0
PAUL YSEBAERT	10	0	1	1	5-	2	0	0	0	0	10	.0
DAREN PUPPA	13	0	1	1	0	0	0	0	0	0	0	.0
ZAC BIERK	1	0	0	0	0	0	0	0	0	0	0	.0
XAVIER DELISLE	2	0	0	0	0	0	0	0	0	0	1	.0
JOHN CULLEN	4	0	0	0	2-	2	0	0	0	0	3	.0
DEREK WILKINSON	5	0	0	0	0	0	0	0	0	0	0	.0
MARIO LAROCQUE	5	0	0	0	4-	16	0	0	0	0	3	.0
KEVIN HODSON	9	0	0	0	0	0	0	0	0	0	0	.0

TEAM RANKINGS

		Conference Rank	League Rank
Record	19-54-9	14	27
Home	12-25-4	14	27
Away	7-29-5	14	27
Versus Own Conference	12-37-8	14	27
Versus Other Conference	7-17-1	13	26
Team Plus\Minus	-88	14	27
Goals For	179	14	27
Goals Against	292	14	27
Average Shots For	25.6	12	24
Average Shots Against	31.7	14	26
Overtime	1-2-9	9	20
One Goal Games	8-14	13	25
Times outshooting opponent	16	14	27
Versus Teams Over .500	8-31-7	14	27
Versus Teams .500 or under	11-23-2	14	27
First Half Record	9-29-3	14	27
Second Half Record	10-25-6	14	26

MISCELLANEOUS STAT LEADERS:
FACEOFFS

Sillinger	57.8%
Gratton	53.9%
Zamuner	47.0%
LeCavalier	40.3%

ICE TIME

Svoboda	23:18
Kubina	22:47
Cross	22:38
Cullimore	20:14
Tucker	19:23

HITS

Cullimore	161
Kubina	156
Cross	127
Tucker	120
Gratton	109

PLAYOFFS

- did not make the playoffs

Toronto Maple Leafs

Okay, the whole season was a shock. Even in Toronto it took the fans a long time to come around and actually believe in this team. Here's a list of some of the surprises.

A 27 point jump in the standings. The following list shows the most improved teams from last year:

	1997-98 Points	1998-99 Points	Improvement
Toronto	69	97	+27
Ottawa	83	103	+20
Anaheim	65	83	+18
Florida	63	78	+15

Now, here's the problem with that. The previous year, the three most improved teams were Boston, Washington and Los Angeles. Boston earned the same number of points, but Washington and Los Angeles suffered the largest point decreases this past season. Most of the time a team with a sudden point increase is doomed to have a sudden point decrease the following year.

That the Leafs were the highest scoring team in the league, and had a 74 goal scored increase. The following show the biggest goal increases:

	1997-98 Points	1998-99 Points	Improvement
Toronto	194	268	74
Ottawa	193	239	46
Tampa Bay	151	179	28
New Jersey	225	248	23

Hard to find a problem with that, especially when their goals against decreased by six. Although they did surrender the seventh most goals in the league, which would have been the most if not for Curtis Joseph.

That the Leafs made it the final four in the playoffs.

That Toronto was +48 at even strength, tops in the league.

That only Dallas had a better record in one-goal games than Toronto's 18-7 mark.

That Toronto had the best overtime record in the league at 6-1-7.

That Toronto had the best team shooting percentage in the league at 11.7%

That the Hockey Annual picked them to finish 25th overall last season, and are never ever wrong.

That Sergei Berezin scored 37 goals, or that

Steve Thomas had 28, or that Steve Sullivan had 20.

That they had a 20-4-2 mark against the Western Conference.

That they had a record over .500 against teams that were over. 500

Go ahead, pick out the most surprising thing, because they all qualify. The Leafs are surely on their way to Stanley Cup glory now. Right?

Not so fast. Making the playoffs won't be easy this year. Here's why.

Teams with big point increases almost always suffer big point decreases the following year.

The Leafs offensive style is being duplicated. Lots of teams this year will be playing a more wide-open game. That means that Toronto won't be so unique in that regard, making it less of a shock to opposing teams. It also means Toronto will be up against teams firing on all cylinders, instead of on just a few.

The team can't possibly have as many things go right for them that did last year.

Quinn managed to make a silk purse out of a sow's ear last season, but may find himself more distracted this year with general manager duties. In addition, new coaches are most effective their first season.

They're not that talented. They just aren't. Honest.

STUFF: The Leafs had 9 shots on goal in a game against St. Louis, the lowest in team history, and still won 4-0.

Mats Sundin had two penalty shots in the playoffs, the first two ever for a Toronto Maple, and the first time in the league that one player has had two the same year.

Lonny Bohonos had three points in his playoff debut, which was tied for the most as long as the NHL stats went back in this category — 10 years. Paul Kariya also earned three points in his playoff debut.

TEAM PREVIEW

GOAL: Curtis Joseph was as responsible for the turnaround of this team as anyone. On his bad nights, he was amazing; on his good nights he was unbeatable. He, along with Dominik Hasek are the only two goalies in the league who can regularly win games for their team.

Nothing wrong with Glenn Healy as a back-up. He can watch Joseph night after night as well as anybody. Plus, when Healy did get into games, he had a knack for winning them. It's a fairly common thing with backup goalies. For one, he hasn't played for a while and is up for the game in a way the number one goalie can't be. For another, the team knows the backup is in the net and do a more defensively than they might otherwise in order to give him better protection.

GOALTENDER	GPI	MINS	AVG	W	L	T	EN	SO	GA	SA	SV %
CURTIS JOSEPH	67	4,001	2.56	35	24	7	4	3	171	1,903	.910
GLENN HEALY	9	546	2.97	6	3	0	1	0	27	257	.895
FELIX POTVIN	5	299	3.81	3	2	0	1	0	19	142	.866
JEFF REESE	2	106	4.53	1	1	0	0	0	8	51	.843
TOR TOTALS	82	4,972	2.79	45	30	7	6	3	231	2,359	.902

DEFENSE: Apart from Bryan Berard, you'd have a hard time coming up with much in trade value on the open market for any of the defensemen. It's just so confusing.

They don't have a top defenseman, they all just seemed to take turns posing as it, and it seemed to work just fine. They couldn't do it consistently, but how can you complain about the job Alexander Karpovtsev did, leading the league with a +39, despite only playing in 59 games. He was supposed to be a chronic underachiever.

Dimtri Yuskevich was a wall at times during the season and in the playoffs. He wasn't supposed to be that good. Danil Markov was on some nights the Leafs top defenseman, hitting everything in sight.

There was also marked inconsistency from all three, but you could probably say the same about every defensemen in the league. Berard may stand out a little more in that area, because he is still a poor defensive player who makes bad decisions, but his offense can be enough if he picks it up in that area, and he can.

Sylvain Cote can still contribute with the man advantage, but he will turn 34 this year, and he doesn't have near the responsibility he had when he first came to Toronto.

Chris McAllister is a big tough guy, but he's also a big, plodding, slow tough guy, and doesn't necessarily fit into the scheme of things here, much the same way that Jason Smith didn't.

The Leafs picked up Greg Andrusak, a career minor leaguer who showed up late in the season for Pittsburgh and made an impression in the playoffs against Toronto.

Toronto was also looking at free agent Mark Tinordi, which would be an excellent pickup except for the fact that he's among the most injury prone players in the league.

Finally, there's Tomas Kaberle, who probably received more praise than any Leaf player for his potential, and deserved very little of it. He has a long long way to go to be a good defenseman in the NHL. He was plunked on the power play and given all kinds of ice-time early in the year, but he looked better than he played.. He should have spent the season in the AHL. And when he was sent to the press box during the season and the playoffs it was for good reason. He might have abundant skills, but he needs to learn how to play the game, and he's not the second coming in any event.

If the Leaf defensemen take turns once again stepping up and playing the role of the team's top defensemen, they'll be okay, but what are the chances of that?

FORWARD: Once again, on paper the Leafs forwards should not have scored so many goals. And they wouldn't on any other team that wasn't designed to play an offensive style.

The team couldn't even find a set number one line, much less a suitable left winger for Mats Sundin and Steve Thomas.

Everybody seemed to overachieve with their scoring stats, except Sundin, who never seems able to do enough, and probably Mike Johnson who suffered a little of the sophomore jinx. You can include Fredrik Modin in there, as well.

Everybody seems to have pretty much given up on Modin, and seemingly with good reason. He's skilled, but he's clueless. Kind of reminds you of another player in the same situation the year before — Sergei Berezin. Berezin jumped from 16 goals to 37. Of course, part of that was because he didn't have to worry about playing defense, which he wasn't going to do anyway, and part of it was because it was his third season in the league.

If a player is going to have a breakout year it is almost always in their third or fourth season. That means Modin has one more year to prove himself.

If Alyn McCauley is recovered from his injuries, he could be the number two centre. He was looking outstanding before getting hurt last season, and could turn out to be a Mike Peca type.

The Leafs have a number of other players who can play centre. They include Steve Sullivan, Todd Warriner, Yannick Perreault and Adam Mair.

The knock against Sullivan is his size, but every time he's on the ice he makes things happen. He seems to pick up every line he's on. Perreault may have a hard time finding ice time on this team, but he's adept at faceoffs and made a big difference in that regard when he came over from Los Angeles. He also had 15 points in 12 regular season games. Adam Mair made a big impression in the playoffs and could go into the season as the team's number four centre.

Of course, there will have to be lots of mixing and matching from the centre to the wings to get the best lineup, but the right side will feature Steve Thomas, Mike Johnson and Tie Domi for starters. Igor Korolev can play there or centre, and playoff hero Lonny Bohonos could be in the lineup somewhere.

Berezin, Modin, Derek King, Kris King and Gary Valk could line up on the left. Valk was re-signed as an unrestricted free agent after proving his worth well beyond his scoring capabilities.

The Leafs also picked up Jason Bonsignore and Jonas Hoglund as free agents. Bonsignore was the fourth overall draft pick in 1994 by Edmonton, but has done absolutely nothing yet to even come close to justifying it. Hoglund was a bust with the Canadiens last year.

The bottom line is there are just too many bodies around, and except for a core of maybe seven forwards — Sundin, Thomas, Berezin, Johnson, Valk, McCauley and Domi — everybody else is fighting for their playing lives.

That's good, but it's also bad, because it means they don't have players good enough to take command of a spot on the team. At the very least they should have depth and competition tends to bring out the best in players.

SPECIAL TEAMS: Most of the year, the power play stunk and most of the year the penalty killing stunk. It's unusual for a team to perform so well in the standings under those circumstances.

The obvious problem for the power play is that they don't have a reliable quarterback. Bryan Berard is supposed to be, and he could still fill that role effectively, but has to be confident he can run things from back there. A little older and a little wiser, he still has a chance to do that. Apart from him, they don't have another bona fide power play point man. The team thinks Kaberle can fill that role eventually, and Cote used to be able to do it but has faded considerably in prominence

Power Play	G	ATT	PCT
Overall	53	361	14.7% (T-15th NHL)
Home	25	174	14.4% (T-19th NHL)
Road	28	187	15.0% (T-13th NHL)

6 SHORT HANDED GOALS ALLOWED (T-7th NHL)

Penalty Killing	G	TSH	PCT
Overall	63	322	80.4% (24th NHL)
Home	34	158	78.5% (27th NHL)

Road   29   164   82.3% (T-18th NHL)

7 SHORT HANDED GOALS SCORED (T-13th NHL)

Penalties	GP	MIN	AVG
MAPLE LEAFS	81	1085	13.4 (6th NHL)

MAPLE LEAFS SPECIAL TEAMS SCORING

Power play	G	A	PTS
THOMAS	11	7	18
BERARD	4	14	18
KING	8	8	16
SUNDIN	4	11	15
BEREZIN	9	3	12
SULLIVAN	4	7	11
KOROLEV	1	9	10
KARPOVTSEV	1	9	10
JOHNSON	5	4	9
YUSHKEVICH	2	7	9
COTE	0	9	9
PERREAULT	4	4	8
MCCAULEY	1	4	5
KABERLE	0	5	5
VALK	1	3	4
WARRINER	1	2	3
TREMBLAY	0	3	3
MODIN	1	1	2

Short handed	G	A	PTS
PERREAULT	3	2	5
JOHNSON	3	0	3
YUSHKEVICH	1	1	2
BEREZIN	1	1	2
KING	1	0	1
SUNDIN	0	1	1
MARKOV	0	1	1
KABERLE	0	1	1

COACHING AND MANAGEMENT: After Murphy's Law, the team experienced Quinn's Law, which is: Everything that can go right, did. Clearly, Quinn's accomplishments as coach were the more remarkable in recent memory, or any memory for that matter. And he didn't even win the Adams Trophy as coach of the year. That went to Jacques Martin in Ottawa.

Now for the silliness that was the Leafs management team. Ken Dryden and Mike Smith were the GM team, although who did what is unclear. Somebody was responsible for hiring Pat Quinn and somebody was responsible for getting Curtis Joseph as a free agent. You can stop right there, because that's what made this team a winner. Getting Bryan Berard for Felix Potvin was certainly an outstanding trade, and you can't argue with getting Karpovtsev for Mathieu Schneider. We don't know who was responsible for what, but they weren't the keys.

By the end of last season Smith and Dryden weren't talking, Smith wanted autonomy as GM, didn't get it and was let go.

Quinn took over as GM, which could be bad news, because his forte is coaching, and the GM job can just be a distraction.

DRAFT: Once again the Maple Leafs attempt to be groundbreakers in draft strategy. Last year, they took a player from Kazakhstan, and this year one from Switzerland.

The obvious reasoning is that they figure they got a deal because everybody else is stupid and they aren't. Or else, they think other teams shied away from them for false reasons.

Either way, it's a strategy best advised for teams piled up with prospects, who can can afford to take a chance on a longshot. The Leafs aren't in that position.

DRAFT

Player	Pos	Rnd	Sel.	Cntry	Team	Lge	Gms	G	A	P	PIM
Luca Cereda	C	1	24	Swi	Ambri	Switz	37	6	10	16	8
Peter Reynolds	D	2	60	Can	London	OHL	59	2	25	27	55
Mirko Morovic	LW	4	108	Can	Moncton	QMJHL	69	21	33	54	60
Jonathan Zion	D	4	110	Can	Ottawa	OHL	60	8	33	41	10
Vaclav Zavaral	D	5	151	Cze	Litvinov Jr	Cze	51	2	12	14	42
Jan Socor	RW	6	161	Cze	Slavia Praha	Cze	48	10	10	20	14
Vladimir Kulkov		7	211	Rus	CSKA Jr	Rus					
Perrie Hedin	D	8	239	Swe	Modo	Swe	41	6	5	11	28
Peter Metcalf	D	9	267	USA	Maine	H.E	33	18	48	66	38

PROGNOSIS: Trouble, Leaf fans. They're not assured of making the playoffs. That may sound ridiculous after a 97 point season, but don't be surprised. Nothing can work again as well as it did last season, so at the very least if they do make the playoffs it will be with a major point reduction.

STAT SECTION

PLAYER	GP	G	A	PTS	+/-	PIM	PP	SH	GW	GT	S	PCTG
MATS SUNDIN	82	31	52	83	22	58	4	0	6	0	209	14.8
STEVE THOMAS	78	28	45	73	26	33	11	0	7	0	209	13.4
SERGEI BEREZIN	76	37	22	59	16	12	9	1	4	0	263	14.1
DEREK KING	81	24	28	52	15	20	8	0	4	0	150	16.0
IGOR KOROLEV	66	13	34	47	11	46	1	0	2	0	99	13.1
MIKE JOHNSON	79	20	24	44	13	35	5	3	2	0	149	13.4
YANIC PERREAULT	76	17	25	42	7	42	4	3	3	0	141	12.1
STEVE SULLIVAN	63	20	20	40	12	28	4	0	5	0	110	18.2
BRYAN BERARD	69	9	25	34	1	48	4	0	5	1	135	6.7
FREDRIK MODIN	67	16	15	31	14	35	1	0	3	1	108	14.8
GARRY VALK	77	8	21	29	8	53	1	0	0	1	93	8.6
SYLVAIN COTE	79	5	24	29	22	28	0	0	1	0	119	4.2
D. YUSHKEVICH	78	6	22	28	25	88	2	1	0	0	95	6.3
A. KARPOVTSEV	58	3	25	28	39	52	1	0	1	0	65	4.6
ALYN MCCAULEY	39	9	15	24	7	2	1	0	1	1	76	11.8
TIE DOMI	72	8	14	22	5	198	0	0	1	0	65	12.3
TOMAS KABERLE	57	4	18	22	3	12	0	0	2	0	71	5.6

Player	GP	G	A	PTS	+/-	PIM	PP	SH	GW	GT	S	PCT
TODD WARRINER	53	9	10	19	6-	28	1	0	1	0	96	9.4
DANIIL MARKOV	57	4	8	12	5	47	0	0	0	1	34	11.8
YANNICK TREMBLAY	35	2	7	9	0	16	0	0	0	0	37	5.4
CURTIS JOSEPH	67	0	5	5	0	6	0	0	0	0	0	.0
KRIS KING	67	2	2	4	16-	105	0	1	1	0	34	5.9
LADISLAV KOHN	16	1	3	4	1	4	0	0	0	0	23	4.3
CHRIS MCALLISTER	48	1	3	4	3-	102	0	0	0	1	18	5.6
LONNY BOHONOS	7	3	0	3	3	4	0	0	0	0	13	23.1
DALLAS EAKINS	18	0	2	2	3	24	0	0	0	0	11	.0
KEVYN ADAMS	1	0	0	0	0	0	0	0	0	0	1	.0
JEFF REESE	2	0	0	0	0	0	0	0	0	0	0	.0
KEVIN DAHL	3	0	0	0	0	2	0	0	0	0	0	.0
GLENN HEALY	9	0	0	0	0	0	0	0	0	0	0	.0

TEAM RANKINGS

		Conference Rank	League Rank
Record	45-30-7	3	5
Home	23-13-5	6	8
Away	22-17-2	3	5
Versus Own Conference	25-26-5	9	16
Versus Other Conference	20-4-2	1	1
Team Plus\Minus	+48	1	1
Goals For	268	1	1
Goals Against	231	10	21
Average Shots For	27.9	5	11
Average Shots Against	28.6	10	17
Overtime	6-1-7	1	1
One Goal Games	18-7	1	2
Times outshooting opponent	36	8	15
Versus Teams Over .500	21-17-4	3	4
Versus Teams .500 or under	24-13-3	3	6
First Half Record	24-15-2	5	7
Second Half Record	21-15-5	3	6

MISCELLANEOUS STAT LEADERS

FACEOFFS

Perreault	62.8%
Sundin	57.3%
McCauley	46.4%
Sullivan	44.4%

ICE TIME

Berard	23:35
Yushkevich	22:20
Cote	21:04
Karpovtsev	21:02
Sundin	20:41

HITS

Yushkevich	169
K.King	116
Domi	100
Valk	99

PLAYOFFS

Results:

Defeated Philadelphia 4-2 in conference quarter-finals

Defeated Pittsburgh 4-2 in conference quarter-finals

Lost to Buffalo 4-1 in conference finals

Record: 9-8

Home: 5-4

Away: 4-4

Goals For: 43 (2.5/game)

Goals Against: 46 (2.7/game)

Overtime: 3-0

Power play: 13.8% (10th)

Penalty Killing: 81.7% (13th)

PLAYER	GP	G	A	PTS	+/-	PIM	PP	SH	GW	OT	S	PCTG
MATS SUNDIN	17	8	8	16	2	16	3	0	2	0	44	18.2
SERGEI BEREZIN	17	6	6	12	0	4	2	0	2	1	65	9.2
STEVE THOMAS	17	6	3	9	1-	12	2	0	1	0	41	14.6
LONNY BOHONOS	9	3	6	9	3	2	0	0	0	0	26	11.5
YANIC PERREAULT	17	3	6	9	6-	6	0	0	2	1	15	20.0
BRYAN BERARD	17	1	8	9	10-	8	1	0	0	0	29	3.4
GARRY VALK	17	3	4	7	1-	22	0	0	1	1	14	21.4
STEVE SULLIVAN	13	3	3	6	3-	14	2	0	0	0	21	14.3
D. YUSHKEVICH	17	1	5	6	7	22	1	0	0	0	17	5.9
DANIIL MARKOV	17	0	6	6	9	18	0	0	0	0	11	.0
MIKE JOHNSON	17	3	2	5	1-	4	0	0	1	0	26	11.5
A. KARPOVTSEV	14	1	3	4	7-	12	1	0	0	0	13	7.7
DEREK KING	16	1	3	4	0	4	0	0	0	0	26	3.8
SYLVAIN COTE	17	2	1	3	3-	10	0	0	0	0	19	10.5
TOMAS KABERLE	14	0	3	3	0	2	0	0	0	0	14	.0
KRIS KING	17	1	1	2	1-	25	0	0	0	0	15	6.7
KEVYN ADAMS	7	0	2	2	2-	14	0	0	0	0	9	.0
TIE DOMI	14	0	2	2	1-	24	0	0	0	0	7	.0
ADAM MAIR	5	1	0	1	1-	14	0	0	0	0	3	33.3
CHRIS MCALLISTER	6	0	1	1	1-	4	0	0	0	0	2	.0
GLENN HEALY	1	0	0	0	0	0	0	0	0	0	0	.0
DALLAS EAKINS	1	0	0	0	0	0	0	0	0	0	0	.0
IGOR KOROLEV	1	0	0	0	0	0	0	0	0	0	0	.0
LADISLAV KOHN	2	0	0	0	0	5	0	0	0	0	0	.0
FREDRIK MODIN	8	0	0	0	2-	6	0	0	0	0	11	.0
TODD WARRINER	9	0	0	0	0	2	0	0	0	0	12	.0
CURTIS JOSEPH	17	0	0	0	0	2	0	0	0	0	1	.0

GOALTENDER	GPI	MINS	AVG	W	L	T	EN	SO	GA	SA	SV %
GLENN HEALY	1	20	.00	0	0	0	0	0	5	10	1.000
CURTIS JOSEPH	17	1,011	2.43	9	8	5	1	0	41	440	.907
TOR TOTALS	17	1,036	2.66	9	8	5	1	0	46	450	.898

Washington Capitals

It was a nightmare season for the Washington Capitals, in almost every conceivable way. Everything that could go wrong, did. If their season was a television series it would be called ER, partly for its drama and partly because that's where most of their players spent some time.

Here's a list of explanations for the Caps terrible season.

Stanley Cup Finalist Jinx. Teams that have lost in the finals, as the Caps did in 1998, almost to a team have had terrible follow-up seasons. Since the conference setup began in 1982, only three of the 17 teams have made it as far as the conference finals the next year. Ten of the 17 either were knocked off in the first round or didn't even make the playoffs.

Injuries. The Caps didn't have a healthy lineup for even one game last year. On some occasions, eight players were scratched due to injuries, and in one game, 10 of them were. In all, the Caps had an incredible 511 man-games lost to injury. Peter Bondra missed 18, Adam Oates 23, Sergei Gonchar 29, Calle Johansson 15, Steve Konowalchuk 37, Jan Bulis 44, Yogi Svejkovsky 57, Chris Simon 59, Mark Tinordi 34, Michal Pivonka 46, Dmitri Mironov 36, and Richard Zednik 33.

Too many Europeans. Actually, it wouldn't matter if they had too many Martians, they were all injured anyway.

Too many older players. They would have been okay, if the younger players had been around, too, but most of them have since departed. That includes Dale Hunter, Kelly Miller, Michal Pivonka, Mark Tinordi, and Brian Bellows.

Coach effectiveness worn off. A coach's effectiveness is so much more significant in their first season, that *The Hockey News* doesn't even recognize first year coaches in their selection of Coach of the Year. It's the second and third seasons, if they last long, that truly define their value as a coach. Mind you, if it weren't for all the injuries, Ron Wilson would have looked like a much better coach.

Bondra and Oates slump. Even when the two of them weren't injured, they were not as effective as they had been in the past. The two did go on a tear after the half-way point for a spell, but it was short-lived, and neither got fully untracked.

Organizational Strength. The Caps annually had one of the best and deepest organizations in hockey when David Poile was the GM. Now, it's run dry, and was ranked 23rd by The Hockey News this year, and that was with Boynton as a prospect, so without him they likely move closer to last.

STUFF: The Caps scored eight times in the second period in a 10-1 win over Tampa Bay, tying a franchise record.

Adam Oates became the the 21st player in NHL history to record 800 career assists.

A quirk in the schedule means that the Caps with play the expansion Atlanta Thrashers three games in a row in early January.

TEAM PREVIEW

GOAL: Olie the Goalie did not have a banner year, but it's hard to tell whether he saved the team from worse humiliation of was part of the problem. Most likely the former.

He has a new backup this year, Craig Billington, who is used to backing up Patrick Roy in Colorado.

DEFENSE: Not long ago, the Washington defense was considered among the best in the league. Not any more. Now, they're old, injury-prone, or have proved their ineffectiveness.

Not that we could tell much from last year, considering how many injuries they had. Surprisingly, it was Ken Klee who was their steadiest rearguard, and he's a regular visitor to the forward lines.

Joe Reekie is a solid defensive defenseman and Enrico Ciccone is a tough-guy enforcer, who didn't do much enforcing. Brendan Witt is a steady defender, but also a steady visitor to the injury list.

Dmitri Mironov was a bust, even before injuries took their toll. He was an ill-advised free agent signing, who did little to help the power play as was expected.

Mark Tinordi was lost to free agency, but it's hard to say they'll miss him because he was injured so often anyway.

Veteran Calle Johansson is an effective power play performer, but it was Sergei Gonchar who shone their the most. Not with any playmaking ability — he only had 10 assists — but with a goal scoring prowess. His 21 goals were second to the 23 Adrian Aucoin of Vancouver earned, but Gonchar missed 29 games. His projected goal total was 32.

Others vying for lineup time include Nolan Baumgartner, Alexei Tezikov, Ken Poapst and Stewart Malgunas.

The group has the potential to be decent, but at the same time have the potential to be very mediocre, not to mention the potential to be injured a lot.

GOALTENDER	GPI	MINS	AVG	W	L	T	EN	SO	GA	SA	SV %
MIKE ROSATI	1	28	.00	1	0	0	0	0	0	12	1.000
RICK TABARACCI	23	1,193	2.51	4	12	3	3	2	50	530	.906
OLAF KOLZIG	64	3,586	2.58	26	31	3	5	4	154	1,538	.900
MARTIN BROCHU	2	120	3.00	0	2	0	0	0	6	55	.891
WSH TOTALS	82	4,959	2.64	31	45	6	8	6	218	2143	.898

FORWARD: Most of the older forwards have been moved out, so it will be up to the kids. Although the Caps can certainly expect a rebound year from Peter Bondra, who averaged exactly 50 goals a season the previous three years before last season's disaster. More from Adam Oates can be expected too, but it should be remembered that he is 37-years-old.

Brian Bellows should not have been the second top scoring forward, with 17 goals, and James Black shouldn't have been third with 16. Both earn full credit for that. Bellows became an unrestricted free agent and Black was rewarded for his surprise season with a new contract.

Steve Konowalchuk is close to being a 20-20 man when he's not injured. Andrei Nikolishin might have been expected to earn more than 35 points, considering he had 14 in 21 games in the previous playoffs. Chris Simon could score a bit and add a lot of toughness, but missed most of the season with injuries, which has become his custom. Mike Eagles, an effective fourth line checker and penalty killer, was re-signed in the summer.

The rest of the scoring is up to unproven kids, big on potential, low on results. That includes Bulis, Svejkovsky, Zednik, Herr, and Benoit Gratton. Gratton is expected to be the fourth line centre and is compared frequently to Dale Hunter, which the Caps hope is not empty praise.

Instead of using veterans to help the kids along, as was the plan last year, the kids are pretty much going to have to help each other along, and that's usually a recipe for disaster.

SPECIAL TEAMS: Thanks to Gonchar the Caps power play was at least respectable. His 13 goals were twice as many as anybody else, except Bellows, who had eight. Bondra, who should be dynamite with the man-advantage, had just six, and was almost as effective short-handced, where he scored three goals.

Fewer injuries would allow the special teams units to operate at a more consistent level.

Power Play	G	ATT	PCT
Overall	52	301	17.3% (9th NHL)
Home	24	151	15.9% (12th NHL)
Road	28	150	18.7% (4th NHL)

7 SHORT HANDED GOALS ALLOWED (T-9th NHL)

Penalty Killing	G	TSH	PCT
Overall	55	353	84.4% (15th NHL)
Home	23	163	85.9% (12th NHL)
Road	32	190	83.2% (T-14th NHL)

8 SHORT HANDED GOALS SCORED (T-8th NHL)

Penalties	GP	MIN	AVG
CAPITALS	82	1281	15.6 (11th NHL)

CAPITALS SPECIAL TEAMS SCORING

Power play	G	A	PTS
OATES	3	18	21
GONCHAR	13	4	17
BONDRA	6	9	15
JOHANSSON	2	13	15
BELLOWS	8	3	11
BULIS	3	7	10
KONOWALCHUK	4	5	9
SVEJKOVSKY	4	3	7
MIRONOV	2	5	7
NIKOLISHIN	0	7	7
BLACK	1	3	4
PIVONKA	2	1	3
KLEE	0	3	3
ZEDNIK	1	1	2
HERR	1	1	2

	G	A	PTS
GRATTON	0	1	1
BOILEAU	0	1	1

Short handed	G	A	PTS
BONDRA	3	1	4
OATES	0	3	3
NIKOLISHIN	1	1	2
GONCHAR	1	1	2
TINORDI	0	2	2
KONOWALCHUK	1	0	1
BLACK	1	0	1
TOMS	0	1	1
MIRONOV	0	1	1
JOHANSSON	0	1	1

COACHING AND MANAGEMENT: Tough to judge Ron Wilson's performance after coming off a Stanley Cup final appearance. He just didn't have the healthy horses and that limits a coach's effectiveness.

George McPhee is a hard working general manager who is big on analysis and big on principle. That forces him to take a hard line on players with unfair contract demands, which is good for the overall game. He might have bitten the bullet, though, on 1997 first rounder Nick Boynton, and caved in to his salary demands instead of letting him go back into the draft. He got a second round compensory pick, but allowed an NHL ready defenseman of whom there are precious few available in the draft, go by the board. He claimed Boynton was on a talented team in Ottawa in the OHL, which made him look better, but if he had watched Boynton consistently he'd know Boynton made the players around HIM look better. Time will tell on this one, but Boynton is slated to be a regular in the Boston Bruins lineup this year.

McPhee doesn't have the magic that former GM David Poile had in building an organization, but he's able to recognize weaknesses and will act accordingly to fix it.

DRAFT: The Caps had five picks in the first 37 selections, which isn't that far off from having five first rounders, especially when you consider three of them were rated in the top 24 in *The Hockey News*.

Kris Beech is the prize, of course. The playmaking centre was slowed down by mononucleosis late

DRAFT

Player	Pos	Rnd	Sel.	Cntry	Team	Lge	Gms	G	A	P	PIM
Kris Beech	C	1	7	Can	Calgary	WHL	68	26	41	67	87
Michal Sivek	C	2	29	Cze	Kladno Jr	Cze	34	4	8	12	24
Charlie Stephens	C	2	31	Can	Guelph	OHL	68	26	32	58	80
Ross Lupaschuk	D	2	34	Can	Prince Albert	WHL	67	8	19	27	127
Nolan Yonkman	D	2	37	Can	Kelowna	WHL	61	1	6	7	129
Roman Tvrdon	F	5	132	Slo	Trencin Jr.	Slov	50	23	25	48	6
Kyle Clark	RW	6	175	USA	Harvard	ECAC	20	0	2	2	30
David Johansson	D	7	192	Swe	AIK Jr.	Swe	33	5	5	10	30
Maxim Orlov	D	8	219	Rus	CSKA Jr	Rus	2	0	0	0	2
Igor Shadilov	D	9	249	Rus	Dynamo	Rus	2	0	0	0	0

in the season. He's considered a two-way player who makes excellent use of his abundant speed.

PROGNOSIS: It would be tempting to suggest that with all the injuries that happened last year, the nightmare season couldn't possibly happen again. That's probably true, but the problem is that much of the team has been dismantled in the meantime, with most of the veterans gone.

Youth is good when there's a proper mix, but there doesn't seem to be one here, and they should suffer for it. There's way too much unproven talent on this team for them to be successful.

They should be better, but they should also fall just short of the playoffs, even if they do have an injury-free season.

STAT SECTION

PLAYER	GP	G	A	PTS	+/-	PIM	PP	SH	GW	GT	S	PCTG
PETER BONDRA	66	31	24	55	1-	56	6	3	5	1	284	10.9
ADAM OATES	59	12	42	54	1-	22	3	0	0	0	79	15.2
BRIAN BELLOWS	76	17	19	36	12-	26	8	0	3	0	166	10.2
ANDREI NIKOLISHIN	73	8	27	35	0	28	0	1	1	0	121	6.6
SERGEI GONCHAR	53	21	10	31	1	57	13	1	3	0	180	11.7
JAMES BLACK	75	16	14	30	5	14	1	1	3	0	135	11.9
CALLE JOHANSSON	67	8	21	29	10	22	2	0	2	1	145	5.5
S. KONOWALCHUK	45	12	12	24	0	26	4	1	2	0	98	12.2
JAN BULIS	38	7	16	23	3	6	3	0	3	0	57	12.3
KEN KLEE	78	7	13	20	9-	80	0	0	1	0	132	5.3
RICHARD ZEDNIK	49	9	8	17	6-	50	1	0	2	0	115	7.8
DMITRI MIRONOV	46	2	14	16	5-	80	2	0	0	0	86	2.3
J. SVEJKOVSKY	25	6	8	14	2-	12	4	0	2	0	50	12.0
MICHAL PIVONKA	36	5	6	11	6-	12	2	0	0	0	30	16.7
CHRIS SIMON	23	3	7	10	4-	48	0	0	0	0	29	10.3
JOE REEKIE	73	0	10	10	11	68	0	0	0	0	81	.0
BENOIT GRATTON	16	4	3	7	1-	16	0	0	0	0	24	16.7
BRENDAN WITT	54	2	5	7	6-	87	0	0	0	0	51	3.9
KELLY MILLER	62	2	5	7	5-	29	0	0	1	0	49	4.1
MIKE EAGLES	52	4	2	6	5-	50	0	0	0	0	41	9.8
JEFF TOMS	21	1	5	6	0	2	0	0	0	0	30	3.3
MARK TINORDI	48	0	6	6	6-	108	0	0	0	0	32	.0
ENRICO CICCONE	59	3	1	4	7-	127	0	0	0	1	52	5.8
MATTHEW HERR	30	2	2	4	7-	8	1	0	0	0	40	5.0
T. HALVERSON	17	0	4	4	5-	28	0	0	0	0	16	.0
OLAF KOLZIG	64	0	2	2	0	19	0	0	0	0	0	.0

Washington Capitals

PATRICK BOILEAU	4	0	1	1	4-	2	0	0	0	0	7	.0
MIKE ROSATI	1	0	0	0	0	0	0	0	0	0	0	.0
PATRICK AUGUSTA	2	0	0	0	0	0	0	0	0	0	4	.0
MARTIN BROCHU	2	0	0	0	0	2	0	0	0	0	0	.0
PATRICE LEFEBVRE	3	0	0	0	2-	2	0	0	0	0	2	.0
N. BAUMGARTNER	5	0	0	0	3-	0	0	0	0	0	1	.0
ALEXEI TEZIKOV	5	0	0	0	1-	0	0	0	0	0	4	.0
STEWART MALGUNAS	10	0	0	0	5-	6	0	0	0	0	2	.0
STEVE POAPST	22	0	0	0	8-	8	0	0	0	0	11	.0
RICK TABARACCI	23	0	0	0	0	2	0	0	0	0	0	.0

TEAM RANKINGS

		Conference Rank	League Rank
Record	31-45-6	10	23
Home	16-23-2	12	23
Away	15-22-4	11	20
Versus Own Conference	26-26-4	8	15
Versus Other Conference	5-19-1	14	27
Team Plus\Minus	-15	10	19
Goals For	200	11	20
Goals Against	218	8	15
Average Shots For	29.0	4	6
Average Shots Against	26.1	5	7
Overtime	2-3-6	10	21
One Goal Games	13-20	12	23
Times outshooting opponent	50	4	7
Versus Teams Over .500	17-26-1	8	14
Versus Teams Under .500	14-19-5	12	24
First Half Record	16-22-3	12	20
Second Half Record	15-23-3	12	23

MISCELLANEOUS STAT LEADERS

FACEOFFS

Oates	59.2%
Nikolishin	52.5%
Bulis	48.9%

ICE TIME

Johansson	23:58
Gonchar	23:55
Reekie	21:53
Bondra	20:35
Oates	20:34

HITS

Klee	248
Reekie	182
Witt	148
Tinordi	133
Konowalchuk	125

PLAYOFFS

- did not make the playoffs

EASTERN CONFERENCE

Anaheim Mighty Ducks

The main storyline with the Mighty Ducks is always the same. Team stinks, overcomes impossible odds, win the championship.

Wait — that's the movie version.

The real-life version stars Teemu Selanne and Paul Kariya, and there aren't a lot of plot twists. The two of them save the world — or at least the team.

The secondary plot involves getting a supporting cast to contribute in an offensive role. That hasn't changed much in recent years, either. The extras are good in their supporting roles, but the Ducks have enough of those and need somebody to step up and steal the show once in a while.

We could debate the issue of the two-man team. After all, the Ducks had a winning record and made the playoffs, although they did bow in four straight to Detroit. And we could point out that many teams don't even have one player as good as either Selanne or Kariya.

But, they're just too much of the offense, as shown by the following chart:

Most Goals Scored by Each Team's Top Two Goal Scorers:

	Goals	Team	Goals	% of Total
Selanne (47) Kariya (39)	Ana	86	215	40.0
LeClair (43) Lindros (40)	Phi	83	231	35.9
Jagr (44) Straka (35)	Pit	79	242	32.6
Yashin (44) McEachern (31)	Ott	75	239	31.3
Sakic (41) Forsberg (30)	Col	71	239	29.7
Demitra (37) Turgeon (31)	StL	68	237	28.7
Berezin (37) Sundin (31)	Tor	68	268	25.4

Another problem, and this may sound awfully strange, but the Ducks were tops in the league on the power play, which is all that saved them from disaster. Maybe more a worry than a problem. They scored 39 percent of their goals with the man-advantage, which was far and away above the league average of 26%. Nobody else was even close.

Highest Percentage of Goals on the Power Play:

Anaheim	38.6%
NY Rangers	32.7%
Dallas	31.4%
Lge. Ave	26.3%

The problem is that Anaheim was not good at even strength. In fact, they scored the fewest even strength goals in the league at 132.

That's a problem in itself, but it gives us the opportunity to figure out statistically how well the second, third, and fourth lines were doing their job.

We'll use Kariya, who conveniently played all 82 regular season games, and we can assume he was on the top line for all of them. Kariya was on the ice for 76 of the even strength goals, as well as 59 against. The Ducks scored 132 at even strength and allowed 146.

If we deduct his totals from the team totals, the other lines had 56 goals for and 87 against at even strength. Of course, it's an approximation because we're not taking into account things such as double-shifting. But, overall, when the number one line wasn't on the ice, the team was a —31.

Seeing as how their job was mostly just to prevent goals, because the top line was doing all their scoring, it doesn't appear they were doing their job well at all.

We hardly needed an illustration to prove that, because it's common knowledge that the Ducks need more scoring, but it does give us another measuring stick to show how the rest of them need to contribute more for the team to be successful.

STUFF

The Ducks had seven 1-0 games, winning three and losing four.

Teemu Selanne was the first winner of the Maurice Richard Trophy for most goals scored.

A seven-game winning streak was the longest in team history. The previous high was six, in 1995-96.

With 327 games, Steve Rucchin is only six away from tying Joe Sacco for the most games played in team history.

The last two playoff series for the Ducks have both been against Detroit, and both were sweep losses.

Selanne was third in Lady Byng Award voting, behind Nicklas Lidstrom and winner, Wayne Gretzky

Selanne was voted to the second all star team at right wing, behind Jaromir Jagr, while Kariya was the first team left winger.

TEAM PREVIEW

GOAL: Guy Herbert has been the number one goalie in Anaheim since the start, and will apparently stay that way, seeing how he signed a long term contract. Considering only Nashville faced more shots than the Ducks, nobody is complaining.

Dominic Roussell is a competent backup. Third on the list, with Patrick Lalime being traded, is Tom Askey.

DEFENSE: The Ducks hit the jackpot when they signed Fredrik Olausson last year. All he did was score 56 points, only one away from the second highest total in the league and just six away from Al MacInnis and the highest.

Not surprisingly, 43 of those points came on the power play, where he teamed with Selanne and Kariya to form the top unit in the league.

Olausson has been up and down in his

GOALTENDER	GPI	MINS	AVG	W	L	T	EN	SO	GA	SA	SV %
GUY HEBERT	69	4,083	2.42	31	29	9	3	6	165	2,114	.922
D. ROUSSEL	18	884	2.51	4	5	4	1	1	37	478	.923
ANA TOTALS	82	4,990	2.48	35	34	13	4	7	206	2,596	.921

career, and was hardly a sure thing when he signed as a free agent with the Ducks last year. Part of the reason for his success in Anaheim is that the Ducks had absolutely nothing else offensively on the defensive front. Olausson had 16 goals, the next highest was two. Mind you, most of the time Olausson was the only actual defenseman playing the point on the power play.

An interesting stat with Olausson is that he doesn't shoot the puck much. Part of the reason for that is that on the power play he was more of a setup man, which makes sense when it's Kariya and Selanne being set up. Olausson had just 121 shots. This is how he compared with the top scoring defensemen in the league.

Top Scoring Defensemen and Shots On Net:

Player	Team	Points	Shots
Al MacInnis	St.L	62	314
Nicklas Lidstrom	Det	57	205
Ray Bourque	Bos	57	262
Frederik Olausson	Ana	56	121*
Brian Leetch	NYR	55	184
Phil Housley	Cgy	54	193

But, the good news is that Olausson made the most of his opportunities. He was tied with Adrian Aucoin for the highest shooting percentage for defensemen with at least 20 points.

Highest Defensemen Shooting Percentages (20 or more points):

Frederik Olausson	ANA	13.2%
Adrian Aucoin	Van	13.2%
Sergei Gonchar	Wsh	11.7%
Kenny Jonsson	NYI	8.6%

Obviously, Olausson was saving his shots for his best opportunities. With the Anaheim power play members, it wasn't necessary for him to blast away at the net and hope somebody was standing in front.

In any event, the Ducks made a draft day coup when they landed Oleg Tverdovsky from Phoenix for their first rounder and Travis Green. It not only gives them two offensive defensemen, but the Ducks are going to be dynamite when they have Kariya, Selanne, Olausson and Tverdovsky out on the ice for the four-on-four overtimes next year.

The Ducks had hoped college star, Mike Crowley, would have been a big help on offense, and still could be, but he needs work on his defensive game. Another year in the minors might help me with that.

With the two offensive types now on the blueline, it makes the rest of the defense look that much better because they're defense-first in thinking. Kevin Haller and Jason Marshall pair together for the prime defensive duo, while Ruslan Salei set up with Olausson last year. The Ducks will need to put a defensive type with both Olausson and Tverdovsky.

Pavel Trnka should be another semi-regular, with Pascal Trepanier showing some excellent progress before getting injured. Jamie Pushor was a regular last season, and was selected by Atlanta in the expansion draft. Dan Trebil is also in the mix in case of injuries

The top prospect is Vitali Vishnevsky, taken fifth overall in the 1998 draft. He was named the top defenseman at the 1999 World Junior Championship. They also expect to have Niklas Havelid in the lineup, a 26-year-old Swede taken in this year's draft.

Last year's defense improved tremendously over the previous season, and the nice thing for the Ducks is that almost all of their defensemen have an upside. With Tverdovsky on board, giving them considerably more balance, in just a few years the Ducks have gone from one of the worst blueline corps to better than average, with the potential to be one of the best in the league.

FORWARD: If the Ducks could play even at even strength, and then pound the opposition on the power play, they'd be ahead in the game.

To that end, three lines of checkers and one line of scoring wouldn't be so bad. But, of course, it isn't likely to work that way. Two scoring lines would take the pressure off the top line and open up more opportunities for the second line, with the opposing checkers busy watching Kariya and Selanne.

Selanne won the inaugural Rocket Richard Trophy as the top goal scorer, but interestingly, was the first player not to score 50 goals and lead the league since the 1969-70 season. Richard, the first player to score 50, did it in 1944-45 when they had just a 50-game season.

Steve Rucchin may be the perfect fit between the two superstars, but the Ducks are always trying to stick somebody else in there. They seem to hold monthly auditions, but it always seems to come back to Rucchin. Mind you, Matt Cullen looked good there for part of last season, and it's likely he'll get more time there again this season.

Rucchin has proven to have value all on his lonesome, without the Big Two, and since nobody else has shown any scoring prowess, having him centre up the second line makes at least some sense. Although, Marty McInnis is the only other scorer of even moderate proportions,

so they don't have a second line, anyway.

Mind you, in some cases it may be difficult to tell if the other players have any scoring prowess because they were shoved on third and fourth lines and asked to check. Especially with some of the younger players.

With Tomas Sandstrom returning home to Sweden, somebody will have to step up and at least play on a potential scoring line. Probably a matter of trial and error in that position, however.

Lots of grinders on board, no shortage of them. Ted Donato, obtained from Ottawa, may be a cut above your average grinder.

Most of the rest of the forwards fill in space or are asked to check. Given the chance, some of them could show something offensively, but it's not a likely scenario on the third and fourth lines. Antii Aalto, Johan Davidsson, Jeff Nielsen, and Ted Drury all fit in there, with tough guys Stu Grimson and Jim McKenzie.

Mike LeClerc might get a longer look this year, along with Jeremy Stevenson and Frank Banham.

The Ducks are most excited about Maxim Balmochnykh, a Russian left winger, who came over to play junior in the Quebec Junior League, but left part way through the year because he didn't think he was improving there. Since that's closest to the style of hockey they play in the NHL, you have to wonder what he'll do if he makes the Ducks. Quit there, too, if he doesn't like it? Hard to get too enthused about a quitter, even if he did feel perfectly justified in his actions.

SPECIAL TEAMS: The following were the league's leading power play point scorers, last season.

Player	Team	Points
Selanne	Ana	54
Jagr	Pit	44
Olausson	Ana	43
Kariya	Ana	43

Since three of the top four are from Anaheim, we can deduce that their power play was one of the best in league. In fact, it was tops, and the margin wasn't even that close.

The year before they were 24th out of 26 teams. The difference? Kariya for the full season, and Olausson for the point.

This year, they'll have Tverdovsky back there as well, which creates an interesting question. Since Kariya was so effective on the point, will he be moved back up to forward? It's not a problem, though, because if it doesn't work, they can just move him back to the point.

Chances are this unit can't miss being the best in the league once again. On paper, with Tverdovsky on board, they have the potential to be even better.

Power Play	G	ATT	PCT
Overall	81	368	22.0% (1st NHL)
Home	49	192	25.5% (1st NHL)
Road	32	176	18.2% (5th NHL)

7 SHORT HANDED GOALS ALLOWED (T-9th NHL)

Penalty Killing	G	TSH	PCT
Overall	58	377	84.6% (T-14th NHL)
Home	27	194	86.1% (11th NHL)
Road	31	183	83.1% (17th NHL)

6 SHORT HANDED GOALS SCORED (T-17th NHL)

Penalties	GP	MIN	AVG
MIGHTY DUCKS	80	1297	16.2 (15th NHL)

MIGHTY DUCKS SPECIAL TEAMS SCORING

Power play	G	A	PTS
SELANNE	25	27	52
OLAUSSON	10	32	42
KARIYA	10	31	41
MCINNIS	11	17	28
RUCCHIN	5	17	22
SANDSTROM	6	5	11
GREEN	3	6	9
SALEI	1	8	9
CULLEN	5	2	7
AALTO	2	1	3
CROWLEY	1	2	3
DAVIDSSON	1	1	2
TREPANIER	0	2	2
MCKENZIE	1	0	1
TRNKA	0	1	1

Short handed	G	A	PTS
KARIYA	2	1	3
MCINNIS	1	1	2
GREEN	1	1	2
RUCCHIN	1	0	1
CULLEN	1	0	1
HALLER	0	1	1

COACHING AND MANAGEMENT: GM Pierre Gauthier may not have many fans in Ottawa after skipping out on them, but he's starting to get some applause in Anaheim. He's a deciple of the patient approach. Let the prospects develop through the system, don't rush them, and keep them coming. Stability within the organization.

All that's fine and dandy, but it's an idealistic approach that doesn't work very often these days. New Jersey is probably the prime successful example of it working, thanks to GM Lou

Lamiorello. Other than that, it's not very common.

What happens is that things tend to fall apart at some point, and that patience goes with it. People have their own jobs to worry about, and sometimes they need to produce quickly, or else. Sometimes , the prospects in the system aren't as good as they thought, and it turns out they were wasting time being patient.

Still, in theory, it's a great idea.

Craig Hartsburg returns as coach. He's always looking at ways to improve — the players, the team, himself. He also seems to communicate with the players, and appears to understand that his best team strategy is to get Selanne and Kariya out on the ice as often as possible.

DRAFT: (see chart) The Ducks traded away their first pick in the Tverdovsky deal, and took an offensive defenseman in the second round. Jordan Leopold isn't very big or very physical or very defensive, which means he better score a heck of a lot.

Third round selection, Niklas Haveldid, is 26 years old and has caught the fancy of — exactly one team. Even so, the Ducks think he'll be in their lineup this year. Either that, or maybe they could trade him to Pittsburgh even up for Jaromir Jagr.

The Ducks went big on the Europeans as usual, and small on Canadians, also as usual.

PROGNOSIS: There's no reason to think the Ducks shouldn't be better than last year. They have very definite weaknesses, one of which was shored up with the acquisition of Tverdovsky. Olausson isn't someone you want to depend on for consistency, because his career is as inconsistent as they come, but Kariya and Selanne are about as dependable as they come.

The only real worry with the Ducks is keeping their stars healthy. If they can do that, and keep filling holes, they're just going to get better and better.

DRAFT

Player	Pos	Rnd	Sel.	Cntry	Team	Lge	Gms	G	A	P	PIM
Jordan Leopold	D	2	44	USA	U. Minn.	WCHA	34	7	13	20	20
Niklas Haveldid	D	3	83	Swe	Malmo	Swe.	50	10	12	22	42
A. Chagodayev	D	4	105	Rus	N/A						
Maxim Rybin	RW	5	141	Rus	Sparak	Rus	41	13	8	21	52
Jan Sandstrom	D	6	173	Swe	AIK	Swe	47	2	7	9	18
Peter Tenkrat	W	8	230	CZE	Kladno	Cze	50	21	14	35	0
Brian Gornick	C	9	258	USA	Air Force	US Col	34	10	11	21	20

STAT SECTION

PLAYER	GP	G	A	PTS	+/-	PIM	PP	SH	GW	GT	S	PCTG
TEEMU SELANNE	75	47	60	107	18	30	25	0	7	1	281	16.7
PAUL KARIYA	82	39	62	101	17	40	11	2	4	0	429	9.1
STEVE RUCCHIN	69	23	39	62	11	22	5	1	5	1	145	15.9
F. OLAUSSON	74	16	40	56	17	30	10	0	2	0	121	13.2
MARTY MCINNIS	81	19	35	54	15-	42	11	1	5	0	146	13.0
T. SANDSTROM	58	15	17	32	5-	42	7	0	2	0	107	14.0
TRAVIS GREEN	79	13	17	30	7-	81	3	1	2	0	165	7.9
MATT CULLEN	75	11	14	25	12-	47	5	1	1	1	112	9.8
RUSLAN SALEI	74	2	14	16	1	65	1	0	0	0	123	1.6
TED DRURY	75	5	6	11	2	83	0	0	0	0	79	6.3
JIM MCKENZIE	73	5	4	9	18-	99	1	0	1	0	59	8.5
JEFF NIELSEN	80	5	4	9	12-	34	0	0	2	0	94	5.3
JOHAN DAVIDSSON	64	3	5	8	9-	14	1	0	1	0	48	6.3
ANTTI AALTO	73	3	5	8	12-	24	2	0	0	0	61	4.9
JASON MARSHALL	72	1	7	8	5-	142	0	0	0	0	63	1.6
KEVIN HALLER	82	1	6	7	1-	122	0	0	0	0	64	1.6
PASCAL TREPANIER	45	2	4	6	0	48	0	0	1	0	49	4.1
MIKE CROWLEY	20	2	3	5	10-	16	1	0	1	0	41	4.9
PAVEL TRNKA	63	0	4	4	6-	60	0	0	0	0	50	.0
STU GRIMSON	73	3	0	3	0	158	0	0	1	0	10	30.0
JAMIE PUSHOR	70	1	2	3	20-	112	0	0	0	0	75	1.3
SCOTT FERGUSON	2	0	1	1	0	0	0	0	0	0	1	.0
GUY HEBERT	69	0	1	1	0	0	0	0	0	0	0	.0
DANIEL TREBIL	6	0	0	0	2-	0	0	0	0	0	1	.0
MIKE LECLERC	7	0	0	0	2-	4	0	0	0	0	1	.0
DOMINIC ROUSSEL	18	0	0	0	0	0	0	0	0	0	0	.0

TEAM RANKINGS

		Conference Rank	League Rank
Record	35-34-13	6	14
Home	21-14-6	4	11
Away	14-20-7	9	19
Versus Own Conference	25-24-8	6	14
Versus Other Conference	10-10-5	7	14
Team Plus\Minus	-14	9	18
Goals For	215	6	11
Goals Against	206	6	12
Average Shots For	28.7	8	13
Average Shots Against	33.7	12	25
Overtime	1-3-13	13	24
One Goal Games	10-14	11	21
Times outshooting opponent	28	11	21
Versus Teams Over .500	9-19-7	10	21
Versus Teams .500 or under	26-15-6	6	13
First Half Record	16-17-8	6	16
Second Half Record	19-17-5	6	10

MISCELLANEOUS STATS
FACEOFFS

	W	L	%
Green	700	625	52.8
Rucchin	965	880	52.3
Drury	215	239	47.9
Cullen	499	548	47.7
McInnis	183	207	46.9
Davidsson	191	325	37.0

ICE TIME PER GAME

Kariya	25.54
Selanne	22.78
Rucchin	22.55
Salei	22.05
Haller	20.66
Olausson	19.78

TOP HITTERS

Salei	154
Marshall	150
Trnka	115
Pushor	110
Green	97
Haller	95

PLAYOFFS

Results:

Lost 4-0 to Detroit in conference quarter-finals

Record: 0-4
Home: 0-2
Away: 0-2
Goals For: 6 (1.5/game)
Goals Against: 17 (4.3/game)
Overtime: 0-0
Power play: 20.0% (3rd)
Penalty Killing: 69.6% (16th)

PLAYER	GP	G	A	PTS	+/-	PIM	PP	SH	GW	OT	S	PCTG
TEEMU SELANNE	4	2	2	4	1-	2	1	0	0	0	7	28.6
PAUL KARIYA	3	1	3	4	0	0	0	0	0	0	11	9.1
STEVE RUCCHIN	4	0	3	3	0	0	0	0	0	0	10	.0
MARTY MCINNIS	4	2	0	2	1-	2	2	0	0	0	12	16.7
FREDRIK OLAUSSON	4	0	2	2	4-	4	0	0	0	0	6	.0
JASON MARSHALL	4	1	0	1	1-	10	1	0	0	0	5	20.0
TRAVIS GREEN	4	0	1	1	4-	4	0	0	0	0	12	.0
PAVEL TRNKA	4	0	1	1	3-	2	0	0	0	0	2	.0
DANIEL TREBIL	1	0	0	0	0	2	0	0	0	0	0	.0
TOM ASKEY	1	0	0	0	0	0	0	0	0	0	0	.0
JOHAN DAVIDSSON	1	0	0	0	0	0	0	0	0	0	0	.0
MIKE LECLERC	1	0	0	0	0	0	0	0	0	0	1	.0
STU GRIMSON	3	0	0	0	0	30	0	0	0	0	0	.0
RUSLAN SALEI	3	0	0	0	4-	4	0	0	0	0	5	.0
KEVIN HALLER	4	0	0	0	1-	2	0	0	0	0	7	.0
GUY HEBERT	4	0	0	0	0	0	0	0	0	0	0	.0
JIM MCKENZIE	4	0	0	0	2-	4	0	0	0	0	5	.0
TOMAS SANDSTROM	4	0	0	0	2-	4	0	0	0	0	9	.0
TED DRURY	4	0	0	0	6-	0	0	0	0	0	4	.0
JEFF NIELSEN	4	0	0	0	6-	2	0	0	0	0	7	.0
JAMIE PUSHOR	4	0	0	0	3-	6	0	0	0	0	6	.0
ANTTI AALTO	4	0	0	0	0	2	0	0	0	0	0	.0
MATT CULLEN	4	0	0	0	2-	0	0	0	0	0	6	.0

GOALTENDER	GPI	MINS	AVG	W	L	T	EN	SO	GA	SA	SV %
*TOM ASKEY	1	30	4.00	0	1	0	0	0	2	11	.818
GUY HEBERT	4	208	4.33	0	3	0	0	0	15	124	.879
ANA TOTALS	4	240	4.25	0	4	0	0	0	17	135	.874

Calgary Flames

It's been 11 years since the Flames last won a playoff series. Mind you, that last playoff series was a Stanley Cup victory.

But, a playoff victory is near at hand. At least according to GM Al Coates, who pronounced last season a 'tremendous success.'

Huh?

Well, we're going to have to look for some evidence of that.

Would it be because they missed the playoffs for the third straight year?

Would it be the fact that they won four more games last year than they did the previous season?

Would it be that they had their first losing season at home in franchise history?

Would it be because they scored the fewest goals in team history for a full season, since their expansion year?

We'll keep looking. Don't worry, we don't give up easily.

Could it have been the eight-game losing streak?

Could it possibly be losing five of their last six games at home, when they still had a chance to make the playoffs, and scoring no more than one goal in any of them?

Was it that they used six different goal-tenders last year?

Was it the seven-game losing streak?

WAIT!!! Found something.

The Flames were tied for the most improved team in the second half of the season!

	W	L	T	GF	GA	Pts
First Half	13	25	3	102	127	29
Second Half	17	15	9	109	107	43

They would have been even better, too, if they hadn't choked down the stretch, and lost most of the important games in their playoff drive.

You have to figure a strong second half is a good indicator, obviously because it's closer to this year, but it might just be an illusion. For one thing, everybody pulled together after the Fleury trade, which isn't uncommon, for example, when a superstar is injured. But, it's rarely a permanent thing, and the water usually returns to its own level.

But, for the record, these are the most improved teams in the second half of last season. We'll see how they fare this year.

	First Half Points	Second Half Points	Improvement Points
Colorado	40	58	18

Calgary	29	43	14
Chicago	28	42	14
San Jose	36	44	8

STUFF

Phil Housley became the all-time leading scorer among Americans, when he surpassed Joe Mullen. Housley has 1,075, while Mullen finished his career with 1,063.

Goalie Fred Braithwaite has scored two goals in his junior and pro career, one with Detroit of the OHL, and one with Manitoba in the IHL.

The Flames have been successful in their last six penalty shot attempts; and have stopped opponents from scoring in their last three, including a stop by Tyler Moss last season against Mike Modano of Dallas.

TEAM PREVIEW

GOAL: Fred Braithwaite's first appearance in the Calgary net was January 5, the Flames' 39th game of the year. All he did was shut out Dallas 1-0.

His life hasn't been the same since. He hadn't even played in the NHL since the 1995-96 season, spending two seasons with the Manitoba Moose, after 40 games over three years with the Edmonton Oilers.

Now, apparently, he's the team's number one goalie, with often injured Ken Wregget gone the free agency route. But, he's going to have to prove last season was no fluke, and he's going to have to do it early, or the Flames are in bigger trouble than they think.

J. S. Gigeure is supposed to be the goalie of the future, but he's not turning too many heads quite yet, so he's got a ways to go.

DEFENSE: Did you ever see that movie: So I Married an Axe Murderer, starring Mike Myers? Well, when his parents have their 50th wedding anniversary (or maybe it was 40th) the old man (a Mike Myers character) stands up and thanks his wife for all their years together — 'because it could have been worse.'

That's kind of the way it is with the Calgary defense. They could be worse.

There are some veterans around: Phil Housley, who still has it on the power play; Tommy Albelin; Steve Smith; and captain Todd Simpson.

And there are some great up and coming stars. Derek Morris is a possible future all-star; hard-hitting Denis Gauthier is going to get better with more playing time; Cale Hulse can be an offensive force if given the chance; and Wade Belak, a former first-rounder obtained from Colorado, gives them some more toughness on the blueline.

So, maybe they're not the greatest defensive unit in the league. But, they could be worse.

GOALTENDER	GPI	MINS	AVG	W	L	T	EN	SO	GA	SA	SV %
F. BRATHWAITE	28	1663	2.45	11	9	7	3	1	68	796	.915
TYLER MOSS	11	550	2.51	3	7	0	0	0	23	295	.922
KEN WREGGET	27	1,590	2.53	0	12	4	2	1	67	712	.906
J GIGUERE	15	860	3.21	6	7	1	2	0	46	447	.897
ANDREI TREFILOV	4	162	4.07	0	3	0	0	0	11	84	.869
TYRONE GARNER	3	139	5.18	0	2	0	0	0	12	74	.838
CGY TOTALS	82	4,990	2.81	30	40	12	7	2	234	2,415	.903

Robyn Regehr, obtained from Colorado, had a bright future with the Flames, but was involved in a devestating car accident over the summer. One of his legs was broken, and pins were put in the other one, making his hockey future in doubt.

FORWARD: Life without Theoren Fleury started off pretty good. The Flames went 7-3-1 in their first 14 games, before the initial adreneline wore off. They were 4-7-1 after that, with many of those games life or death for the playoffs.

Cory Stillman had eight points in the first four games after Fleury left, Jarome Iginla had seven, and Valeri Bure had six.

But, let's face it. They have a tough time putting the puck in the net, and that's likely to continue.

Newcomer Marc Savard is more of a playmaker type centre, maybe along the lines of Andrew Cassels, who had trouble getting points in Calgary. Cassels, a free agent, signed with Vancouver, and we'll see if he fares better there, and whether or not it was the Flames or him.

Without Fleury, it's difficult to see the Flames as having a legitimate number one line. They're closer to having an outstanding second line.

That's not to say that Stillman hasn't been remarkable. Especially when it looked as if he wouldn't amount to much in his earlier years with the Flames. He had 27 goals this season, which is good on this team. Bure had 28 goals and Iginla had 26.

That's where the scoring ends, however, with nobody else even getting as many as 15. If they could find a 30-goal man somewhere they'd be in much better shape. Mind you, every team would be in better shape with a 30-goal scorer, so it's easier said than done.

The two top prospects are Daniel Tkaczuk and Rico Fata, neither of whom are likely to light up the scoreboard very quickly. Fata played 20 games with the Flames last year, earning just one point, before being sent back to junior. Tkaczuk had 105 points on a star-laden team in Barrie in the OHL, and was signed just before the draft so he wouldn't be a re-entry. He should get a chance with the Flames this year, but as a third or fourth line centre, he's going to probably have to earn his keep by playing a defensive game to start.

The Flames already have a couple good defensive centres behind Savard and Stillman, in Jeff Shantz and Clarke Wilhelm.

Rene Corbet, who once scored 79 goals in junior, has been a third or fourth liner in Colorado and didn't get the quality ice-time that he should receive on the left wing in Calgary. It's not out of the realm of possibility that he could become a surprise scorer.

It probably is for Jason Wiemer, though. At one time he looked as if he could be a legitimate power forward, who could score goals, and he's shown some flashes, but it appears time is up for him in that department. Andrei Nazarov also patrols the left side, and is a good tough guy to have on your team, when he's not injured, which seems like most of the time. Dave Roche is more or less a fill-in, who will score on occasion, and play and honest tough contest. Hnat Dominichelli could be ready to break loose and show some of the scoring he showed in junior and the minors. He hasn't fared too well in previous auditons, but put him on one of the top two lines and he could break out.

Bure, Iginla and Steve Dubinsky are scheduled for the right side, but Sutter has moved a lot of players around by position and would probably wish he didn't have to.

The key for the Flames will be down the middle. If they can get production from that position, it will extend to the wingers, and the Flames will have some more scoring punch.

SPECIAL TEAMS: Only Nashville was worse at penalty killing than the Flames. And there weren't a lot of teams worse on the power play.

The Flames didn't have one particular guy doing the sniping on the power play, although that's not necessarily bad. The bad part is that they just don't have a major sniper, period.

Obviously, some improvement would be nice in this area, but there doesn't seem to be any cause for optimism.

Housley is good on the point, along with Morris, and the upfront players seem largely a matter of power play by committee.

Power Play	G	ATT	PCT
Overall	49	351	14.0% (19th NHL)
Home	20	167	12.0% (25th NHL)
Road	29	184	15.8% (10th NHL)
5 SHORT HANDED GOALS ALLOWED (T-4th NHL)			

Penalty Killing	G	TSH	PCT
Overall	77	380	79.7% (26th NHL)
Home	37	173	78.6% (26th NHL)
Road	40	207	80.7% (T-22nd NHL)
12 SHORT HANDED GOALS SCORED (T-3rd NHL)			

Penalties	GP	MIN	AVG
FLAMES	80	1,377	17.2 (T-19th NHL)

FLAMES SPECIAL TEAMS SCORING

Power play	G	A	PTS
HOUSLEY	4	19	23
STILLMAN	9	10	19
BURE	7	12	19
IGINLA	6	9	15
CASSELS	4	10	14
MORRIS	3	7	10
CORBET	3	7	10
WIEMER	1	3	4
DOMENICHELLI	3	0	3
NAZAROV	0	3	3
SMITH	0	2	2
WILM	1	0	1
SHANTZ	1	0	1
ROCHE	1	0	1
ST. LOUIS	0	1	1
HULSE	0	1	1

Short handed	G	A	PTS
CASSELS	1	3	4
STILLMAN	3	0	3
DUBINSKY	2	1	3
WILM	2	0	2
SHANTZ	1	1	2
SIMPSON	0	1	1
GAUTHIER	0	1	1
ALBELIN	0	1	1

COACHING AND MANAGEMENT: Brian Sutter is armed with a new contract, but not a new approach to the game. The Flames play a trapping type defense, and have problems turning on the charm at goal scoring time.

GM Al Coates got a good booty for giving up Theoren Fleury to Colorado, but got aced at the draft when he made a trade with the Rangers switching draft positions from 7th to 9th, and losing out on Jamie Lundmark, who was still available. Mind you, the trade, which netted Marc Savard, looked good until Lundmark was still there.

DRAFT

Player	Pos	Rnd	Sel.	Cntry	Team	Lge	Gms	G	A	P	PIM
Oleg Saprykin	F	1	11	Rus	Seattle	WHL	66	47	46	93	107
Dan Cavanaugh	F	2	38	USA	Boston U	H.E.	33	6	7	13	54
Craig Andersson	G	3	77	USA	Guelph	OHL	3.10	.903			
Roman Rozakov	D	4	106	Rus	Togliatti	Rus	0	0	0	0	0
Matt Doman	RW	5	135	USA	Wisconsin	WCHA	32	5	3	8	50
Jesse Cook	D	5	153	USA	Denver	WCHA	30	0	9	9	22
Cory Pecker	C	6	166	Can	S.S. Marie	OHL	68	25	34	59	24
Matt Underhill	G	6	170	Can	Cornell	ECAC	2.95	.902			
Blair Stayzer	LW	7	190	Can	Windsor	OHL	62	12	19	31	140
Dimitri Kirilenko	C	9	252	Rus	CSKA	Rus	37	4	4	8	22

DRAFT: (see chart) Oleg Saprykin can put the puck in the net, no doubt about that, with 47 goals in his first season in the WHL. The Russian born player is considered an obnoxious type on the ice, and could fit in well with the Flames in a few years if he continues his scoring prowess.

PROGNOSIS: Don't expect any miracles out of the Flames this year, despite the optimism that may be floating around. They're not exceptionally strong at any position, and while they're not exceptionally weak, either, it's no reason for optimism.

If they can pick up a sniper in free agency or through a trade, it could make a world of difference. Come to think of it, though, Fleury could score goals and he couldn't make the Flames winners. Without him, it's going to be tougher.

Don't look for the Flames to make the playoffs, unless some of their younger unproven players, actually prove something and have spectacular years.

STAT SECTION

PLAYER	GP	G	A	PTS	+/-	PIM	PP	SH	GW	GT	S	PCTG
CORY STILLMAN	76	27	30	57	7	38	9	3	5	1	175	15.4
PHIL HOUSLEY	79	11	43	54	14	52	4	0	1	0	193	5.7
VALERI BURE	80	26	27	53	0	22	7	0	4	0	260	10.0
JAROME IGINLA	82	28	23	51	1	58	7	0	4	1	211	13.3
ANDREW CASSELS	70	12	25	37	12-	18	4	1	3	0	97	12.4
DEREK MORRIS	71	7	27	34	4	73	3	0	2	2	150	4.7
RENE CORBET	73	13	18	31	1	68	3	0	1	0	127	10.2
JEFF SHANTZ	76	13	17	30	14	44	1	1	3	0	82	15.9
JASON WIEMER	78	8	13	21	12-	177	1	0	1	0	128	6.3
CLARKE WILM	78	10	8	18	11	53	2	2	0	0	94	10.6

ANDREI NAZAROV	62	7	9	16	4-	73	0	0	2	1	71	9.9
STEVE SMITH	69	1	14	15	3	80	0	0	0	0	42	2.4
STEVE DUBINSKY	62	4	10	14	7-	14	0	2	0	0	70	5.7
CALE HULSE	73	3	9	12	8-	117	0	0	0	0	83	3.6
H. DOMENICHELLI	23	5	5	10	4-	11	3	0	0	0	45	11.1
TODD SIMPSON	73	2	8	10	18	151	0	0	0	0	52	3.8
ED WARD	68	3	5	8	4-	67	0	0	0	0	56	5.4
DENIS GAUTHIER	55	3	4	7	3	68	0	0	0	0	40	7.5
DAVE ROCHE	36	3	3	6	1-	44	1	0	2	0	30	10.0
TOMMY ALBELIN	60	1	5	6	11-	8	0	0	0	0	54	1.9
BOB BASSEN	41	1	2	3	13-	35	0	0	0	0	47	2.1
GREG PANKEWICZ	18	0	3	3	0	20	0	0	0	0	10	.0
TOM CHORSKE	26	0	3	3	8-	8	0	0	0	0	44	.0
MARTIN ST. LOUIS	13	1	1	2	2-	10	0	0	0	0	14	7.1
FRED BRATHWAITE	28	0	2	2	0	2	0	0	0	0	0	.0
ERIC LANDRY	3	0	1	1	1	0	0	0	0	0	1	.0
CHRIS O'SULLIVAN	10	0	1	1	1-	2	0	0	0	0	10	.0
TYLER MOSS	11	0	1	1	0	0	0	0	0	0	0	.0
ERIC CHARRON	12	0	1	1	6-	14	0	0	0	0	9	.0
J GIGUERE	15	0	1	1	0	4	0	0	0	0	0	.0
RICO FATA	20	0	1	1	0	4	0	0	0	0	13	.0
KEN WREGGET	27	0	1	1	0	8	0	0	0	0	0	.0
WADE BELAK	31	0	1	1	1	94	0	0	0	0	7	.0
LEE SOROCHAN	2	0	0	0	3-	0	0	0	0	0	5	.0
ROCKY THOMPSON	3	0	0	0	0	25	0	0	0	0	0	.0
TYRONE GARNER	3	0	0	0	0	0	0	0	0	0	0	.0
ANDREI TREFILOV	5	0	0	0	0	0	0	0	0	0	0	.0

TEAM RANKINGS

		Conference Rank	League Rank
Record	30-40-12	9	20
Home	15-20-6	11	22
Away	15-20-6	8	18
Versus Own Conference	21-25-9	9	20
Versus Other Conference	9-15-3	11	24

Team Plus\Minus	+4	8	15
Goals For	211	7	14
Goals Against	234	10	22
Average Shots For	28.5	7	11
Average Shots Against	29.5	9	19
Overtime	3-1-12	3	6
One Goal Games	14-18	9	19
Times outshooting opponent	34	9	17

Versus Teams

Over .500	12-22-5	8	17
Versus Teams .500			
or under	17-18-7	11	22
First Half Record	13-25-3	12	24
Second Half Record	17-15-9	7	13

MISCELLANEOUS STAT LEADERS
FACEOFFS

	W	L	%
Fleury	306	211	59.2
Cassels	675	647	51.1
Shantz	538	574	48.4
Dubinsky	104	119	46.7
Stillman	249	286	46.5
Wiemer	355	512	41.0
Wilm	249	360	40.9

ICE TIME

Smith	22:33
Housley	20:52
Morris	20:44
Albelin	19:08
Cassels	18:58

HITS

Wiemer	171
Gauthier	162
Dubinsky	162
Stilman	128
Ward	122
Iginla	119

PLAYOFFS
- did not make the playoffs

Chicago Blackhawks

You could get excited about the upcoming season if you're a Blackhawks fan. Here a few reasons.

They cut seat prices in the upper reaches of the United Centre. How often do you see that?

They won their last six games of the season.

They won their last nine at home.

They had the best record in the league over their last 10 games, at 8-1-1.

The Hawks won the draft lottery, which allowed them to move up the draft order, and trade the pick, getting Bryan McCabe and a first rounder from Vancouver.

Owner Bill Wirtz had his fingers crossed when he had a handshake agreement not to trade Chris Chelios. This allowed Chicago to get Anders Eriksson and two first round draft picks.

Depth.

Alexei Zhamnov is changing his jersey number to 13, which is a good luck number in Europe.

The Hawks were 13-6-4 under new coach, Lorne Molleken, and more importantly, were a happy group, and wanted to play for him.

Goalie Jocelyn Thibault didn't allow more than two goals in his last eight starts of the season.

The Hawks had the worst penalty-killing in the league, but that's something that can be reversed through coaching. In their last 10 games of the season, they didn't give up any power play goals in seven of them.

The Hawks were 11-24-6 in the first half of last season, and 18-17-6 in the second half, making the second largest improvement behind Colorado.

They should be a more exciting team to watch this year with Molleken's more wide open approach.

The Blackhawks will score more often, and are stronger on defense, so will also allow fewer goals.

The Blackhawks were — 61 in power play opportunities for and against in the 59 games Graham coached, and were only — 9 in 23 games under Molleken. A disciplined approach should mean less time killing penalties.

They have one of the better groups of young defensemen in the league, with Brad Brown, Anders Eriksson and Bryan McCabe.

No more Chris Chelios trade rumors.

They have a potential rookie-of-the-year in J.P. Dumont.

STUFF

A nine-game home winning streak to end the season tied with Pittsburgh for longest of the year.

Bob Probert scored the last goal ever at Maple Leaf Gardens.

TEAM PREVIEW: Jocelyn Thibault didn't set the world on fire until late in the season when he got a little help from his friends. But, he was considerably better than Jeff Hackett, who did, however, go on to have a successful campaign with Montreal.

Steve Passmore, last of Edmonton, was signed after Mark Fitzpatrick was lost to free agency.

DEFENSE: Take the top six defensemen on the Blackhawks and you'd be hard-pressed to find a better group, with more potential or toughness, anywhere in the league.

Boris Mironov is a premier offensive threat; Bryan McCabe is tough, good at handling the puck, and can take a spot on the power play; Nobody much likes hanging around the Chicago net when Dave Manson's around, and he can play on the power play when asked; Anders Ericksson is a young upwardly mobile defenseman who should also contribute offensively; Brad Brown is tough and punishing and an intimidating force on the ice; and Jamie Allison was hampered by injuries most of last season.

On the periphery is Doug Zmolek, Radim Bicanek, Remi Royer, and Bryan Muir.

Blackhawks fans like tough guys, and they'll find lots of them on the blueline. Consider five of the top six defensemen, excluding Eriksson, and their career penalty minutes per 82 games:

Brown	252
Manson	232
Allison	160
McCabe	159
Mironov	125

FORWARD: By the way the Hawks were playing under new coach, Molleken, we should expect them to score a ton more goals this year. That's darn good news for this bunch, because they're offensive-minded anyway and should never have been playing a defensive system.

The whole bunch of them are just so darn happy, they may run out and shoot the lights out.

The only problem is setting them up so it all works properly. That may involve some position shifts, such as moving Doug Gilmour to left wing. He's been a centre forever and teaching an old dog new tricks won't be easy, but he could line up on the left side of Alexei Zhamnov and Tony Amonte.

Josef Marha looked good late in the season centring Eric Daze and J.P. Dumont, but it could just be an illusion

Also to fit in on the right side is tough guy, Ryan Vandenbussche; tough guy, Chris Murray; and tough guy Ty Jones.

At centre, Dean McAmmond plays there, along with left wing; Mark Janssens is a fourth line shift disturber, and Mark Bell could make the grade out of Ottawa in the OHL. Todd White played some there last season, as well.

GOALTENDER	GPI	MINS	AVG	W	L	T	EN	SO	GA	SA	SV %
J. THIBAULT	52	3,014	2.71	21	26	5	6	4	136	1,435	.905
M. FITZPATRICK	27	1,403	2.74	6	8	6	2	0	64	682	.906
JEFF HACKETT	10	524	3.78	2	6	1	3	0	33	256	.871
ANDREI TREFILOV	1	25	9.60	0	1	0	0	0	4	20	.800
CHI TOTALS	82	4,989	2.98	29	41	12	11	4	248	2,404	.897

The left-side is short on scoring, hence the possible Gilmour move. After him, is Jean-Yves Leroux, Bob Probert, Reid Simpson and possible Dan Cleary.

A lot depends on whether Dumont can come through like he did late in the season. He's a front-runner for Calder Trophy as rookie-of-the-year, with the Blackhawks conveniently ensuring he didn't go over the number of games allowed to remain a rookie.

Is Molleken's offensive style for real? Let's consider some of the scoring since he took over and project it over 82 games.

| | Graham as Coach (59 games) | | | | Molleken as Coach (23 games) | | | |
	Gm	G	A	P	Gm	G	A	P
Gilmour	59	14	33	37	13	2	7	9
Amonte	59	29	21	50	23	15	10	25
Zhamnov	53	11	22	33	23	9	18	27
Daze	49	13	9	22	23	7	11	18
Marha	12	0	1	1	20	2	5	7
Dumont	7	0	0	0	18	9	6	15

Projected for 82 games using same rate as when Molleken took over:

	G	A	P
Zhamnov	32	64	96
Amonte	53	36	89
Dumont	41	27	68
Gilmour	13	44	57
Daze	25	39	64
Marha	8	21	29

Now, you don't want to get carried away, because the numbers under Molleken could have just been the initial adreneline, but maybe it's not. We'll see.

The numbers do show what Dumont is capable of, if he stays at the same rate, as well as 53 goals for Amonte, and a return to form by Zhamnov, who clearly was much more relaxed under Molleken.

SPECIAL TEAMS: The penalty killing was much better after Molleken took over, so we'll assume that carries over into the season. Despite averaging almost a goal a game against all season, they didn't allow any in six of their last eight games.

As for the power play, there's no reason that shouldn't improve as well. They've got Mironov for the full season on the point, and they've got some snipers up front, led by Amonte. As well, the Hawks have a decent second power play unit they can stick on the ice.

Power Play	G	ATT	PCT
Overall	49	327	15.0% (14th NHL)
Home	26	180	14.4% (T-19th NHL)
Road	23	147	15.6% (11th NHL)

10 SHORT HANDED GOALS ALLOWED (T-19th NHL)

Penalty Killing	G	TSH	PCT
Overall	80	399	79.9% (25th NHL)
Home	37	185	80.0% (24th NHL)
Road	43	214	79.9% (25th NHL)

8 SHORT HANDED GOALS SCORED (T-8th NHL)

BLACKHAWKS SPECIAL TEAMS SCORING

Power play	G	A	PTS
AMONTE	14	12	26
MIRONOV	5	20	25
ZHAMNOV	8	16	24
GILMOUR	7	13	20
DAZE	8	9	17
MANSON	2	6	8

MCAMMOND	1	4	5
WHITE	2	2	4
OLCZYK	1	2	3
ERIKSSON	0	3	3
PROBERT	0	2	2
SIMPSON	1	0	1
MARHA	1	0	1
ZMOLEK	0	1	1
LEROUX	0	1	1
DUMONT	0	1	1

Short handed	G	A	PTS
AMONTE	3	1	4
ZHAMNOV	1	1	2
OLCZYK	1	0	1
GILMOUR	1	0	1
ERIKSSON	0	1	1

COACHING AND MANAGEMENT: Lorne Molleken was like a breath of fresh air when he took over from Dirk Graham, who was clearly out of his element coming into the job with no coaching experience. The offensive approach suits this team and the players love it, so their commitment level will be much better than it was using a system that didn't agree with them.

Bob Murray has learned a few lessons while GM of Chicago, such as don't hire a coach without any experience, but he's also maybe taught a few, too. He's pulled off some excellent deals and he's on the right path to lead this team back to respectability.

DRAFT: (see chart) McCarthy is an offensive defenseman, who went later than projected. There were some concerns about his size and skating, although the latter was debatable. He has been compared a lot to Dallas defenseman, Darryl Sydor.

The Blackhawks are in good shape at the draft table, with four first-rounders over the next two years.

PROGNOSIS: If the late season surge last year was any indication, the Hawks are going to be an outstanding team this year. If it was just a mirage, we can at least look for some improvement and a playoffs spot.

The defense is good, the goaltending adequate, and the forwards could use another offensive type.

It all bodes to a good season by the Blackhawks, and possibly the most improved team.

DRAFT

Player	Pos	Rnd	Sel.	Cntry	Team	Lge	Gms	G	A	P	PIM
Steve McCarty	D	1	23	Can	Kootenay	WHL	57	19	33	52	79
Dimitri Levinski	RW	2	46	Kaz	Cherepovic	Rus	85	47	23	70	42
Stepan Mokhov	D	2	63	Kaz	Cherepovic	Rus	1	0	0	0	0
Michael Jacobsen	D	5	134	Can	Belleville	OHL	68	5	27	32	33
Michael Leighton	G	6	165	Can	Windsor	OHL	4.84	.867			
M. Wennerberg	C	7	194	Swe	Modo Jr.	Swel	43	13	12	25	0
Yorick Treille	RW	7	195	Fra	Mass-Lowell	H.E.	30	6	5	11	24
Andrew Carver	D	8	223	Can	Hull	QMJHL	65	2	15	17	104

STAT SECTION

PLAYER	GP	G	A	PTS	+/-	PIM	PP	SH	GW	GT	S	PCTG
TONY AMONTE	82	44	31	75	0	60	14	3	8	0	256	17.2
ALEXEI ZHAMNOV	76	20	41	61	10-	50	8	1	2	1	200	10.0
DOUG GILMOUR	72	16	40	56	16-	56	7	1	4	0	110	14.5
BORIS MIRONOV	75	11	38	49	13	131	5	0	4	1	173	6.4
ERIC DAZE	72	22	20	42	13-	22	8	0	2	3	189	11.6
DEAN MCAMMOND	77	10	20	30	8	38	1	0	1	0	138	7.2
ED OLCZYK	61	10	15	25	3-	29	2	1	2	0	88	11.4
DAVE MANSON	75	6	17	23	1	155	2	0	0	0	145	4.1
BOB PROBERT	78	7	14	21	11-	206	0	0	3	0	87	8.0
ANDERS ERIKSSON	72	2	18	20	11	34	0	0	1	0	79	2.5
J.-P. DUMONT	25	9	6	15	7	10	0	0	2	0	42	21.4
DOUG ZMOLEK	62	0	14	14	1	102	0	0	0	0	33	.0
TODD WHITE	35	5	8	13	1-	20	2	0	0	0	43	11.6
REID SIMPSON	53	5	4	9	2	145	1	0	0	0	23	21.7
DANIEL CLEARY	35	4	5	9	1-	24	0	0	0	0	49	8.2
JEAN-YVES LEROUX	40	3	5	8	7-	21	0	0	0	0	47	6.4
JOSEF MARHA	32	2	6	8	1	4	1	0	1	0	45	4.4
BRAD BROWN	66	1	7	8	4-	205	0	0	0	1	26	3.8
CHRIS MURRAY	42	1	6	7	2-	79	0	0	0	0	37	2.7
BRYAN MUIR	54	1	4	5	1	50	0	0	0	0	82	1.2
JAMIE ALLISON	39	2	2	4	0	62	0	0	0	0	24	8.3
MARK JANSSENS	60	1	0	1	11-	65	0	0	0	0	27	3.7
MARK FITZPATRICK	27	0	1	1	0	8	0	0	0	0	0	.0
JOCELYN THIBAULT	62	0	1	1	0	2	0	0	0	0	0	.0
R. VANDENBUSSCHE	6	0	0	0	0	17	0	0	0	0	3	.0
SYLVAIN CLOUTIER	7	0	0	0	1-	0	0	0	0	0	3	.0
CRAIG MILLS	7	0	0	0	2-	2	0	0	0	0	1	.0
TY JONES	8	0	0	0	1-	12	0	0	0	0	3	.0
DENNIS BONVIE	11	0	0	0	4-	44	0	0	0	0	1	.0
RADIM BICANEK	14	0	0	0	4-	10	0	0	0	0	13	.0
REMI ROYER	18	0	0	0	10-	67	0	0	0	0	24	.0
TRENT YAWNEY	20	0	0	0	6-	32	0	0	0	0	11	.0

TEAM RANKINGS

		Conference Rank	League Rank
Record	29-41-12	10	21
Home	20-17-4	6	15
Away	9-24-8	12	18
Versus Own Conference	21-25-9	9	20
Versus Other Conference	11-12-5	6	15
Team Plus\Minus	-16	10	20
Goals For	202	9	19
Goals Against	248	11	24
Average Shots For	25.6	12	23
Average Shots Against	28.7	8	18
Overtime	1-2-12	9	18
One Goal Games	13-12	5	13
Times outshooting opponent	31	10	20
Versus Teams Over .500	12-26-6	11	22
Versus Teams .500 or under	17-15-6	9	20
First Half Record	11-24-6	13	25
Second Half Record	18-17-6	8	14

MISCELLANEOUS STAT LEADERS
FACEOFFS

	W	L	%
Janssens	594	344	57.9
White	208	244	56.6
Gilmour	867	752	53.6
Zhamnov	635	664	48.9
Olczyk	229	212	51.9
Marha	140	135	50.9

ICE TIME

Mirinov	25:40
Gilmour	22:29
Amonte	22:12
Manson	21:50
Zhamnov	21:30

HITS

Mironov	174
Brown	146
Manson	141
McAmmond	138
Probert	105

PLAYOFFS

- Did Not Make the Playoffs.

Colorado Avalanche

The Avalanche came that close to going to the Stanley Cup finals and possibly bringing home another Cup. A seventh game loss to Dallas in the conference finals was all that stood in their way.

But, they're in upheavel now, and the road to the Stanley Cup next year, will be covered in snow.

Maybe that's why GM Pierre Lacroix went for the marbles last year, giving up some good young players for Theoren Fleury. It was worth a try. Fleury was outstanding during the regular season, and was okay in the playoffs until the conference finals against Dallas, where he and some others, did not play well.

Fleury's gone to free agency, along with Valeri Kamensky and Sylvain Lefebvre. Peter Forsberg will probably miss the first month of the season after undergoing shoulder surgery.

With the ownership situation in doubt, and despite the fact that they will be moving into the new Pepsi Centre next year, it's not economically viable to have too many high-priced players. They already have Forsberg, Joe Sakic, Patrick Roy, and Sandis Ozolinsh.

Signing Fleury to a five-year deal, with a no-trade clause, isn't a wise move for any team unless they've got money to burn. And even if they do, it doesn't help the rest of the league or the smaller market teams that are trying to exercise some fiscal responsibility.

If the Avs could afford everybody, they could be a dynasty for a long time, just like the old days when a team such as Montreal, or Edmonton, or the NY Islanders could build a strong nucleus and keep it together.

Teams can only keep a strong unit together for a couple years now. Players are less interested in winning than they used to be, and more interested in making as much money as they can. So, would almost all of us put into the same situation. It's just the nature of the game, now. The players want their piece of the pie and they don't care who gives it to them.

Eventually there won't be any pie left, and some places now are only offering crumbs.

The greed from the players' associations is justifiable because that's their job. They don't care about the game as much as they do the people who are paying their salaries. In the meantime, they want to ensure that owners make no money, and that the paying public is bled to the saturation point. They're getting there.

The NHL has a fair system of free agency right now and they're not like the NBA and Major League baseball where players change teams so easily and frequently that there is no continuity on any particular club. Could anyone even picture Ray Bourque or Jaromir Jagr in different uniforms? It shouldn't have to happen.

Teams have to do so much of their planning over money. It's not whether so-and-so would be a good fit on the left wing. It's whether so-and-so would be a good fit on the left wing, with the salary he's making.

There doesn't seem any way of fixing something like that. Until it's too late. And we're not that far away. Ticket prices are so ridiculous now that îregularî people can't afford to go to the game, much less a family. When you see empty seats in a place such as Chicago, that's why.

There's no level playing field anymore. Edmonton or other small market teams have a hard time being competetive. And if they are, it's because they don't have a lot of big-name stars, such as in Buffalo.

The fans are the ones paying the freight, which they don't seem to realize when they advocate paying a lot of money for a free agent. Although, even when you listen to the radio talk shows, much of the conversation is about team finances, and whether so and so is worth it. You have to turn down the radio to quiet the grumbling. They're getting fed up.

You might call all this the free market economy. You might someday call it the death of sports.

While we're ranting and raving, another thing the NHL should do is change the trading deadline. It's too close to the end of the season. We've played most of the games, and then all of a sudden, they pop in some stars who are on their way to free agency when the season is over. It just magnifies how much the game has become about money.

Enough of that already.

STUFF

Patrick Roy became the all-time NHL career victory, playoffs and regular season, leader.

A 10-game road unbeaten streak was a franchise record.

A 12-game winning streak was the longest in the league and a franchise record.

The Avalanche became only the seventh team in NHL history to come back from a five-goal deficit, when they fell behind 5-0 to Florida, before eventually winning it 7-5.

The Panthers did not have any successful penalty shots in the first five years of their existence, but managed two in one month, with both Pavel Bure and Ray Whitney scoring.

A 9-1 loss to Toronto was the biggest margin of defeat in team history.

11 shots in a game versus Ottawa were tied for the fewest in team history, but the Panthers still won the game 2-0.

Became only the 12th team in NHL playoff history to lose the first two games at home, and still win the series, when they defeated Detroit 4-2 in the conference semi-finals.

TEAM PREVIEW

GOAL: Are there cracks starting to show in Patrick Roy's armor? Well a 2.29 GAA and four shutouts would suggest not, but he definitely struggled at the start of last season. Mind you, the whole team struggled.

Marc Denis is pencilled in as the future of the franchise in net, but it's tough for him to get any playing time at the NHL level. It's going to have to happen soon, though. He didn't set the world on fire at Hersey in the AHL last year, but the Avalanche traded Craig Billington, so he will be the backup this season.

DEFENSE: The Avs need some toughness at this position.

They already have one of the best offensive threats in Sandis Ozolinsh, one of the best all-round defensemen in Adam Foote, and one of the better young prospects in Martin Skoula.

What they don't have is a big, tough, physical presence to intimidate opposing forwards. What they do have is lot of fifth defensemen.

They've got Aaron Miller, Greg deVries, Eric Messier, Jon Klemm, and Cam Russell, although Miller played very well in the playoffs. Sergei Gusarov became an unrestricted free agent, but was re-signed by the team.

None are going to make the all-star team any time soon. And none are going to scare anybody into giving up the puck.

Ozolinsh's return to the lineup after his holdout made a big difference with the Avalanche power play.

	PP's	Goals	%
Before Ozolinsh	192	31	16.1%
With Ozolinsh	183	40	21.9%

The difference is even more pronounced when you pro-rate it over the entire season. Since Ozolinsh played about half the games, it would give them 62 without him, 80 with him. That's a big, big difference.

The Avs don't have any prospects of note, other than Skoula, so Lacroix will likely have to make a deal to get the physical presence that will make everybody else that much more effective.

FORWARD: Theoren Fleury is gone, Valeri Kamensky is gone, and Forsberg is expected to miss the first month or so of he season. That means replacements will be needed.

The Avs forwards are good at mixing and matching, cause they're always moving around from position to position.

Last year, they had an unexpected bonus when they had two of the top rookies in the league.

Chris Drury won the Calder Trophy, with Hejduk coming third.

The voting went like this for the top five, with points weighted from first to fifth place on a ballot:

Chris Drury	Colorado	448
Marian Hossa	Ottawa	269
Milan Hejuk	Colorado	184
Mark Parrish	Florida	168
Brendan Morrison	New Jersey	163

The interesting thing about the above list is that Mark Parrish was also property of the Avalanche at one time, which means three of the top four products were theirs.

GOALTENDER	GPI	MINS	AVG	W	L	T	EN	SO	GA	SA	SV %
PATRICK ROY	61	3648	2.29	32	19	8	4	5	139	1673	.917
MARC DENIS	4	217	2.49	1	1	1	0	0	9	110	.918
C. BILLINGTON	21	1086	2.87	11	8	1	1	0	52	492	.894
COL TOTALS	82	4974	2.47	44	28	10	5	5	205	2280	.910

Forsberg won't be available at the start of the season, while he recovers from shoulder surgery, so that means even more juggling. Let's see what we can piece together.

You have to figure on Joe Sakic, Claude Lemieux, Adam Deadmarsh, Drury and Hejduk occupying space on the top two lines, with maybe Alex Tanguay filling in for Forsberg.

Tanguay actually made the team out of training camp last year, but couldn't agree on a contract. He's signed for this year and is almost sure to play.

After the above six, you can put in checking and penalty-killing duo with Stephane Yelle and Shjon Podein. After them, fill in with tough guys Jeff Odgers and/or Scott Parker; possibly minor-league scorer, Christian Matte; and the most maligned (fairly and unfairly) role-player in the league, Shean Donovan.

One more point about Fleury. The Avs were 8-5-2 when he was in the lineup after being acquired from Calgary. He was phenomenal, with 24 points in 15 games. But, nine of the games were versus opponents that didn't make the play-offs, and 14 of them were against teams with records under .500. Don't know what that means, but there it is. Plus, players heading into unrestricted free agency seem to play remarkably well.

The Avs aren't that bad off at forward. If you discount Fleury, who only joined the team late, then they're really just losing Kamensky, who was showing signs of slowing down, anyway.

SPECIAL TEAMS: The chart in the Defense section showed the contribution Ozolinsh made to the power play. With the Avs firepower, they should be up there with the league leaders. One problem they have, however, is that they give up a lot of shorthanded goals. One of the reasons is that they have to use a forward on defense most of the time, and the other is that Ozolinsh is always moving in from his point position, which means essentially they have five forwards on the ice. It's a tradeoff, but it appears that it's worth it, as long as the power play is clicking.

Power Play	G	ATT	PCT
Overall	71	375	18.9% (5th NHL)
Home	44	207	21.3% (T-3rd NHL)
Road	27	168	16.1% (9th NHL)
12 SHORT HANDED GOALS ALLOWED (25th NHL)			

Penalty Killing	G	TSH	PCT
Overall	63	386	83.7% (17th NHL)
Home	36	197	81.7% (22nd NHL)
Road	27	189	85.7% (9th NHL)
7 SHORT HANDED GOALS SCORED (T-15th NHL)			

Penalties	GP	MIN	AVG
AVALANCHE	82	1619	19.7 (25th NHL)

AVALANCHE SPECIAL TEAMS SCORING

Power play	G	A	PTS
FORSBERG	9	28	37
SAKIC	12	22	34
LEMIEUX	11	14	25
FLEURY	8	17	25
OZOLINSH	4	17	21
DEADMARSH	10	10	20
DRURY	6	7	13
KAMENSKY	2	10	12
HEJDUK	4	7	11
FOOTE	3	5	8
GUSAROV	1	3	4
MILLER	1	1	2
DONOVAN	1	1	2
YELLE	1	0	1

ODGERS	1	0	1
MESSIER	1	0	1
HUNTER	0	1	1

Short handed	G	A	PTS
SAKIC	5	1	6
FORSBERG	2	4	6
FLEURY	3	2	5
LEMIEUX	0	1	1
LEFEBVRE	0	1	1
HUNTER	0	1	1
DEADMARSH	0	1	1

COACHING AND MANAGEMENT: With the ownership situation up in arms it makes it difficult for Lacroix to make moves based on financial necessity. The team was sold to the Laurie family, but then questions came up about the legitimacy of the sale. A new bidding process was scheduled to take place at the end of July.

Lacroix is making a reputation for himself as somewhat of a wizard. He's been questioned for letting some good people leave in the past, but if he doesn't give his reasons in public, you can bet they're sound, and that he usually ends up being right.

Getting Fleury for the playoff run was another great move. It almost worked and was worth it. Almost every team would have liked to get Fleury, but it was the Avalanche who had put themselves into position to get him through a strong organization that keeps turning up prospects.

Lacroix should get credit, as well, for not signing Fleury to a ridiculous contract. Of course, he would have liked to get him, but not on ridiculous terms that hurt the franchise over the long run.

Bob Hartley had a decent year as a rookie NHL coach. He would have looked better, earlier, if Ozolinsh had been on board from the start, but making it to within one game of the Stanley Cup finals has to be considered a tremendous success.

DRAFT: Mikail Kuleshov is said to have a lot of talent, but very little intensity. In other words, he won't be playing in the NHL unless he smartens up. Mind you, there are more than a few NHLers in the exact same situation, so you never know.

DRAFT

Player	Pos	Rnd	Sel.	Cntry	Team	Lge	Gms	G	A	P	PIM
Mihail Kulesov	LW	1	25	Rus	Cherepovic	Rus	15	2	0	2	8
Martin Grenier	D	2	45	Can	Quebec	QMJHL	60	7	8	25	479
Branko Radivojevic	RW	3	93	Slo	Belleville	OHL	68	20	38	58	61
Sanny Lindstrom	D	4	112	Swe	Huddinge	Swe	23	3	2	5	45
Kristian Kovac	RW	4	122	Slo	Kosice	Slo	34	33	32	65	30
William Magnuson	D	5	142	USA	Lake Superior	CCHA	30	0	1	1	42
J. Krestanovich	LW	5	152	Can	Calgary	WHL	62	6	13	19	10
Anders Lovdahl	C	6	158	Swe	HV 71	Swe					
Riku Hahl	C	6	183	Fin	Hameenlinna	Fin	28	0	1	1	0
Radim Vrbata	RW	7	212	Cze	Hull	QMJHL	54	22	38	60	16
Jeff Finger	D	8	240	USA	Green Bay	USHL	55	11	28	39	199

PROGNOSIS: It won't be any easier for the Avs this year, after losing so many veterans to free agency. It's easy to forget they still have some of the top players in the game, and they've got prospects moving up.

They don't look as if they're going to tear up the league, but they don't look they're still not going to be one of the top three teams in the Western Conference, along with Detroit and Dallas, both of which are likely to take some baby steps backward, as well.

STAT SECTION

PLAYER	GP	G	A	PTS	+/-	PIM	PP	SH	GW	GT	S	PCTG
PETER FORSBERG	78	30	67	97	27	108	9	2	7	0	217	13.8
JOE SAKIC	73	41	55	96	23	29	12	5	6	1	255	16.1
THEOREN FLEURY	75	40	53	93	26	86	8	3	5	2	301	13.3
CLAUDE LEMIEUX	82	27	24	51	0	102	11	0	8	1	292	9.2
ADAM DEADMARSH	66	22	27	49	2-	99	10	0	3	1	152	14.5
MILAN HEJDUK	82	14	34	48	8	26	4	0	5	0	178	7.9
CHRIS DRURY	79	20	24	44	9	62	6	0	3	1	138	14.5
VALERI KAMENSKY	65	14	30	44	1	28	2	0	2	0	123	11.4
SANDIS OZOLINSH	39	7	25	32	10	22	4	0	3	0	81	8.6
ADAM FOOTE	64	5	16	21	20	92	3	0	0	0	83	6.0
SYLVAIN LEFEBVRE	76	2	18	20	18	48	0	0	0	0	64	3.1
SHEAN DONOVAN	68	7	12	19	4	37	1	0	1	0	81	8.6
AARON MILLER	76	5	13	18	3	42	1	0	2	0	87	5.7
STEPHANE YELLE	72	8	7	15	8-	40	1	0	0	0	99	8.1
ALEXEI GUSAROV	54	3	10	13	12	24	1	0	0	0	28	10.7
DALE HUNTER	62	2	9	11	7-	119	0	0	0	0	24	8.3
SHJON PODEIN	55	3	6	9	5-	24	0	0	0	0	75	4.0
ERIC MESSIER	31	4	2	6	0	14	1	0	1	0	30	13.3
JEFF ODGERS	75	2	3	5	3-	259	1	0	0	0	39	5.1
GREG DE VRIES	73	1	3	4	7-	64	0	0	0	0	57	1.8
JON KLEMM	39	1	2	3	4	31	0	0	0	0	28	3.6
CAM RUSSELL	42	1	2	3	4-	94	0	0	0	0	15	6.7
CHRISTIAN MATTE	7	1	1	2	2-	0	0	0	0	0	9	11.1
WARREN RYCHEL	28	0	2	2	3	63	0	0	0	0	15	.0
PATRICK ROY	61	0	2	2	0	28	0	0	0	0	0	.0
MICHAEL GAUL	1	0	0	0	0	0	0	0	0	0	1	.0
SERGE AUBIN	1	0	0	0	0	0	0	0	0	0	1	.0
BRIAN WHITE	2	0	0	0	0	0	0	0	0	0	0	.0
CHRIS DINGMAN	3	0	0	0	2-	24	0	0	0	0	1	.0

MARC DENIS	4	0	0	0	0	0	0	0	0	0	0	.0
JEFF BUCHANAN	6	0	0	0	1	6	0	0	0	0	1	.0
DAN SMITH	12	0	0	0	5	9	0	0	0	0	6	.0
CRAIG BILLINGTON	21	0	0	0	0	2	0	0	0	0	0	.0
SCOTT PARKER	27	0	0	0	3-	71	0	0	0	0	3	.0

TEAM RANKINGS

		Conference Rank	League Rank
Record	44-28-10	2	4
Home	21-14-6	4	11
Away	23-14-4	2	4
Versus Own Conference	29-19-8	3	6
Versus Other Conference	15-9-2	2	5
Team Plus\Minus	+26	2	6
Goals For	239	2	6
Goals Against	205	5	11
Average Shots For	28.0	6	10
Average Shots Against	27.8	7	14
Overtime	2-0-10	2	4
One Goal Games	15-12	3	9
Times outshooting opponent	40	6	11
Versus Teams Over .500	15-14-4	2	5
Versus Teams .500 or under	29-14-6	3	4
First Half Record	18-19-4	515	
Second Half Record	26-9-6	1	1

MISCELLANEOUS STATS LEADERS
FACEOFFS

	W	L	%
Forsberg	487	408	54.4
Sakic	886	837	51.4
Yelle	615	586	51.2
Drury	196	222	46.8
Deadmarsh	285	336	45.9

ICE TIME

Sakic	25:35
Foote	24:50
Forsberg	23:29
Fleury	23:20
Ozolinsh	22:06
Miller	21:49
Lemieux	21:14
Lefebvre	20:56
Deadmarsh	20:46

HITS

Yelle	136
Foote	125
Deadmarsh	121
Lefebvre	120
Miller	115
Lemieux	110
Forsberg	108

PLAYOFFS
Results:

Defeated San Jose 4-2 in conference quarter-finals

Defeated Detroit 4-2 in conference semi-finals

Loss to Dallas 4-3 in conference finals

Record: 11-8

Home: 3-6

Away: 8-2

Goals For: 56 (2.9/game)

Goals Against: 54 (2.8/game)

Overtime: 2-2

Power play: 14.6% (9th)

Penalty Killing: 82.1% (11th)

PLAYER	GP	G	A	PTS	+/-	PIM	PP	SH	GW	OT	S	PCTG
PETER FORSBERG	19	8	16	24	7	31	1	1	0	0	54	14.8
JOE SAKIC	19	6	13	19	2-	8	1	1	1	0	56	10.7
THEOREN FLEURY	18	5	12	17	2-	20	2	0	0	0	56	8.9
CLAUDE LEMIEUX	19	3	11	14	5	26	1	0	0	0	69	4.3
ADAM DEADMARSH	19	8	4	12	2	20	3	0	0	0	44	18.2
MILAN HEJDUK	16	6	6	12	3	4	1	0	3	2	38	15.8
SANDIS OZOLINSH	19	4	8	12	5-	22	3	0	1	0	56	7.1
VALERI KAMENSKY	10	4	5	9	5	4	1	0	1	0	18	22.2
CHRIS DRURY	19	6	2	8	2	4	0	0	4	1	40	15.0
AARON MILLER	19	1	5	6	8	10	0	0	0	0	22	4.5
ADAM FOOTE	19	2	3	5	3	24	1	0	0	0	28	7.1
DALE HUNTER	19	1	3	4	0	38	0	0	0	0	10	10.0
SHJON PODEIN	19	1	1	2	1-	12	0	0	0	0	33	3.0
PATRICK ROY	19	0	2	2	0	4	0	0	0	0	1	.0
GREG DE VRIES	19	0	2	2	3	22	0	0	0	0	7	.0
JEFF ODGERS	15	1	0	1	0	14	0	0	1	0	3	33.3
STEPHANE YELLE	10	0	1	1	1-	6	0	0	0	0	18	.0
WARREN RYCHEL	12	0	1	1	1-	14	0	0	0	0	6	.0
SYLVAIN LEFEBVRE	19	0	1	1	6	12	0	0	0	0	16	.0
JON KLEMM	19	0	1	1	1	10	0	0	0	0	11	.0
CRAIG BILLINGTON	1	0	0	0	0	0	0	0	0	0	0	.0
ERIC MESSIER	3	0	0	0	1-	0	0	0	0	0	1	.0
ALEXEI GUSAROV	5	0	0	0	1	2	0	0	0	0	2	.0
SHEAN DONOVAN	5	0	0	0	0	2	0	0	0	0	1	.0

GOALTENDER	GPI	MINS	AVG	W	L	T	EN	SO	GA	SA	SV %
PATRICK ROY	19	1173	2.66	11	8	1	1	0	52	650	.920
C. BILLINGTON	1	9	6.67	0	0	0	0	0	1	6	.833
COL TOTALS	19	1185	2.73	11	8	1	1	0	54	657	.918

Dallas Stars

Once all is said and done, there's only one thing for the Stanley Cup champions to think about now. Can they do it again this year?

YES — They've still got an excellent coach, Ken Hitchock, who has the players behind him and his system. And they have excellent management in Bob Gainey.

NO — Compacency often sets in after a Stanley Cup victory, and although Detroit managed it twice in a row, it's difficult to duplicate the same drive and determination it takes to win it the first time.

MAYBE — They've got so many "character" type players that they can push each other on.

YES — They're still among the best teams in the league.

NO — A lot of that talent is aging, or aged too much and is at the end of their careers.

MAYBE — A lot of that older talent has been let loose, via free agency, and a host of good young players are ready to take their place.

NO — They may have too many young players coming into the lineup at once.

YES — If everything goes right for them again.
NO — If everything doesn't go right for them again, and it does for a different team.
MAYBE — If enough things go right.

NO — League is stepping up offensively, and sometimes the Stars don't know how to play that game when they need to.

YES — None of the other top teams, Detroit and Colorado, figure to be improved.

NO — The Rangers may have bought up all the best free agents in the league.

YES — The Stars have balance, meaning if one player falters there are plenty of others to pick up the slack.

NO — The Stars fought through their injuries in the playoffs, with incredible determination and fortitude. They may not have the same motivation this year.

YES — Anybody can win the Stanley Cup in any given year.

NO — Anybody can win the Stanley Cup in any given year.

STUFF

The 12 shots Dallas allowed against Buffalo tied a finals record for fewest shots.

The Stars were the first team to lead the regular season in points and also win the Cup since the New York Rangers in 1994.

TEAM PREVIEW

GOAL: Just between you and me, just about any goalie in the league last year could have won with the Stars. At least during the regular season. In the playoffs, where it counts most anyway, Ed Belfour was pretty close to being the MVP.

It's no coincidence that Roman Turek had almost the exact same goals against average and the exact same save percentage. Goaltending, for the most part, is more of a team thing.

Roman Turek was traded to the Blues, and the backup role with be the winner of the Manny Fernandez and Marty Turco battle in training camp. Both had outstanding seasons for different teams in the IHL, but Turco could use one more year, so maybe Fernandez has a good chance at the job.

DEFENSE: The Dallas defense isn't old. Some of the other positions on the team, yes, but not the defense. In fact, almost all the defensemen are in their prime. Their ages are in brackets.

Derian Hatcher (27) showed, especially during that playoffs, that he is one of the premier defensemen in the league. Sergei Zubov (29) and Darryl Sydor (27) are two of the premier offensive and power play point men in the league. Hard-hitting Richard Matvichuk (26) is as good a fourth defenseman as there is in the league, if that's what he is, and youngster Brad Lukowich (22) is set to make a regular appearance in the lineup.

Craig Ludwig and Shawn Chambers combined with the first four to give Dallas the top blueline in the league, but Ludwig is a free agent and wasn't sure whether or not he'd be playing again this year. The Stars would re-sign him if he wanted.

The Stars are kind of thin on defense prospects in the minors, with Richard Jackman, the fifth overall pick in 1996, being the best bet. He's on offensive type who is still learning the game in the minors.

The Stars did pick up Jamie Pushor from Atlanta, and signed free agent Mark Wotton, last of Vancouver.

FORWARD: One of the criticisms of the Dallas Stars last year was that they were so defensive-minded that they wouldn't be able to turn on the offense when it was needed.

The Stars weren't that low scoring, with their

GOALTENDER	GPI	MINS	AVG	W	L	T	EN	SO	GA	SA	SV %
ED BELFOUR	61	3,536	1.99	35	15	9	0	5	117	1,373	.915
E. FERNANDE	1	60	2.00	0	1	0	0	0	2	29	.931
ROMAN TUREK	26	1,382	2.08	16	3	3	1	1	48	562	.915
DAL TOTALS	82	4,986	2.02	51	19	12	1	6	168	1,965	.915

236 goals fourth in the Western Conference and eighth in the league. What we have here is a chicken and egg type thing. The Stars didn't score more goals because they didn't need to.

They were so adept at holding leads that they didn't need to score more goals once they got that lead.

Okay, almost every team wins the vast majority of their games when they have the lead going into the third period, and Dallas was no different. Their record in that circumstance was 38-2-5. But, nobody led more often going into the third period.

Let's consider the Dallas scoring by period, followed by their ranking overall for goals scored

	Goals For	Scored Against	Ranking
First Period	84	56	3 (tied)
Second Period	91	48	2
Third Period	58	63	27

So, Dallas was one of the top scoring teams in the league in the first and second period — third overall in the first period, second overall in the second. Suddenly, in the third period, they were the lowest scoring team in the entire league, worse than everybody, including Tampa Bay.

Because we know they were leading the most often going into the third period, then we also know they needed to score the fewest goals in the third to win. In other words they were adept at holding their lead and didn't score because they didn't need to.

Okay, let's see how they did when they were tied going into the third period, because that would show us if they were able to turn it on and score when they had to. The Stars had the best

record in the league in that circumstance, with a record of 12-3-5.

They didn't come from behind very often in the third, but that statistic isn't conclusive because they didn't have to come from behind very often.

To sum it up, if Dallas wasn't so good offensively in the first and second periods, then they'd have to be better in the third. Consequently, they'd have more goals, be ranked higher in that category, and we wouldn't be saying they can't score when they have to.

Okay, this is a group that has aged. Big time. They had eight regular forwards in the playoffs last year who were at least 32 years of age. Guy Carbonneau was 39.

But, Carbonneau, Dave Reid (35) Pat Verbeek (35), and Tony Hrkac (32) were all allowed to go via the free agent route. It's possible one or two could be re-signed, particularly Carbonneau, if he wants to play another year.

Down the middle the stars are in good shape, with Mike Modano, Playoff MVP Joe Nieuwendyk, Brian Skrudland, and Derek Plante, or Carbonneau if he comes back.

On the left side is Jere Lehtinen, one of the best two-way players in the game, and the Selke Trophy winner as best defensive forward. He's followed by defensive specialist and leader Mike Keane, and returnee Juha Lind. Lind couldn't score his first time in Dallas, went back to Europe for a year, and is said to be much improved. He has speed, which is an area the Stars were lacking. You might also see Jon Sim over there, a feisty little guy who got into a couple playoff games.

On the right side is Brett Hull, Jamie Langenbrunner, Blake Sloan, Grant Marshall, and perhaps Warren Luhning.

Jamie Wright, Jason Botterill, and Aaron Gavey will also have the opportunity to show they belong.

SPECIAL TEAMS: The Stars have everything they need to remain among the elite teams on the power play, including two of the best power play point men in the league, a sniper in Hull, a setup man and scorer in Modano, and Niewendyk, Lehtinen and Langenbrunner, all of whom could score on an power play.

Penalty killing is among the best two, because the Stars have more than their share of two-way players.

Power Play	G	ATT	PCT
Overall	74	393	18.8% (6th NHL)
Home	47	213	22.1% (2nd NHL)
Road	27	180	15.0% (T-12th NHL)

4 SHORT HANDED GOALS ALLOWED (T-1st NHL)

Penalty Killing	G	TSH	PCT
Overall	43	319	86.5% (6th NHL)
Home	22	166	86.7% (8th NHL)
Road	21	153	86.3% (T-5th NHL)

6 SHORT HANDED GOALS SCORED (T-21st NHL)

Penalties	GP	MIN	AVG
STARS	82	1108	13.5 (T-6th NHL)

STARS SPECIAL TEAMS SCORING

Power play	G	A	PTS
SYDOR	9	26	35
MODANO	6	21	27
ZUBOV	5	22	27
HULL	15	6	21
NIEUWENDYK	8	10	18
LEHTINEN	7	10	17
LANGENBRUNNER	4	12	16
VERBEEK	8	6	14
HRKAC	2	4	6
HATCHER	3	2	5
MARSHALL	2	3	5
HOGUE	2	3	5
CHAMBERS	1	4	5
PLANTE	1	3	4
KEANE	1	3	4
MATVICHUK	1	1	2
REID	1	0	1
CARBONNEAU	0	1	1

Short handed	G	A	PTS
MODANO	4	1	5
HOGUE	0	3	3
LEHTINEN	1	1	2
LUDWIG	0	2	2
KEANE	1	0	1
SKRUDLAND	0	1	1
PLANTE	0	1	1
MATVICHUK	0	1	1
HATCHER	0	1	1

COACHING AND MANAGEMENT: It's one thing to go out and get some free agents as the Stars have done the previous couple years, it's another to make sure they fit the team and can be molded into winners.

What more could be expected from both GM Bob Gainey and coach Ken Hitchcock?

DRAFT: (see chart) High schooler, Michael Ryan, is a long ways away from the NHL, but the Stars, who didn't have a first round pick, can afford to wait. His best asset is his speed. He'll be attending university this year.

DRAFT

Player	Pos	Rnd	Sel.	Cntry	Team	Lge	Gms	G	A	P	PIM
Michael Ryan	C	2	32	USA	B.C. H.S	US HS	21	20	24	44	22
Dan Jancevski	D	2	66	Can	London	OHL	68	2	12	14	115
Mathias Tjarnqvist	C	3	96	Swe	Rogle	Swe					
Jeff Bateman	C	4	126	Can	Brampton	OHL	68	23	35	58	27
G. Baumgartner	C	5	156	Aut	Acadie-Bath.	QMJHL					
Justin Cox	RW	6	184	Can	Prince George	WHL	72	9	13	22	51
Brett Draney	LW	6	186	Can	Kamloops	WHL	58	10	7	17	48
Jeff MacMillan	D	7	215	Can	Oshawa	OHL	65	3	18	21	109
Brian Sullivan	RW	8	243								
Jamie Chamberlain	RW	9	264	Can	Peterborough	OHL	68	15	24	39	26
Mihail Donika	D	9	272	Rus	Yaroslavl	Rus	37	0	1	1	10

PROGNOSIS: There are just so many variables than can affect a Stanley Cup win. There are fewer variables, however, to determine an excellent regular season, and there's little doubt the Stars will remain among the elite.

They're moving in some of the younger players, which is good for the regular season, but may not help in the playoffs.

And of course, once they get to the post-season, they may not have the same hunger to win as they had last year. But, they might.

STAT SECTION

PLAYER	GP	G	A	PTS	+/-	PIM	PP	SH	GW	GT	S	PCTG
MIKE MODANO	77	34	47	81	29	44	6	4	7	1	224	15.2
BRETT HULL	60	32	26	58	19	30	15	0	11	0	192	16.7
JOE NIEUWENDYK	67	28	27	55	11	34	8	0	8	1	157	17.8
JERE LEHTINEN	74	20	32	52	29	18	7	1	2	0	173	11.6
SERGEI ZUBOV	81	10	41	51	9	20	5	0	3	0	155	6.5
DARRYL SYDOR	74	14	34	48	1-	50	9	0	2	1	163	8.6
J. LANGENBRUNNER	75	12	33	45	10	62	4	0	1	0	145	8.3
PAT VERBEEK	78	17	17	34	11	133	8	0	2	1	134	12.7
GRANT MARSHALL	82	13	18	31	1	85	2	0	4	0	112	11.6
DERIAN HATCHER	80	9	21	30	21	102	3	0	2	0	125	7.2
BENOIT HOGUE	74	12	17	29	10-	54	2	0	3	0	121	9.9
MIKE KEANE	81	6	23	29	2-	62	1	1	1	0	106	5.7
TONY HRKAC	69	13	14	27	2	26	2	0	2	2	67	19.4
DEREK PLANTE	51	6	14	20	4	16	1	0	0	0	90	6.7

DAVE REID	73	6	11	17	0	16	1	0	1	0	81	7.4
GUY CARBONNEAU	74	4	12	16	3-	31	0	0	2	0	60	6.7
R. MATVICHUK	64	3	9	12	23	51	1	0	0	0	54	5.6
SHAWN CHAMBERS	61	2	9	11	6	18	1	0	1	0	82	2.4
CRAIG LUDWIG	80	2	6	8	5	87	0	0	0	0	39	5.1
BRIAN SKRUDLAND	40	4	1	5	2	33	0	0	1	0	33	12.1
BRAD LUKOWICH	14	1	2	3	3	19	0	0	0	0	8	12.5
BRENT SEVERYN	30	1	2	3	2-	50	0	0	0	0	22	4.5
JONATHAN SIM	7	1	0	1	1	12	0	0	0	0	8	12.5
KELLY FAIRCHILD	1	0	0	0	0	0	0	0	0	0	4	.0
E. FERNANDEZ	1	0	0	0	0	0	0	0	0	0	0	.0
PETR BUZEK	2	0	0	0	0	2	0	0	0	0	0	.0
AARON GAVEY	7	0	0	0	1-	10	0	0	0	0	4	.0
JAMIE WRIGHT	11	0	0	0	3-	0	0	0	0	0	10	.0
BLAKE SLOAN	14	0	0	0	1-	10	0	0	0	0	7	.0
DOUG LIDSTER	17	0	0	0	0	10	0	0	0	0	7	.0
JASON BOTTERILL	17	0	0	0	2-	23	0	0	0	0	8	.0
ROMAN TUREK	26	0	0	0	0	0	0	0	0	0	0	.0
ED BELFOUR	61	0	0	0	0	26	0	0	0	0	0	.0

TEAM RANKINGS

		Conference Rank	League Rank
Record	51-19-12	1	1
Home	29-8-4	1	1
Away	22-11-8	1	2
Versus Own Conference	35-14-7	1	1
Versus Other Conference	16-5-5	1	2
Team Plus\Minus	+37	1	5
Goals For	236	4	8
Goals Against	168	1	1
Average Shots For	27.6	9	5
Average Shots Against	24.0	2	3
Overtime	3-1-12	3	6
One Goal Games	22-7	1	1
Times outshooting opponent	54	2	5
Versus Teams Over .500	20-10-6	2	1
Versus Teams .500 or under	31-9-6	1	1
First Half Record	27-7-7	1	1
Second Half Record	24-12-5	2	3

MISCELLANEOUS LEADERS
FACEOFFS

	W	L	%
Modano	804	768	51.1
Nieuwendyk	740	430	63.2
Carbonneau	562	593	53.3
Hrkac	320	346	48.0
Skrudland	122	152	44.5

ICE TIME

Hatcher	24:44
Zubov	24:14
Matvichuk	21:19
Sydor	21:16
Modano	20:50

HITS

Hatcher	204
Matvichuk	186
Marshall	172
Ludvig	151
Verbeek	130
Langenbrunner	129
Keane	126
Hogue	120

PLAYOFFS

Results:

Defeated Edmonton 4-0 in Conference Quarter-finals

Defeated St. Louis 4-2 in Conference Semi-Finals

Defeated Colorado 4-3 in Conference Finals

Defeated Buffalo 4-2 in Stanley Cup Finals

Record: 16-7

Home: 9-3

Away: 7-4

Goals For: 64 (2.8/game)

Goals Against: 44 (1.9/game)

Overtime: 4-4

Power play: 12.1% (12th)

Penalty Killing: 90.5% (2nd)

PLAYER	GP	G	A	PTS	+/-	PIM	PP	SH	GW	OT	S	PCTG
MIKE MODANO	23	5	18	23	6	16	1	1	1	1	83	6.0
JOE NIEUWENDYK	23	11	10	21	7	19	3	0	6	2	72	15.3
J. LANGENBRUNNER	23	10	7	17	7	16	4	0	3	0	46	21.7
BRETT HULL	22	8	7	15	3	4	3	0	2	1	86	9.3
JERE LEHTINEN	23	10	3	13	8	2	1	1	0	0	55	18.2
SERGEI ZUBOV	23	1	12	13	13	4	0	0	0	0	46	2.2
DARRYL SYDOR	23	3	9	12	8	16	1	0	1	0	49	6.1
DAVE REID	23	2	8	10	4	14	0	0	0	0	30	6.7
MIKE KEANE	23	5	2	7	1-	6	0	1	1	0	41	12.2
PAT VERBEEK	18	3	4	7	4	14	0	0	1	0	33	9.1
DERIAN HATCHER	18	1	6	7	4	24	0	0	0	0	28	3.6
GUY CARBONNEAU	17	2	4	6	0	6	0	0	1	0	29	6.9
R. MATVICHUK	22	1	5	6	4	20	0	0	0	0	26	3.8
CRAIG LUDWIG	23	1	4	5	2	20	0	0	0	0	6	16.7
GRANT MARSHALL	14	0	3	3	1	20	0	0	0	0	23	.0
TONY HRKAC	5	0	2	2	3	4	0	0	0	0	3	.0
BENOIT HOGUE	14	0	2	2	1-	16	0	0	0	0	20	.0
SHAWN CHAMBERS	17	0	2	2	1-	18	0	0	0	0	19	.0
BRIAN SKRUDLAND	19	0	2	2	0	16	0	0	0	0	10	.0

BLAKE SLOAN	19	0	2	2	1-	8	0	0	0	0	7	.0
DEREK PLANTE	6	1	0	1	0	4	0	0	0	0	8	12.5
BRAD LUKOWICH	8	0	1	1	3	4	0	0	0	0	6	.0
DOUG LIDSTER	4	0	0	0	0	2	0	0	0	0	1	.0
JONATHAN SIM	4	0	0	0	1-	0	0	0	0	0	1	.0
ED BELFOUR	23	0	0	0	0	4	0	0	0	0	0	.0

GOALTENDER	GPI	MINS	AVG	W	L	T	EN	SO	GA	SA	SV %
ED BELFOUR	23	1544	1.67	16	7	1	3	0	43	617	.930
DAL TOTALS	23	1547	1.71	16	7	1	3	0	44	618	.929

Detroit Red Wings

The Red Wings won their first six games of the playoffs, and at the time it appeared conceivable that they would win every game and take home their third consecutive Stanley Cup.

Four games later, they were finished for the season, and Colorado had moved on to face Dallas in the conference finals. In those four games the Wings were outscored 19-7.

Some of the top players didn't score, there were injury problem to key players, and assorted other excuses for why Detroit failed to advance. It could even bet that Colorado just plain outplayed them and deserved the win.

The Red Wings didn't have a great regular season, but that's sort of their nature. They save their A game for the playoffs, which makes the most sense, because they won't burn themselves out. The air-lift at the trading deadline obviously didn't help either, although you'd expect the character-type players they brought in, including Chris Chelios, to be positive factors in team chemistry.

Something in particular thing stands out, however, when comparing their statistics from the previous Stanley Cup winning season.

One way to tell how good a team is going to be during the post-season is to see how well they play in important games during the regular sea-son — the ones they have to get up for and know they have to play at a higher level to win.

When the Wings won the Stanley Cup in 1998, they were 18-12-6 versus teams with records over .500. Last year, they were 13-21-4.

We should see if that really is an important factor.

Let's consider the four conference finalists and how they did at that particular stat during the regular season.

Versus Teams Over .500:

	Team Record	League Rank
Dallas	20-10-6	2
Buffalo	16-15-12	6
Toronto	21-17-4	4
Colorado	15-14-4	5

So, the top four playoff teams were in the top six in this particular stat. Not likely a coincidence. Only seven teams had a winning record versus the over. 500 teams during the season. Mind you, the top team, New Jersey, and the third team, Ottawa, were bounced early.

In the playoffs, teams are playing almost exclusively versus teams with over. 500 records, so the stat shows that teams had better have a game that can compete with the best. Detroit didn't.

STUFF

Steve Yzerman needs eight goals for 600 for his career.

Larry Murphy became the all-time leader in games played by a defenseman.

TEAM PREVIEW

GOAL: Chris Osgood will have some new back-ups this season, after Norm Maracle was taken by Atlanta in the expansion draft, Bill Ranford was released, and Kevin Hodson was traded.

Ken Wregget should inherit the number one backup spot. The veteran is better suited to part-time play at this stage of his career and with his extensive history of injuries. Third in line is Manny Legace, signed as a free agent during the off-season. He made a bit of a splash last year when he filled in for injured Kings in Los Angeles.

DEFENSE: The Wings have a couple ongoing sagas.

Will Niklas Lidstrom go back to Sweden?

Will Uwe Krupp be able to come back from career threatening injuries?

The answer to both of them appears to be no, at this point.

Lidstrom talks longingly of his homeland, and seems sincere. You'd hope it wasn't some kind of bargaining ploy, but if it is, it's a good one. The difference in salary is staggering, however. If he wanted his kids educated in Sweden, he could bring over a team of tutors with the difference in salary.

Krupp is not recovering well from his back problems, and very likely could miss all of this season.

The defense will line up with other returnees, Chelios, Larry Murphy, Aaron Ward and Mathieu Dandenault, who can also play forward.

That leaves some rookies with a chance to stick. Jesse Wallin, a first-round choice in 1996, is almost sure to be one of them. He's a stay-at-home type who had a good season in Adirondack in the AHL, and is ready for full-time NHL duty.

Jiri Fischer made tremendous strides last year for Hull in the QMJHL, and his offensive game came around, with 78 points. He's a big guy, with a big shot.

Yan Golubovsky was supposed to be a regular by now, but so far, he's been a disappointment and may have played himself out of an NHL career.

If Lidstrom returns, everybody else is better. If he doesn't, the Wings are too dependant on aging veterans and unproven rookies.

FORWARD: During the first part of last season, everybody was lauding the accomplishments of

GOALTENDER	GPI	MINS	AVG	W	L	T	EN	SO	GA	SA	SV %
BILL RANFORD	4	244	1.97	3	0	1	0	0	8	98	.918
NORM MARACLE	16	821	2.27	6	5	2	1	0	31	379	.918
CHRIS OSGOOD	63	3,691	2.42	34	25	4	4	3	149	1,654	.910
KEVIN HODSON	4	175	3.09	0	2	0	0	0	9	79	.886
DET TOTALS	82	4,962	2.44	43	32	7	5	3	202	2,215	.909

Darren McCarty and Brendan Shanahan, while wondering what happened to Slava Kozlov and Sergei Fedorov.

On the Wings, much as to do with opportunity. The Yzerman-Shanahan-McCarty troika played so well at the start that they got all the prime scoring opportunities, including the power play.

Then Shanahan slumped, McCarty fell off the face of the earth, and Kozlov and Fedorov surged.

During Kozlov's first 18 games, he had just five points. Later in the season, during one five game stretch, he had 13 points. In a 15-game stretch before missing time with an injury late in the season, McCarty's cumulative point total was exactly one. He finished the season on the fourth line.

The only change, at this point, on the Detroit forward lines, is that late-season acquisition, Wendel Clark, became a free agent.

Otherwise, it's the same cast of characters, with Yzerman, Fedorov, Larionov, Draper and Roest at centre, and Shanahan, Kozlov, Martin Lapointe, Thomas Holmstrom, Doug Brown, McCarty, Kirk Maltby, Brent Gilchrist, and Joey Kocur on the wings.

The worries the Wings have is that some of the supporting cast is aging, and some of the primary cast is inconsistent.

SPECIAL TEAMS: The Wings power play should have been better than the mediocre showing they had, because they have so much offensive talent that if one guy falters another can move in easily. On the points, you will probably see Murphy's time being reduced, with Chelios and Lidstrom as the prime pointmen with the extra man.

Power Play	G	ATT	PCT
Overall	67	412	16.3% (11th NHL)
Home	38	211	18.0% (10th NHL)
Road	29	201	14.4% (15th NHL)

7 SHORT HANDED GOALS ALLOWED (T-9th NHL)

Penalty Killing	G	TSH	PCT
Overall	45	352	87.2% (4th NHL)
Home	21	170	87.6% (T-6th NHL)
Road	24	182	86.8% (4th NHL)

14 SHORT HANDED GOALS SCORED (2nd NHL)

Penalties	GP	MIN	AVG	
RED WINGS	81	1196	14.8	(10th NHL)

RED WINGS SPECIAL TEAMS SCORING

Power play	G	A	PTS
LIDSTROM	6	23	29
MURPHY	5	21	26
YZERMAN	13	11	24
LARIONOV	4	18	22
KOZLOV	6	14	20
FEDOROV	6	13	19
SHANAHAN	5	11	16
CLARK	11	4	15
HOLMSTROM	5	9	14
CHELIOS	3	11	14
MCCARTY	6	3	9
LAPOINTE	7	1	8
BROWN	3	1	4
SAMUELSSON	0	2	2
GILL	1	0	1
ROEST	0	1	1
MALTBY	0	1	1
KRUPP	0	1	1
DANDENAULT	0	1	1

Short handed	G	A	PTS
LIDSTROM	2	2	4

LARIONOV	2	2	4
DRAPER	1	3	4
YZERMAN	2	1	3
KOZLOV	1	2	3
BROWN	1	2	3
FEDOROV	2	0	2
MURPHY	1	1	2
CHELIOS	1	1	2
SHANAHAN	0	2	2
MALTBY	1	0	1
LAPOINTE	1	0	1
WARD	0	1	1
MCCARTY	0	1	1

COACHING AND MANAGEMENT: Bowman's annual coaching question was answered early this year, when he decided to go for another season. He probably doesn't like being aced by a rookie coach for Colorado in the conference semi-finals.

GM has a little more work to do this year. He's got to find a way to move some younger players onto the forward lines, and the Wings don't have much in the way of prospects. His late-season airlift to win the Cup looked good at the time, but didn't work out for him, so he may reconsider that approach next time.

DRAFT: (see chart) The Wings traded away all their top draft picks in an attempt to win the Stanley Cup last year. It would be a major surprise to see any of the above players in the NHL.

PROGNOSIS: No reason to think the Wings won't be among the better teams once again, and a Stanley Cup contender. Their collapse last year may even help this year. They're not really a regular season type team, but they are a playoff team, and will be on somewhat of a mission this year after being zoned by Colorado.

DRAFT

Player	Pos	Rnd	Sel.	Cntry	Team	Lge	Gms	G	A	P	PIM
Jari Toulsa	C	4	120	Swe	Frolunda	Swe	35	16	21	37	51
Andrei Maximenko	LW	5	149	Rus	Krylja Sovetev	Rus	15	0	1	1	16
Kent McDonnell	RW	6	181	Can	Guelph	OHL	60	31	38	69	60
Henrik Zetterberg	LW	7	210	Swe	Timra	Swe	24	13	12	25	10
Anton Borodkin	LW	8	238	Rus	Kamloops	WHL	71	8	29	37	98
Ken Davis	RW	9	266	Can	Portland	WHL	72	13	14	27	76

STAT SECTION

PLAYER	GP	G	A	PTS	+/-	PIM	PP	SH	GW	GT	S	PCTG
STEVE YZERMAN	80	29	45	74	8	42	13	2	4	0	231	12.6
SERGEI FEDOROV	77	26	37	63	9	66	6	2	3	0	224	11.6
IGOR LARIONOV	75	14	49	63	13	48	4	2	2	1	83	16.9
B. SHANAHAN	81	31	27	58	2	123	5	0	5	0	288	10.8
V. KOZLOV	79	29	29	58	10	45	6	1	4	2	209	13.9
NICKLAS LIDSTROM	81	14	43	57	14	14	6	2	3	0	205	6.8
LARRY MURPHY	80	10	42	52	21	42	5	1	2	0	168	6.0
WENDEL CLARK	77	32	16	48	24-	37	11	0	3	1	215	14.9
DARREN MCCARTY	69	14	26	40	10	108	6	0	1	1	140	10.0
CHRIS CHELIOS	75	9	27	36	1	93	3	1	1	1	187	4.8
T. HOLMSTROM	82	13	21	34	11-	69	5	0	4	0	100	13.0
MARTIN LAPOINTE	77	16	13	29	7	141	7	1	4	0	153	10.5
DOUG BROWN	80	9	19	28	5	42	3	1	1	0	180	5.0
KRIS DRAPER	80	4	14	18	2	79	0	1	1	0	78	5.1
KIRK MALTBY	53	8	6	14	6-	34	0	1	2	0	76	10.5
MA. DANDENAULT	75	4	10	14	17	59	0	0	0	0	94	4.3
STACY ROEST	59	4	8	12	7-	14	0	0	1	0	50	8.0
ULF SAMUELSSON	71	4	8	12	5	99	0	0	0	0	39	10.3
AARON WARD	60	3	8	11	5-	52	0	0	0	0	46	6.5
JAMIE MACOUN	69	1	10	11	1-	36	0	0	0	0	62	1.6
TODD GILL	51	4	5	9	10-	27	1	0	1	1	61	6.6
JOEY KOCUR	39	2	5	7	0	87	0	0	0	0	20	10.0
UWE KRUPP	22	3	2	5	0	6	0	0	0	0	32	9.4
CHRIS OSGOOD	63	0	3	3	0	8	0	0	0	0	0	.0
BRENT GILCHRIST	5	1	0	1	1-	0	0	0	1	0	4	25.0
PETR KLIMA	13	1	0	1	3-	4	0	0	1	0	12	8.3
DOUG HOUDA	3	0	1	1	2-	0	0	0	0	0	1	.0
YAN GOLUBOVSKY	17	0	1	1	4	16	0	0	0	0	10	.0
DARRYL LAPLANTE	3	0	0	0	0	0	0	0	0	0	0	.0
PHILIPPE AUDET	4	0	0	0	2-	0	0	0	0	0	3	.0
NORM MARACLE	16	0	0	0	0	0	0	0	0	0	0	.0
BILL RANFORD	36	0	0	0	0	2	0	0	0	0	0	.0

TEAM RANKINGS

		Conference Rank	League Rank
Record	43-32-7	3	6
Home	27-12-2	2	2
Away	16-20-5	6	14
Versus Own Conference	30-20-4	2	5
Versus Other Conference	13-12-3	4	10
Team Plus\Minus	+21	3	8
Goals For	245	1	3
Goals Against	202	4	9
Average Shots For	31.7	1	1
Average Shots Against	26.8	5	11
Overtime	2-1-7	5	9
One Goal Games	12-8	2	7
Times outshooting opponent	47	4	8
Versus Teams Over .500	13-21-4	7	15
Versus Teams .500 or under	30-11-3	2	2
First Half Record	21-18-2	3	10
Second Half Record	22-14-5	3	5

MISCELLANEOUS STAT LEADERS
FACEOFFS

	W	L	%
Yzerman	911	689	56.9
Draper	484	403	54.6
Fedorov	731	683	51.7
Larionov	432	435	49.8

ICE TIME

Chelios	26:40
Lidstrom	26:31
Murphy	24:15
Yzerman	21:35
Samulesson	20:19
Fedorov	19:21

HITS

McCarty	217
Samuelsson	176
Lapointe	167
Ward	133
Maltby	129
Shanahan	119

PLAYOFFS

Results:

Defeated Anaheim 4-0 in Conference Quarter-Finals

Lost to Colorado 4-2 in Conference Semi-Finals

Record: 6-4

Home: 2-3

Away: 4-1

Goals For: 31 (3.1/game)

Goals Against: 27 (2.7/game)

Overtime: 1-0

Power play: 23.7% (1st)

Penalty Killing: 82.0% (12th)

PLAYER	GP	G	A	PTS	+/-	PIM	PP	SH	GW	OT	S	PCTG
STEVE YZERMAN	10	9	4	13	2	0	4	0	2	0	41	22.0
NICKLAS LIDSTROM	10	2	9	11	0	4	2	0	0	0	29	6.9
B. SHANAHAN	10	3	7	10	2	6	1	0	1	0	31	9.7
SERGEI FEDOROV	10	1	8	9	3	8	0	0	0	0	38	2.6
V. KOZLOV	10	6	1	7	3-	4	3	0	0	0	28	21.4
T. HOLMSTROM	10	4	3	7	2	4	2	0	1	0	26	15.4
WENDEL CLARK	10	2	3	5	1-	10	1	0	0	0	29	6.9
DOUG BROWN	10	2	2	4	0	4	1	0	1	0	15	13.3
CHRIS CHELIOS	10	0	4	4	6-	14	0	0	0	0	21	.0
ULF SAMUELSSON	9	0	3	3	1	10	0	0	0	0	6	.0
DARREN MCCARTY	10	1	1	2	1-	23	0	0	0	0	15	6.7
IGOR LARIONOV	7	0	2	2	1-	0	0	0	0	0	3	.0
LARRY MURPHY	10	0	2	2	2	8	0	0	0	0	14	.0
MARTIN LAPOINTE	10	0	2	2	0	20	0	0	0	0	14	.0
KIRK MALTBY	10	1	0	1	2-	8	0	0	1	1	13	7.7
TODD GILL	2	0	1	1	0	0	0	0	0	0	3	.0
AARON WARD	8	0	1	1	2	8	0	0	0	0	6	.0
KRIS DRAPER	10	0	1	1	1-	6	0	0	0	0	9	.0
M. DANDENAULT	10	0	1	1	0	0	0	0	0	0	15	.0
JAMIE MACOUN	1	0	0	0	1-	0	0	0	0	0	1	.0
NORM MARACLE	2	0	0	0	0	0	0	0	0	0	0	.0
BRENT GILCHRIST	3	0	0	0	2-	0	0	0	0	0	2	.0
BILL RANFORD	4	0	0	0	0	0	0	0	0	0	0	.0
CHRIS OSGOOD	6	0	0	0	0	0	0	0	0	0	0	.0

GOALTENDER	GPI	MINS	AVG	W	L	T	EN	SO	GA	SA	SV %
CHRIS OSGOOD	6	358	2.35	4	2	0	1	0	14	172	.919
NORM MARACLE	2	58	3.10	0	0	0	0	0	3	22	.864
BILL RANFORD	4	183	3.28	2	2	0	1	0	10	105	.905
DET TOTALS	10	604	2.68	6	4	0	2	0	27	299	.910

Edmonton Oilers

Wayne Gretzky will always be remembered primarily as an Edmonton Oiler , not a Ranger, or a St. Louis Blue, or a Los Angeles King.

The same, actually, with Mark Messier, Paul Coffey, Esa Tikkanen, Jari Kurri, and Glen Anderson.

The longevity of those stars is a constant reminder of just how unbelievably good those Oiler teams of the 1980's were.

It's also a reminder that it can't happen again. At least the way the NHL is structured now. Oh, a team might be able to build a team of stars, but they're not going to stay together for long. With free agency and high salaries, there's no loyalty either way. Decisions are based on financial considerations.

With free agency and high salaries, the best anyone can hope for is to build a team without stars, similar to what Buffalo has been able to do. And similar to what the Oilers have been trying to do for so long now.

Trades are exciting for the game and create interest. But, maybe not when it's almost every player on a team, such as has been the case in Edmonton.

Thirty players played for the Oilers in the 1996-97 season. Only five remain.

Of the top 14 scorers at the end of the 1997-98 season, eight of them weren't with the team one year later.

It seems there are two ways of going about building a successful small market team. One is the Oilers way. That involves getting lots of young players and prospects and holding onto them until they get too good and command high salaries. Then, they're traded away for more young prospects and the cycle begins again. The Oilers do this through volume, hoping that even a couple of their prospects work out and are useful to them for a couple years.

Also involved in this process is trying out guys that nobody else wants, hoping to find a $100 bill in a garbage dump. Occasionally, they find at least a $20 bill, but invariably they discover why the player was discarded in the first place.

Also in the plan is holding on to a couple key players and paying them accordingly. But, they had better produce or its off they go for some young prospects.

This method allows the team to be respectable on occasion, but it will never allow them to be one of the top teams in the league.

Now, there's the other way. Another small market team, the Buffalo Sabres, seems to work this to perfection. Mind you, if they didn't have Dominik Hasek in net, it wouldn't work for them.

But anyway, it's the no-stars approach. You get a group of hard-working, devoted, hungry, team-oriented players who are never going to be superstars. Maybe two-way types, like Mike Peca. Or the Dixon Ward's of the world.

You draft for character and talent, rather than just if somebody can skate fast, like the Oilers seem to do. They probably would have passed over Gretzky at the draft because he wasn't a great skater.

You work young guys into the system with the veterans and allow them to see what it takes to be successful.

And you probably don't airlift everybody out every season. Maybe you build your stability by building a strong third line and a strong second line. You can build loyalty both ways there, too, because you don't have to pay them so much.

Finally, you find yourself a great goalie and pay him.

I'd go with the Buffalo approach, for the simple reason that the Edmonton style just doesn't work.

TEAM PREVIEW
GOAL: One thing the Oilers have always had is great goaltending. At least until now, anyway.

Grant Fuhr, Bill Ranford, Curtis Joseph, and Andy Moog, have all made their mark as great goalies.

The same fate isn't likely in the cards for Tommy Salo, who isn't the type of goalie to make a weak team good. He's already tried it once for the NY Islanders.

The Oilers didn't have a backup at press time, but one name being mentioned was Bill Ranford, who is well past his prime, undesired elsewhere, and will probably come cheap.

Bob Essensa could be re-signed, but it might be too late, and you have to wonder why he just didn't take what he was offered by the Oilers. He isn't exactly in a bargaining position.

DEFENSE: The Edmonton defense was going to be explosive, with Roman Hamrlik, Boris Mironov, Janne Niinimaa and Tom Poti. Explosive was hardly the word.

Mironov was traded, Hamrlik was good, but no Norris Trophy winner and looks to be on the trading block, and Niinimaa was impotent offensively until late in the season after Mironov left. Poti, however, looks to be the real thing.

There's no point having all that offensive power on the blueline if they're not going to use it. It did nothing for the power play, which stunk, or the goals against, which also wasn't good.

The law of diminishing returns suggests that two offensive types is plenty. When you have a surplus, you can deal, because teams are always looking for offensive help on the blueline or power play.

GOALTENDER	GPI	MINS	AVG	W	L	T	EN	SO	GA	SA	SV %
TOMMY SALO	13	700	2.31	8	2	2	0	0	27	279	.903
M. SHTALENKO	34	1,819	2.67	12	17	3	2	3	81	782	.896
BOB ESSENSA	39	2,091	2.75	12	14	6	2	0	96	974	.901
STEVE PASSMORE	6	362	2.82	1	4	1	1	0	17	183	.907
EDM TOTALS	82	4,997	2.71	33	37	12	5	3	226	2223	.898

They need defensive types, which is why they acquired Jason Smith. They have a couple good prospects, too, including Chris Hajt, Brad Norton and Alex Henry.

Christian LaFlamme should be a regular, Todd Reirden has a shot, and Sean Brown will be the gunslinger.

FORWARD: Doug Weight's season was a write-off, so he should benefit from having a full season and starting at the start. That won't help Josef Berenek, though, who benefitted from Weight's absence by playing on the top line.

Bill Guerin should benefit from having the top centre there for a full season, but he scored more when Weight wasn't there, starting off the season with eight of his 30 goals in the first eight games. Ryan Smyth doesn't benefit unless he's the top right winger and is on the power play.

Alexander Selivanov would benefit from sitting on the bench and learning about intensity. Or from watching Pat Falloon who made a great comeback from the retread pile. Or Mike Grier, a defensive forward who had a great offensive season.

Rem Murray would benefit from playing on the top line, because he was still the team's second leading goal scorer.

Todd Marchant would benefit from slowing down some so he wouldn't be moving faster than his ability to play the game.

Chad Kilger and Ethan Moreau would benefit from something, but it's hard to say what.

Boyd Devereaux and Daniel Cleary would benefit from playing for a full season.

George Laraque will punch your lights out if you tell him he needs to benefit from something.

SPECIAL TEAMS: Special teams should be a product of the coach. Good power play and penalty killing systems can be taught. On the power play, the Oilers had the personnel, and on the penalty killing, Lowe's assistant coach, Craig MacTavish, might be of help.

One thing that speed does for the Oilers is draw penalties. In recent years, they've been among the league leaders in power play advantages.

These are the top teams from last season:

	Power Play Advantages
Edmonton	438
Detroit	415
San Jose	399
Ottawa	397
Dallas	393
Lge. Ave.	359

Power Play	G	ATT	PCT
Overall	62	434	14.3% (18th NHL)
Home	30	203	14.8% (19th NHL)
Road	32	231	13.9% (T-17th NHL)

10 SHORT HANDED GOALS ALLOWED (T-19th NHL)

Penalty Killing	G	TSH	PCT
Overall	66	370	82.2% (T-21st NHL)
Home	34	168	79.8% (25th NHL)
Road	32	202	84.2% (T-11th NHL)

7 SHORT HANDED GOALS SCORED (T-13th NHL)

Penalties	GP	MIN	AVG
OILERS	81	1355	16.7 (T-17th NHL)

OILERS SPECIAL TEAMS SCORING

Power play	G	A	PTS
GUERIN	13	9	22

BERANEK	7	10	17
HAMRLIK	3	14	17
WEIGHT	1	15	16
FALLOON	8	7	15
SMYTH	6	6	12
SELIVANOV	2	8	10
NIINIMAA	2	8	10
MURRAY	4	5	9
POTI	2	7	9
MARCHANT	3	2	5
GRIER	2	2	4
LAFLAMME	0	4	4
KILGER	2	1	3
BROWN	2	1	3
MOREAU	0	2	2
REIRDEN	0	1	1

Short handed	G	A	PTS
BUCHBERGER	2	0	2
MURRAY	1	1	2
KILGER	1	1	2
MARCHANT	1	0	1
GRIER	1	0	1
DEVEREAUX	1	0	1
NIINIMAA	0	1	1

COACHING AND MANAGEMENT: The Oilers tend to look in low places for their coaches. Or is that Lowe places? When Ron Low refused the low contract the Oilers offered him, Kevin Lowe was awarded with his own low contract.

Lowe, who scored the first goal in franchise history, has no head coaching experience, which usually spells disaster in the NHL today. He's been looking to coaching for a while now, and appears to be well-prepared to make this a permanent career choice.

The pre-requisite for being the Oilers' coach, anyway, is to accept a low salary, with little prospects for a raise.

GM Glen Sather didn't pull off any miracles this year and probably never will. It appeared as if he was going to give team chemistry a chance to develop when he made no moves well into the season. But, then he started his usual airlift. Either way, it wasn't going anywhere.

Sather doesn't have much of a budget to work with, as we're reminded constantly, so whatever he's able to accomplish with this team, should be considered a bonus, at least according to him.

But, Sather doesn't just get rid of salaries. He operates on the trial-and-error basis, seeing how a player looks once he's an Oiler. Then, they're often discarded. Maybe better pre-scouting would save everyone a lot of trouble.

Same with the amateur scouting. They make lousy picks, year after year, and still keep their jobs. They must work cheap.

DRAFT: (see chart) First round pick Jani Rita can forget about being successful in the NHL. Most of the Oiler's picks are doomed to failure, maybe because they got more than their share in 1979 and 1980 when they got Kevin Lowe, Mark Messier, Glenn Anderson, Paul Coffey, Jari Kurri and Andy Moog. Since then, their first round picks qualify as members of the Who's Not listing of NHL players.

Rita is a Finn, and the Oilers have been successful with their Finns, with Jari Kurri and Esa Tikkanen, as well as Reijo Ruotsalainen, Risto Siltanen, Matti Hagman and Raimo Summanen. Nobody knows if Rita can put the puck in the net, but if he can't he's been projected as a power forward. That's just where you want to get your power forwards from — Finland, where they

DRAFT

Player	Pos	Rnd	Sel.	Cntry	Team	Lge	Gms	G	A	P	PIM
Jani Rita	RW	1	13	Fin	Jokerit	Fin	41	3	2	5	39
Alexei Semenov	D	2	36	Rus	Sudbury	OHL	28	0	3	3	28
Tony Salmelainen	LW	2	41	Fin	HIFK Helsinki	Fin	21	13	10	23	45
Adam Huaser	G	3	81	USA	Minnesota	WCHA	3.54	.873			
Mike Comrie	C	3	91	Can	Michigan	CCHA	36	17	22	39	30
Jonathan Fauteux	D	5	139	Can	Val D'or	QMJHL	59	15	33	48	139
Chris Legg	C	6	171	Can	London Jr.b	OHA	52	38	40	78	28
Christian Chartier	D	7	199	Can	Saskatoon	WHL	62	2	14	16	71
Tomas Groschl	W	9	256								

don't do any hitting in their games.

No wonder the Oilers can't draft. Good thing Wayne Gretzky didn't have to be drafted.

PROGNOSIS: The Oilers just barely made the playoffs last year, and aren't improved any for this season.

A full season without major injuries or excuses, however, and they could slip into the playoffs. It's not likely, however, because other teams, such as Los Angeles, have made big steps to improve.

STAT SECTION

PLAYER	GP	G	A	PTS	+/-	PIM	PP	SH	GW	GT	S	PCTG
BILL GUERIN	80	30	34	64	7	133	13	0	2	1	261	11.5
JOSEF BERANEK	66	19	30	49	6	23	7	0	2	0	160	11.9
MIKE GRIER	82	20	24	44	5	54	3	2	1	0	143	14.0
PAT FALLOON	82	17	23	40	4-	20	8	0	2	0	152	11.2
REM MURRAY	78	21	18	39	4	20	4	1	4	1	116	18.1
DOUG WEIGHT	43	6	31	37	8-	12	1	0	0	1	79	7.6
TODD MARCHANT	82	14	22	36	3	65	3	1	2	0	183	7.7
A. SELIVANOV	72	14	19	33	8-	42	2	0	1	0	177	7.9
ROMAN HAMRLIK	75	8	24	32	9	70	3	0	0	0	172	4.7
RYAN SMYTH	71	13	18	31	0	62	6	0	2	2	161	8.1
JANNE NIINIMAA	81	4	24	28	7	88	2	0	1	0	142	2.8
CHAD KILGER	77	15	12	27	4-	34	2	1	1	1	81	18.5
ETHAN MOREAU	80	10	11	21	3-	92	0	0	2	0	96	10.4
TOM POTI	73	5	16	21	10	42	2	0	3	0	94	5.3
JASON SMITH	72	3	12	15	9-	51	0	0	0	0	68	4.4
BOYD DEVEREAUX	61	6	8	14	2	23	0	1	4	1	39	15.4

C. LAFLAMME	73	2	12	14	3-	70	0	0	0	0	68	2.9
K. BUCHBERGER	52	4	4	8	6-	68	0	2	1	0	29	13.8
SEAN BROWN	51	0	7	7	1	188	0	0	0	0	27	.0
KEVIN BROWN	12	4	2	6	2-	0	2	0	0	0	13	30.8
G. LARAQUE	39	3	2	5	1-	57	0	0	0	0	17	17.6
TODD REIRDEN	17	2	3	5	1-	20	0	0	0	0	26	7.7
MARTY MCSORLEY	46	2	3	5	5-	101	0	0	0	0	29	6.9
FRANK MUSIL	39	0	3	3	0	34	0	0	0	0	9	.0
V. VOROBIEV	2	2	0	2	1	2	0	0	0	0	5	40.0
CRAIG MILLAR	24	0	2	2	6-	19	0	0	0	0	18	.0
CHRIS FERRARO	2	1	0	1	1	0	0	0	0	0	1	100.0
STEVE PASSMORE	6	0	1	1	0	2	0	0	0	0	0	.0
BOB ESSENSA	39	0	1	1	0	0	0	0	0	0	0	.0
JIM DOWD	1	0	0	0	0	0	0	0	0	0	1	.0
JOE HULBIG	1	0	0	0	1	2	0	0	0	0	2	.0
BILL HUARD	3	0	0	0	0	0	0	0	0	0	2	.0
DAN LACOUTURE	3	0	0	0	1	0	0	0	0	0	0	.0
DANIEL LACROIX	4	0	0	0	0	13	0	0	0	0	5	.0
F. LINDQUIST	8	0	0	0	2-	2	0	0	0	0	6	.0
TOMMY SALO	64	0	0	0	0	12	0	0	0	0	0	.0

TEAM RANKINGS

		Conference Rank	League Rank
Record	33-37-12	8	16
Home	17-19-5	10	21
Away	16-18-7	4	8
Versus Own Conference	25-24-6	6	13
Versus Other Conference	8-13-6	10	22
Team Plus\Minus	+8	7	13
Goals For	230	5	10
Goals Against	226	9	18
Average Shots For	28.9	4	8
Average Shots Against	26.7	3	9
Overtime	3-5-12	11	22
One Goal Games	11-16	12	22
Times outshooting opponent	51	3	6
Versus Teams Over .500	15-21-7	5	12
Versus Teams .500 or under	18-16-5	9	20
First Half Record	16-19-6	7	17
Second Half Record	17-18-6	9	15

MISCELLANEOUS STATS LEADERS
FACEOFFS

	W	L	%
Beranek	633	628	50.2
Marchant	725	724	50.0
Weight	422	431	49.5
Murray	487	526	48.1
Devereaux	175	234	42.8

ICE TIME

Niinimaa	23:54
Hamrlik	23:49
Weight	19:51
Guerin	19:42
Poti	19:33

HITS

Grier	188
LaFlamme	176
Kilger	157
Smith	148
Hamrlik	144
Niinimaa	144
Moreau	139
Marchant	133
Guerin	131

PLAYOFFS

Results:

Lost in conference quarter-finals 4-0 to Dallas

Record: 0-4
Home: 0-2
Away: 0-2
Goals For: 7 (1.8/game)
Goals Against: 11 (2.8/game)
Overtime: 0-1
Power play: 11.8% (13th)
Penalty Killing: 90.9% (1st)

PLAYER	GP	G	A	PTS	+/-	PIM	PP	SH	GW	OT	S	PCTG
RYAN SMYTH	3	3	0	3	1-	0	2	0	0	0	7	42.9
ETHAN MOREAU	4	0	3	3	3	6	0	0	0	0	6	.0
DOUG WEIGHT	4	1	1	2	3-	15	0	0	0	0	4	25.0
REM MURRAY	4	1	1	2	1-	2	0	0	0	0	6	16.7
TODD MARCHANT	4	1	1	2	2	12	0	0	0	0	10	10.0
MIKE GRIER	4	1	1	2	3	6	0	0	0	0	9	11.1
BILL GUERIN	3	0	2	2	4-	2	0	0	0	0	8	.0
A. SELIVANOV	2	0	1	1	0	2	0	0	0	0	3	.0
PAT FALLOON	4	0	1	1	0	4	0	0	0	0	6	.0
JASON SMITH	4	0	1	1	0	4	0	0	0	0	1	.0
C. LAFLAMME	4	0	1	1	4-	2	0	0	0	0	5	.0
TOM POTI	4	0	1	1	3-	2	0	0	0	0	9	.0
FRANK MUSIL	1	0	0	0	1-	2	0	0	0	0	2	.0
VLADIMIR VOROBIEV	1	0	0	0	1-	0	0	0	0	0	1	.0
SEAN BROWN	1	0	0	0	0	10	0	0	0	0	0	.0
BOYD DEVEREAUX	1	0	0	0	0	0	0	0	0	0	3	.0
JOSEF BERANEK	2	0	0	0	1-	4	0	0	0	0	0	.0
MARTY MCSORLEY	3	0	0	0	1	2	0	0	0	0	3	.0
ROMAN HAMRLIK	3	0	0	0	1	2	0	0	0	0	1	.0

	GP	G	A	PTS	+/-	PIM	PP	SH	GW	OT	S	%
KELLY BUCHBERGER	4	0	0	0	4-	0	0	0	0	0	2	.0
JANNE NIINIMAA	4	0	0	0	2-	2	0	0	0	0	5	.0
TOMMY SALO	4	0	0	0	0	0	0	0	0	0	0	.0
CHAD KILGER	4	0	0	0	2-	4	0	0	0	0	1	.0
GEORGES LARAQUE	4	0	0	0	2-	2	0	0	0	0	1	.0

GOALTENDER	GPI	MINS	AVG	W	L	T	EN	SO	GA	SA	SV %
TOMMY SALO	4	296	2.23	0	4	0	0	0	11	149	.926
EDM TOTALS	4	298	2.21	0	4	0	0	0	11	149	.926

Los Angeles Kings

There's good news and bad news.

Bad News: The Kings had high hopes for progress at the start of last year, based on their previous season. It didn't work out, of course.
Good News: They've got high hopes for this year, too.

Bad News: Larry Robinson was fired because the players didn't respond to him.
Good News: Robinson was replaced as coach.
Bad News: The players should have responded to him, because he treated them well, and gave them every opportunity to show their appreciation.

Bad News: Had a losing record of 18-20-3 at home.
Good News: The Great Western Forum won't be their home next year, as they move into the Staples Centre.

Bad News: Were decimated by injuries last season.
Good News: It can't be that bad again.

Bad News: Josef Stumpel was a complete bust last season.

Good News: He was hampered by injuries, for one, and this year he'll be playing alongside Zigmund Palffy.

Bad News: The Kings were only 6-18-0 versus their own Pacific Division.
Good News: They were almost .500 against the rest of the league at 26-27-5.

Good News: The Kings got Zigmund Palffy to help them make the playoffs.
Bad News: Palffy has been in North America for six years and has never been in even one playoff game.

Good News: Luc Robitaille is coming off a great season in which he scored 39 goals.
Bad News: He will turn 34 this year, and his goal scoring high in the previous three seasons was 24.

Bad News: Only five teams gave up more shots than the Kings.
Good News: Eleven teams had worse goals against averages.

Bad News: Veterans Ray Ferraro, Russ Courtnall, Doug Bodger and Dave Babych are no longer with the team.

Good News: Some younger players will get a chance to play.
Bad News: There's no guarantee the younger players will work out.

Good News: Rob Blake should be recovered from his injuries and return to form as one of the premier defensemen.
Bad News: The Kings still probably have one of the worst defense units in the league.

Bad News: The Kings were 4-16 in games that Blake was out of the lineup.
Good News: They were 28-29-5 when he was in the lineup.

Good News: The Kings obtained Zigmund Palffy from the Islanders.
Bad News: There's no bad news.

STUFF

The 189 goals scored by the Kings were the fewest (in a full season) since 1969-70 when they had 168.

The Kings have an 18-game current winless streak against Dallas over four years, with a record of 0-12-6.

Doug Bodger became the 130th player to play in 1,000 games.

TEAM PREVIEW

GOAL: This is one position in which the Kings are in good shape — as long as there aren't injuries. Last year, they had plenty to their two number ones, Jamie Storr and Stephane Fiset.

Manny Legace looked good when he was needed as an injury fill-in, although both he and Ryan Bach were lost to free agency. The Kings did pick up Marcel Cousineau from the Islanders in the Palffy deal for insurance.

It's rare for teams to have two such good goalies at one time, or at least rare to be playing them both. With the money teams shell out for their number one man, they want him playing, and playing a lot.

Also, it's somewhat of an unnecessary luxury in the NHL these days, and one or the other could be a decent bargaining chip for a trade. Storr, at 23, is six years younger than Fiset, so you'd figure on Fiset going first, if Storr shows he can handle the full load.

DEFENSE: The Kings look to have a lousy defense, but they should at least be mobile. Much depends on newcomer Frantisek Kaberle, who was voted the best defenseman in Sweden last year; Finn Jere Karahlati whom the Kings drafted six years ago; and whether or not they can re-sign Aki Berg, who played in Europe last season after refusing to sign a contract.

GOALTENDER	GPI	MINS	AVG	W	L	T	EN	SO	GA	SA	SV %
JAMIE STORR	28	1525	2.40	12	12	2	3	4	61	724	.916
MANNY LEGACE	17	899	2.60	2	9	2	5	0	39	439	.911
STEPHANE FISET	42	2,403	2.60	18	21	1	2	3	104	1217	.915
RYAN BACH	3	108	4.44	0	3	0	0	0	8	66	.879
L.A TOTALS	82	4,960	2.69	32	45	5	10	8	222	2,456	.910

STEPHANE FISET and MANNY LEGACE shared a shutout vs N.J on Oct 28, 1998

So, they have a number one combination that works well together in Blake and Mattias Norstrom, but after that it's anything but solid.

Kaberle and Karahlati could adapt well, or might not adapt well. Philippe Boucher has to show he deserves to play full-time. Sean O'Donnell is a defensive defenseman and the resident fighter, which leaves Gary Galley for spot duty, perhaps on the power play.

And there's also Berg if he signs and maybe Jaroslav Modry as the seventh or eighth defenseman.

After Blake, they need help offensively, and that's where Kaberle and Karahlati need to show they can contribute.

They key, of course, is having Blake healthy, because that's the key difference. But, that's easier said than done. Let's look at his career record for games played.

	Played	Missed
1989-90	4	-
1990-91	75	5
1991-92	57	23
1992-93	76	8
1993-94	84	0
1994-95	24	24
1995-96	6	76
1996-97	62	20
1997-98	81	1
1998-99	62	20
Total	531	177

Blake has missed exactly one-quarter of his games since becoming a regular in the NHL. On this team, he's the difference between winning and losing.

FORWARD: It's an 82-game season, and Luc Robitaille played all 82 of them. Incredibly, only one other Los Angeles forward played as many as 70.

Robitaille scored 39 goals. Incredibly, no one else had more than 18.

Okay, both problems should be solved this year. Injuries can't possibly be as bad, there appear to be more set regulars, and they've added some scoring.

Robitaille might have a hard time duplicating those numbers at 34-years-old, but he will likely start on the top line with Palffy and Stumpel. If Robitaille is up to it, this line should be one of the best in the league.

Stumpel just had an off-year. He was injured right from the start, and never really got into the swing of things. He should rebound nicely.

Palffy will be a fan favourite in Los Angeles after about two shifts, and better yet, few players in the league have been consistently as good the last couple years. He's coming off an bad year, too, precipitated by a contract holdout at the start of the season, and ending with a team going nowhere.

The chart below shows the players who have had more than one 40-40 season over the last four years.

40-40 men the last foure seasons:
Zigmund Palffy 3 (only player in 1997-98)
Jaromir Jagr   3
John LeClair   3
Teemu Selanne 3
Joe Sakic   2
Eric Lindros   2
Theoren Fleury 2
Paul Kariya   2
Mario Lemieux   2

If Palffy hadn't been a holdout, there's a good chance he would have been the only player to accomplish the 40-40 feat over each of the last four years.

Having Palffy and a renewed Stumpel opens up the second and third lines to scoring now, as well.

Bryan Smolinski could have a comeback season quite easily, too, so they've got him, Glenn Murray, coming off an injury season, and Donald Audette, who also missed much of last season by being a holdout.

And there's still some scoring potential, with Vladimir Tsyplakov and Craig Johnson coming off poor scoring seasons and looking to rebound. Plus, they've imported Marko Tuomainen, a seasoned veteran; have Pavel Rosa ready to break out; and have Jason Blake, who looked outstanding in his one game audition at the end of last season, even scoring a goal.

Defensively, they've got centre Ian Laperriere, and humungous Steve McKenna to handle the rough stuff.

The only way the Kings can blow this is they try to play a defensive system.

Of course, the other worry is that all the players who need to rebound from poor season, actually won't.

SPECIAL TEAMS: Steve Duchesne was supposed to be the pointman the Kings needed for the power play when they signed him to a big free agent contract before the start of last year. He wasn't even close.

The Kings brought in some offensive type defensemen to help in that area, and have more snipers up front. Palffy should make a big difference on the power play, which should be revamped anyway under a new coach and new system.

Power Play	G	ATT	PCT
Overall	43	327	13.1% (24th NHL)
Home	26	177	14.7% (19th NHL)
Road	17	150	11.3% (T-23rd NHL)

11 SHORT HANDED GOALS ALLOWED (T-23rd NHL)

Penalty Killing	G	TSH	PCT
Overall	47	330	85.8% (9th NHL)
Home	25	175	85.7% (T-13th NHL)
Road	22	155	85.8% (8th NHL)

12 SHORT HANDED GOALS SCORED (T-3rd NHL)

Penalties	GP	MIN	AVG
KINGS	82	1383	16.9 (T-18th NHL)

KINGS SPECIAL TEAMS SCORING

Power play	G	A	PTS
ROBITAILLE	11	10	21
AUDETTE	6	9	15
BLAKE	5	6	11
GALLEY	3	4	7
FERRARO	4	2	6
MURRAY	3	3	6
JOKINEN	3	3	6
STUMPEL	1	5	6
BABYCH	2	3	5
BODGER	0	5	5
BOUCHER	1	3	4
O'DONNELL	0	4	4
ROSA	0	3	3
CONVERY	0	3	3
JOHNSON	2	0	2
TSYPLAKOV	0	2	2
GREEN	1	0	1
MOGER	0	1	1
MODRY	0	1	1
LAPERRIERE	0	1	1
LAFAYETTE	0	1	1

Short handed	G	A	PTS
MURRAY	3	0	3
TSYPLAKOV	2	1	3
COURTNALL	1	1	2
BLAKE	1	1	2
STUMPEL	0	2	2
GALLEY	0	2	2
NORSTROM	1	0	1
LAFAYETTE	1	0	1
JOKINEN	1	0	1
VISHEAU	0	1	1
O'DONNELL	0	1	1
LAPERRIERE	0	1	1
FERRARO	0	1	1
BODGER	0	1	1

COACHING AND MANAGEMENT: Andy Murray is the new coach, fresh off a season of coaching high school hockey in Minnesota. That's not too big a deal. He has plenty of experience, including a two-year stint as Canada's national team coach, which won a gold medal at the world championships.

Murray is considered to be very well prepared and very demanding, which will be a change from Larry Robinson. Robinson had the mistaken notion that these were professionals and should be giving one hundred percent effort all the time without being disciplined.

Murray says he wants the players to be creative offensively, without ignoring their defensive responsibilities.

GM Dave Taylor appears to have done a great job in giving this team the opportunity to turn it around right away. He gave up some prospects to get Palffy, Smolinski and Cousineau, including Olli Jokinen, Martin Biron, Josh Green and a first rounder, but there are few players around more productive than Palffy, so it was a great deal.

Plus, he's brought in NHL ready players, he hopes, that can contribute right away.

DRAFT: (see chart) The Kings traded away their first round pick, and couldn't care less about it. That's because they got Zigmund Palffy from the Islanders, and few draft picks are ever going to compare to him. Besides, they're used to not having a top draft pick, and have only had one in four of the last 10 years.

DRAFT

Player	Pos	Rnd	Sel.	Cntry	Team	Lge	Gms	G	A	P	PIM
Andrei Shefer	LW	2	43	Rus	Cherepovic	Rus	82	31	18	49	0
Jason Crain	D	3	74	USA	Ohio St.	CCHA	37	3	13	16	16
Frantisek Kaberle	D	3	76	Cze	Modo	Swe	45	15	18	33	4
Cory Campbell	G	3	92	Can	Belleville	OHL	3.49	.888			
Brian McGrattan	RW	4	104	Can	Sudbury	OHL	59	8	13	21	168
Daniel Johansson	C	4	125	Swe	Modo Jr.	Swe	43	10	19	29	0
J-F Nogues	G	5	133	Can	Victoriaville	QMJHL	4.17	.863			
Kevin Baker	RW	7	193	Can	Belleville	OHL	68	44	37	81	66
George Parros	RW	8	222	USA	Chicago	NAHL	53	30	20	50	124
Noah Clarke	LW	9	250	USA	Des Moines	USHL					

PROGNOSIS: The defense is suspect and so many players are being counted on to have turn-around years. That's the bad news. The good news is that it looks as if the Kings will be able to shoot out the lights and score lots of goals.

They could very well be this year's surprise success story. At the very least they can't be as bad as last year.

STAT SECTION

PLAYER	GP	G	A	PTS	+/-	PIM	PP	SH	GW	GT	S	PCTG
LUC ROBITAILLE	82	39	35	74	1-	54	11	0	7	0	292	13.4
DONALD AUDETTE	49	18	18	36	7	51	6	0	2	0	152	11.8
ROB BLAKE	62	12	23	35	7-	128	5	1	2	0	216	5.6
JOZEF STUMPEL	64	13	21	34	18-	10	1	0	1	0	131	9.9
GLEN MURRAY	61	16	15	31	14-	36	3	3	3	0	173	9.2
RAY FERRARO	65	13	18	31	0	59	4	0	4	0	84	15.5
V. TSYPLAKOV	69	11	12	23	7-	32	0	2	2	0	111	9.9
OLLI JOKINEN	66	9	12	21	10-	44	3	1	1	0	87	10.3
CRAIG JOHNSON	69	7	12	19	12-	32	2	0	2	0	94	7.4
RUSS COURTNALL	57	6	13	19	9-	19	0	1	1	0	77	7.8
PAVEL ROSA	29	4	12	16	0	6	0	0	0	0	61	6.6
GARRY GALLEY	60	4	12	16	9-	30	3	0	0	0	77	5.2
DOUG BODGER	65	3	11	14	1	34	0	0	0	0	67	4.5
SEAN O'DONNELL	80	1	13	14	1	186	0	0	0	0	64	1.6
IAN LAPERRIERE	72	3	10	13	5-	138	0	0	1	0	62	4.8
BRANDON CONVERY	15	2	7	9	4	12	0	0	1	0	14	14.3
DAVE BABYCH	41	2	6	8	2-	22	2	0	0	0	49	4.1
PHILIPPE BOUCHER	45	2	6	8	12-	32	1	0	0	0	87	2.3
M. NORSTROM	78	2	5	7	10-	36	0	1	0	0	61	3.3
SANDY MOGER	42	3	2	5	9-	26	0	0	2	0	28	10.7
N. LAFAYETTE	33	2	2	4	0	35	0	1	1	0	42	4.8
JOSH GREEN	27	1	3	4	5-	8	1	0	0	0	35	2.9
MARK VISHEAU	28	1	3	4	7-	107	0	0	0	0	10	10.0
SEAN PRONGER	29	0	4	4	1-	8	0	0	0	0	14	.0
MATT JOHNSON	49	2	1	3	5-	131	0	0	0	0	14	14.3
JASON BLAKE	1	1	0	1	1	0	0	0	0	0	5	20.0
JAN NEMECEK	6	1	0	1	1-	4	0	0	1	0	8	12.5
STEVE MCKENNA	20	1	0	1	3-	36	0	0	0	0	12	8.3
JAROSLAV MODRY	5	0	1	1	1	0	0	0	0	0	11	.0
MANNY LEGACE	17	0	1	1	0	0	0	0	0	0	0	.0

JAMIE STORR	28	0	1	1	0	6	0	0	0	0	0	.0
RYAN BACH	3	0	0	0	0	0	0	0	0	0	0	.0
DAN BYLSMA	8	0	0	0	1-	2	0	0	0	0	3	.0
JASON PODOLLAN	10	0	0	0	3-	5	0	0	0	0	9	.0
STEPHANE FISET	42	0	0	0	0	2	0	0	0	0	0	.0

TEAM RANKINGS

		Conference Rank	League Rank
Record	32-45-5	11	22
Home	18-20-3	9	19
Away	14-25-2	10	21
Versus Own Conference	21-32-4	11	23
Versus Other Conference	11-13-1	9	18
Team Plus\Minus	-29	11	21
Goals For	189	13	25
Goals Against	222	8	16
Average Shots For	28.3	5	9
Average Shots Against	30.0	11	22
Overtime	5-2-5	1	3
One Goal Games	16-19	8	18
Times outshooting opponent	36	7	14
Versus Teams Over .500	12-30-2	13	26
Versus Teams .500 or under	20-15-3	7	18
First Half Record	15-22-4	9	21
Second Half Record	17-23-1	11	22

MISCELLANEOUS STATS LEADERS
FACOFFS

	W	L	%
Stumpel	802	682	54.0
Ferraro	468	511	47.8
Laperriere	304	339	47.3
Jokinen	342	437	43.9

ICE-TIME

Blake	24:52
Murray	20:33
Norstrom	20:20
Stumpel	19:44
Bodger	19:27
Robitaille	19:11
O'Donnell	19:10

HITS

Norstrom	236
Laperriere	149
O'Donnell	133
Blake	132
Jokinen	109
Galley	100

PLAYOFFS

- did not make the playoffs

Nashville Predators

The good news is that the Nashville Predators had the fifth best record among the 12 modern expansion teams. They were a respectable team that was only eliminated from the playoff race with four games remaining. Three teams had worse records.

The bad news is that it's not going to get any better this year. At least that's what history tells us. And the more successful they were in their initial season the more likely they are to fall back.

The chart below shows the winning percentages for the 11 previous expansion teams, not including the WHA additions or the original expansion. They're listed in order of first year winning percentage.

Of the 11 previous teams, six of them had worse records in their second season. A couple of them couldn't have possibly been any worse in their second season, so to look at it another way, six of the best eight expansion teams had a dropoff in their second season..

Record Comparison — Expansion Teams

	Year	First Year	Second Year	%
Florida	1993-94	.494	.479	down
Anaheim	1993-94	.423	.385	down
Atlanta (Cgy)	1972-73	.417	.474	up
Buffalo	1970-71	.404	.327	down
Nashville	1998-99	.384	?	
Vancouver	1970-71	.359	.308	down
Tampa Bay	1992-93	.315	.423	up
Kansas City (NJ)	1974-75	.256	.225	down
San Jose	1991-92	.244	.143	down
NY Islanders		1972-73	.192	.359 up
Ottawa	1992-93	.143	.220	up
Washington	1974-75	.131	.200	up

Logically, you'd expect a team to improve as they went along, but there are some good reasons for the second year drop, or at least they seem to be good reasons.

1. The initial adrenaline has worn off. Everything is new and exciting the first year, both for the players, management and the fans. Everybody on the team is trying just a little bit harder to make a good impression.

2. Players are a little more comfortable with their spot on the team in their second season, and aren't motivated to make an impression. They

may still be motivated to play well, of course, but the first season everything is up for grabs and everybody has to prove themselves.

3. Interest in the team from the public is always highest in the first season. The second year it wanes some and it's conceivable it also affects the players. When the love affair starts to fade, then more criticism comes out, followed by more pressure.

4. Depth within the organization starts to show. Rather, the lack of it. The Predators did quite well with all their injuries last season, but that tends to catch up

5. Opponents don't take them as lightly. The Predators were quick to establish they were a decent team last year, but there was always that knowledge that they were an expansion team.

6. They start to develop prospects, and start thinking about trying to get them into the lineup for the future. Then, the veterans, who were always only thought of as a stopgap to make the team respectable, are eased out of the lineup.

STUFF

Andrew Brunette had the first goal in team history, Greg Johnson and Joel Bouchard the first assists.

Tom Fitzgerald had the first penalty, Patrick Cote the first fight.

Mike Dunham was credited with their first win, in their second game of the season.

TEAM PREVIEW

GOAL: Mike Dunham was thought to be some type of goaltending god for the first part of last season. But, then he got injured and replacement Tomas Vokoun turned out to be every bit as good, and even better at times.

Vokoun was actually third on the depth chart behind Eric Fichaud at the start of the season, but Fichaud got injured and Vokoun took over.

Dunham is still the number one goalie this year, but Vokoun should still get plenty of work.

Overall, this is probably the strongest position for the team, unless there are injuries. They surrendered the most shots in the league, 2709, and still Dunham and Vokoun managed to keep their team in almost every game.

Their future star, Brian Finley, taken sixth overall in this year's draft is a couple years away.

DEFENSE: The Predators have a little bit of everything on their defense. The key word there is little.

They're fairly tough with Bob Boughner back there, but for the most part they're not very physical, not very big, and have little in the way of an offensive threat.

GOALTENDER	GPI	MINS	AVG	W	L	T	EN	SO	GA	SA	SV %
TOMAS VOKOUN	37	1,954	2.95	12	18	4	4	1	96	1,041	.908
MIKE DUNHAM	44	2,472	3.08	16	23	3	3	1	127	1,387	.908
ERIC FICHAUD	9	447	3.22	0	6	0	1	0	24	229	.895
CHRIS MASON	3	69	5.22	0	0	0	0	0	6	44	.864
NSH TOTALS	82	4,964	3.15	28	47	7	8	2	261	2,709	.904

Their top point-getter on the blueline was Jamie Heward, with a whopping 18 points. He's gone, as is John Slaney, who had 16 points. Neither was offered a contract for this season.

Drake Berehowsky isn't exactly your protypical offensive defenseman, although he was projected as one back in 1990-91 when he scored 82 points in junior and joined the Toronto Maple Leafs. Nashville is his fourth NHL team, and he's played for five minor league teams. He apparently has learned something along the way, though, because he was fairly solid, and second on the team in ice-time behind Joel Bouchard, who was probably the team's best defenseman.

Dan Keczmer won't score much, but he showed a lot of savvy on the bluline, and gives them a veteran presence.

The Predators are hoping Kimmo Timonen can fill more of an offensive role, or perhaps Jan Vopat. Both are timid when it comes to the physical game, but both are decent puck handlers.

Jay More is another veteran, but his career is still in limbo after he suffered a concussion last year and was slow in recovering.

The prospects wouldn't be prospects already for most teams, but they have Richard Lintner, Karlis Skrastins, and tough-guy Marc Moro. They'll all probably get into the lineup at one time or another during the season.

FORWARD: Cliff Ronning might have been the best acquisition the Predators made last season. He's a good playmaker who could make more plays if he had some more snipers on the wing. But, he's also 34-years-old, and his career was pretty much considered over before he came to Nashville.

If he's the number one centre again, behind him are Greg Johnson, Darren Turcotte, Sebastien Bordeleau, and David Legwand.

Greg Johnson turned out to be a good versatile two-way player and should be the second line centre, while Turcotte was injured most of the season, and Bordeleau won't be ready at the start of the year after having to undergo spinal surgery after suffering a fractured vertebrae in his neck.

Legwand, the second overall pick in last year's draft, is coming off a comparatively poor season in the OHL. He contracted mononucleosis during training camp, however, which is one excuse, and then said he didn't score as many goals because he was working on the defensive aspects of his game. He dropped from 54 goals to 31, in just four fewer games.

On the wing, Sergei Krivokrasov was one of the biggest surprises. He'd never shown much offensive promise before, but he led the team with 25 goals, and pumped in 10 of those on the power play.

Ville Peltonen was injured for almost all of last year, but still had 10 points in 14 games, so if he's healthy, you could see him as the first line left winger.

The Predators are way overloaded with non-physical forwards, but potential scoring threats in that category include Patric Kjellberg and Vitali Yachmenev.

Scott Walker gives them feistiness and versatility, Patrick Cote is the resident tough guy, Tom Fitzgerald is the defensive specialist, and they have a couple bruisers in Denny Lambert and newcomer Phil Crowe.

Amont the other candidates, they're mostly fringe type players as opposed to serious prospects. Rob Valicevic played well in a limited appearance, as did Mark Mowers. Petr Sykora is also given a chance, but there might be too many players ahead of him.

If this is progress, then it's going very slowly. Legwand is at least a year away from making a serious contribution and you have to look very hard to find a physical force on the top three lines.

They might score more goals this year, but it's hardly a certainty. They're not improved over last year.

SPECIAL TEAMS: Not surprising that they were among the worst in the league at special teams. Often expansion clubs, however, are at least decent at penalty killing.

On the power play, there is no quarterback for the power play. In fact they don't even have a candidate worthy of being called a backup quarterback. That's a position, however, that can often be easily filled. Some teams get tired of players on the blueline who aren't good defensively. In fact, that's what happened to Jamie Heward and John Slaney.

The Predators will certainly pick up a veteran to help them out in this area.

There are few natural snipers on the Predators, however, although Ronning is a good playmaker, so somebody will have to step up in order for there to be any improvement.

Power Play	G	ATT	PCT
Overall	40	316	12.7% (25th NHL)
Home	24	178	13.5% (22nd NHL)
Road	16	138	11.6% (22nd NHL)

9 SHORT HANDED GOALS ALLOWED (T-15th NHL)

Penalty Killing	G	TSH	PCT
Overall	72	348	79.3% (27th NHL)
Home	29	171	83.0% (21st NHL)
Road	43	177	75.7% (27th NHL)

7 SHORT HANDED GOALS SCORED (T-13th NHL)

Penalties	GP	MIN	AVG
PREDATORS	80	1372	17.2 (T-19th NHL)

PREDATORS SPECIAL TEAMS SCORING

Power play	G	A	PTS
RONNING	10	13	23
KRIVOKRASOV	10	7	17
BRUNETTE	7	6	13
JOHNSON	2	11	13
HEWARD	4	7	11
KJELLBERG	2	8	10
TIMONEN	1	5	6
SLANEY	0	6	6
BORDELEAU	1	3	4
BEREHOWSKY	0	4	4
PELTONEN	1	2	3
WALKER	0	2	2
FITZGERALD	0	2	2
BOUCHARD	0	2	2
LAMBERT	1	0	1
VOPAT	0	1	1

Short handed	G	A	PTS
JOHNSON	3	1	4
BORDELEAU	2	0	2
WALKER	1	1	2
FITZGERALD	0	2	2
YACHMENEV	1	0	1
VOPAT	0	1	1
SLANEY	0	1	1
BOUGHNER	0	1	1
BOUCHARD	0	1	1
BEREHOWSKY	0	1	1

COACHING AND MANAGEMENT: You can't criticize coach Barry Trotz, because he did an excellent job of pulling together the retreads and never-have-beens into a respectable outfit. His job won't be any easier this year, however.

GM David Poile is one of the best in the business and made the Washington Capitals a winning franchise for 15 years. It's going to take him some time, but he will eventually do the same thing in Nashville.

DRAFT: (see chart) There was no disputing that Brian Finley was the best goalie available in the draft. He's got good size, great quickness, and does everything well, including stopping the puck. Give him a couple years.

Keep an eye on the Predators last pick. Darren (Mini) Haydar is from Milton, Ontario (the same as the author) and at every level he's played at he's been considered too small (at first) before having to prove himself. In Tier II Junior A he set all kinds of scoring records. He also put up outstanding numbers at New Hampshire in his freshman year and helped them to the finals of the NCAA tournament. He's listed at 5-9, 160.

PROGNOSIS: Not a good outlook for the Predators. As explained earlier, the team is due for a fall in its second season. Apart from that they're not improved in any area, anyway. It should be a long season, with games against the Atlanta Thrashers providing their best highlights.

They could slip ahead of the Vancouver Canucks, but that's about the best they can hope for.

DRAFT

Player	Pos	Rnd	Sel.	Cntry	Team	Lge	Gms	G	A	P	PIM
Brian Finley	G	1	6	Can	Barrie	OHL	2.66	.913			
Jonas Andersson	RW	2	33	Swe	AIK	Swe	16	3	7	10	18
Adam Hall	RW	2	52	USA	Mich. St.	CCHA	31	10	5	15	72
A. Hutchinson	D	2	54	USA	Mich. St.	CCHA	33	1	11	12	20
Ed Hill	D	2	61	USA	Barrie	OHL	53	7	17	24	42
Jan Lasak	G	2	65	Slo	Zvolen Jr	Slov	2.60				
Brett Angel	D	2	72	Can	North Bay	OHL	55				
Yevgeny Pavlov	F	4	121	Rus	Togliatti	Rus	9	5	9	14	139
Alexandr Krevsun	RW	4	124	Rus	Samara	Rus	5	0	1	1	2
Kontantin Panov	RW	5	131	Rus	Kamloops	WHL	62	0	2	2	4
Timo Helbling	D	6	162	Swi	Davos	Switz	22	33	30	63	2
Martin Erat	LW	7	191	Cze	Zlin Jr.	Cze	35	21	23	44	0
Kyle Kettles	G	7	205	Can							
Miroslav Durak	D	8	220	Slo	Bratislava	Slo					
Darren Haydar	RW	9	248	Can	U. N.H.	H.E.	36	29	23	52	12

STAT SECTION

PLAYER	GP	G	A	PTS	+/-	PIM	PP	SH	GW	GT	S	PCTG
CLIFF RONNING	79	20	40	60	3-	42	10	0	4	0	257	7.8
GREG JOHNSON	68	16	34	50	8-	24	2	3	0	0	120	13.3
S. KRIVOKRASOV	70	25	23	48	5-	42 1	0	0	6	1	208	12.0
S. BORDELEAU	72	16	24	40 1	4-	26	1	2	3	0	168	9.5
SCOTT WALKER	71	15	25	40	0	103	0	1	2	0	96	15.6
TOM FITZGERALD	80	13	19	32	18-	48	0	0	1	0	180	7.2
PATRIC KJELLBERG	71	11	20	31	13-	24	2	0	2	0	103	10.7
ANDREW BRUNETTE	77	11	20	31	10-	26	7	0	1	0	65	16.9
JAMIE HEWARD	63	6	12	18	24-	44	4	0	1	0	124	4.8
VITALI YACHMENEV	55	7	10	17	10-	10	0	1	2	0	83	8.4
D. BEREHOWSKY	74	2	15	17	9-	140	0	0	0	0	79	2.5
DENNY LAMBERT	76	5	11	16	3-	218	1	0	0	0	66	7.6
JOEL BOUCHARD	64	4	11	15	10-	60	0	0	0	0	78	5.1
JOHN SLANEY	46	2	12	14	12-	14	0	0	1	0	84	2.4
BOB BOUGHNER	79	3	10	13	6-	137	0	0	1	0	59	5.1
KIMMO TIMONEN	50	4	8	12	4-	30	1	0	0	0	75	5.3
JAN VOPAT	55	5	6	11	0	28	0	0	0	0	46	10.9
VILLE PELTONEN	14	5	5	10	1	2	1	0	0	0	31	16.1
DARREN TURCOTTE	40	4	5	9	11-	16	0	0	1	0	73	5.5
ROBERT VALICEVIC	19	4	2	6	4	2	0	0	2	0	23	17.4
MARK MOWERS	30	0	6	6	4-	4	0	0	0	0	24	.0
JEFF DANIELS	9	1	3	4	1-	2	0	0	0	0	8	12.5
JEFF NELSON	9	2	1	3	1-	2	0	0	0	0	8	25.0
PATRICK COTE	70	1	2	3	7-	242	0	0	0	0	21	4.8
JAY MORE	18	0	2	2	2	18	0	0	0	0	24	.0
DOUG FRIEDMAN	2	0	1	1	0	14	0	0	0	0	3	.0
KARLIS SKRASTINS	2	0	1	1	0	0	0	0	0	0	0	.0
TOMAS VOKOUN	37	0	1	1	0	6	0	0	0	0	1	.0
DAN KECZMER	38	0	1	1	5-	34	0	0	0	0	24	.0
DAVID LEGWAND	1	0	0	0	0	0	0	0	0	0	2	.0
ROB ZETTLER	2	0	0	0	2-	2	0	0	0	0	0	.0
PETR SYKORA	2	0	0	0	1-	0	0	0	0	0	2	.0
MATT HENDERSON	2	0	0	0	1-	2	0	0	0	0	0	.0
BRAD SMYTH	3	0	0	0	1-	6	0	0	0	0	5	.0
CHRIS MASON	3	0	0	0	0	0	0	0	0	0	0	.0
ERIC FICHAUD	9	0	0	0	0	0	0	0	0	0	0	.0
MIKE DUNHAM	44	0	0	0	0	4	0	0	0	0	0	.0

TEAM RANKINGS

		Conference Rank	League Rank
Record	28-47-7	12	24
Home	15-22-4	12	26
Away	13-25-3	11	23
Versus Own Conference	21-30-4	10	22
Versus Other Conference	7-17-3	13	25
Team Plus\Minus	-36	12	24
Goals For	190	12	24
Goals Against	261	13	26
Average Shots For	26.4	10	18
Average Shots Against	32.2	13	27
Overtime	1-3-13	11	23
One Goal Games	16-17	6	14
Times outshooting opponent	19	13	26
Versus Teams Over .500	12-28-3	12	25
Versus Teams .500 or under	16-19-4	12	23
First Half Record	14-23-4	11	23
Second Half Record	16-19-4	12	23

MISCELLANEOUS STAT LEADERS

FACEOFFS

Bordeleau	57.1%
Johnson	53.6%
Fitzgerald	52.3%
Ronning	47.7%

ICE TIME

Bouchard	22:34
Berehowsky	21:43
Slaney	20:38
Johnson	19:26
Ronning	19:19
Timonen	19:04

HITS

Boughner	233
Berehowsky	140
Bouchard	109

PLAYOFFS

- Did not make the playoffs

Phoenix Coyotes

Everything was going along so nicely. Their start made them the talk of the league.

So did their collapse.

On December 10, they were first overall, their penalty killing was tops overall, and they were first in goals against with a GAA of 1.66. Nothing could go wrong.

Here are the standings in the Western Conference, before and after December 10.

Western Conference
Through December 10

	W	L	T	Pts
Phoenix	16	3	3	35
Dallas	15	5	4	34
Detroit	15	9	1	31
Colorado	13	11	2	28
Edmonton	13	12	2	28
St. Louis	9	8	6	24
Anaheim	9	11	6	24
Vancouver	10	13	4	24
Nashville	10	14	2	22
Chicago	9	15	3	21
Calgary	9	15	2	20
San Jose	5	14	7	17
Los Angeles	7	17	3	17

After December 10

	W	L	T	Pts
Dallas	36	14	8	80
Colorado	31	17	8	70
St. Louis	28	24	7	63
San Jose	26	19	11	63
Detroit	28	23	6	62
Anaheim	26	23	7	59
Phoenix	23	28	9	55
Calgary	21	25	10	52
Los Angeles	25	28	2	52
Edmonton	20	25	10	50
Chicago	20	26	9	49
Nashville	18	33	5	41
Vancouver	13	34	8	32

Either their start was a fluke or their finish was a fluke. There's more evidence to suggest the former. Although most teams go through a hot streak, they're rarely as long as Phoenix's. But sometimes a team can get on a roll and gain confidence. The same thing can happen when they start to lose.

STUFF

The Coyotes have lost in the first round in their last eight playoff appearances

Eight shutouts by Nikolai Khabibulin were the most in team history.

TEAM PREVIEW

GOAL: Khabibulin broke his team shutout mark with eight, and generally had an outstanding year. He was in the top six in every goaltending category. He needs to be rested though, and for a couple years, Jimmy Waite has done a good job in that regard. Now the backup duties fall to Mikhail Shtalenkov, who has a history of being very good in that role.

DEFENSE: This is a veteran defense, but they're also very mobile, which should fit in well with the new offensive system the team is expected to play.

They won't miss Oleg Tverdovsky, who was traded on draft day to Anaheim, but they're probably going to look bad for trading him because he's likely to put up big numbers in Anaheim. Minding the point on a power play with Paul Kariya and Teemu Selanne tends to do that. His biggest cheer in Phoenix came when it was announced he was a scratch for game seven in last year's first round series with St. Louis.

Todd Gill was signed as a free agent to go along with Teppo Numminen, Jyrki Lumme, Keith Carney, Deron Quint, Stan Neckar, and J. J. Daigneault.

There isn't a serious physical force among them, unless you count Neckar, who was passed around like a baton last season from Ottawa to the Rangers to Phoenix, frequently spending his time as a healthy scratch. Gill can hit, but isn't that big, and Carney can take the body, as well. They should score more points though, and if Quint gets the power play time, it's possible this could be a breakout season for him.

FORWARD: The big news during the summer was that Robert Reichel was threatening to play in Europe if he didn't get the contract he wanted. Unlike other Europeans and their agents, who use the ploy as an idle threat, he's actually done it before when he was with Calgary.

There's no way he can make near the same amount of money playing in Europe, or be able to make it up if he comes back the next year, but at least he'll have an easy time of it, which seems like a matter of importance to him. That's why he's been a streaky scorer — because he plays when he feels like it. Makes you wonder if his value as a scorer is worth bothering with in the interest of team cohesiveness.

The Coyotes have a couple other guys with chips on their shoulders, but they also have more than their share of character players, too, at least at forward.

GOALTENDER	GPI	MINS	AVG	W	L	T	EN	SO	GA	SA	SV %
N. KHABIBULIN	63	3,657	2.13	32	23	7	6	8	130	1,681	.923
M. SHTALENKOV	4	243	2.22	1	2	1	1	0	9	104	.913
JIM WAITE	16	898	2.74	6	5	4	0	1	41	390	.895
ROBERT ESCHE	3	130	3.23	0	1	0	0	0	7	50	.860
SCOTT LANGKOW	1	35	5.14	0	0	0	0	0	3	17	.824
PHX TOTALS	82	4,985	2.37	39	31	12	7	9	197	2,249	.912

Look for Keith Tkachuk to have a big season. He slipped to 36 goals, mostly because of injuries, but with a more offensive system, look for him to get back to the 50-goal plateau.

Jeremy Roenick is coming off his best season since hitting for 100 points for three years in a row, early in the decade. He was a key loss for the playoffs when he broke his jaw late in the season, and could have been the difference between a seventh game loss and a seventh game win.

Dallas Drake played frequently on the right side of the top line with Tkachuk and Roenick, and while he's not a gifted scorer, his other qualities make him fit well there.

Down the middle, after Roenick and Reichel, if he signs, the Coyotes have Travis Green, who is a good two-way player, who should more than replace Bob Corkum, who was lost to free agency.

Daniel Briere should get more ice-time this season. He was a disappointment when he didn't pile up the points in his rookie year. Most players have their breakout season in their third or fourth year, but that's only if the team is patient with them, and keeps playing them. The third or fourth line isn't a bad place for him until he matures as a hockey player.

The Coyotes are hardly stacked on the wing, with two aged veterans holding down spots on the second line. Rick Tocchet had a great season, however, and Greg Adams managed to stay healthy for one of the few times in his career. Both are a month-long slump away from ending their careers.

Other wingers include Shane Doan, who might be ready to add some scoring to his repetoire, defensive type Yuha Ylonen, toughnik Louie DeBrusk, Mike Sullivan, and grinder Tavis Hansen.

There's very little in the way of prospects, but Trevor Letowski led Springfield in scoring and didn't look out of place in a short audition with the Coyotes.

SPECIAL TEAMS: The brutal power play should be fixed by new coach, Bobby Francis. With the Coyotes concentrating so much on defense, sometimes it's hard to turn it on at will, even on the power play. Some type of system should be set up to get sniper Tkachuk the puck, and if Reichel signs, he's adept with the man advantage.

Power Play	G	ATT	PCT	
Overall	40	337	11.9%	(26th NHL)
Home	19	172	11.0%	(27th NHL)
Road	21	165	12.7%	(20th NHL)

5 SHORT HANDED GOALS ALLOWED (T-4th NHL)

Penalty Killing	G	TSH	PCT	
Overall	45	341	86.8%	(5th NHL)
Home	21	167	87.4%	(7th NHL)
Road	24	174	86.2%	(6th NHL)

8 SHORT HANDED GOALS SCORED (T-8th NHL)

Penalties	GP	MIN	AVG
COYOTES	81	1350	16.7 (T-17th NHL)

COYOTES SPECIAL TEAMS SCORING

Power play	G	A	PTS
REICHEL	7	23	30
ROENICK	4	19	23
TKACHUK	11	6	17
TOCCHET	6	9	15
NUMMINEN	1	14	15
ADAMS	5	5	10
LUMME	1	9	10
TVERDOVSKY	2	4	6
QUINT	2	4	6

BRIERE	2	2	4
YLONEN	2	0	2
STAPLETON	0	2	2
DRAKE	0	2	2
DAIGNEAULT	1	0	1
DOAN	0	1	1

Short handed	G	A	PTS
TKACHUK	2	2	4
CARNEY	2	1	3
STAPLETON	2	0	2
SULLIVAN	1	1	2
ROENICK	0	2	2
NUMMINEN	0	2	2
TOCCHET	1	0	1
REICHEL	1	0	1
LUMME	0	1	1
CORKUM	0	1	1
ADAMS	0	1	1

COACHING AND MANAGEMENT: Jim Schoenfeld didn't seal his fate when he guaranteed a win in game seven of the playoffs versus St. Louis. He'd have pretty much have had to win the Stanley Cup for him not to be fired. It's amazing how a coach can go so quickly from a genius, as Schoenfeld did after the team sagged following their quick start.

His problem was that he wouldn't listen to GM Bobby Smith's suggestions when things were going badly. Smith is definitely a hands-on management type, unless things are going well. So, new coach Bobby Francis had better listen.

Francis is expected to improve the special teams and have the team play a more offensive style. He was an assistant coach the last two years with Boston and was credited with making their special teams among the best in the league.

DRAFT: (see chart) Scott Kelman is considered a character-type two way player, who's more of a playmaker than a scorer. The Coyote's second first round pick is a defensive defenseman who was considered by some to be the best defenseman in the draft.

PROGNOSIS: The Coyotes will be playing a new offensive style this season. That's not going to make them winners, however. Much of their personnel is more suited to a defensive style, or at least more of a two-way game.

They're not improved over last year, and

DRAFT

Player	Pos	Rnd	Sel.	Cntry	Team	Lge	Gms	G	A	P	PIM
Scott Kelman	C	1	15	Can	Seattle	WHL	66	19	54	63	95
Kiril Safranov	D	1	19	Rus	St. Petersburg	Rus	35	1	1	2	26
Brad Ralph	LW	2	53	Can	Oshawa	OHL	67	31	44	74	93
Jason Jaspers	F	3	71	Can	Sudbury	OHL	68	28	33	62	81
Ryan Lauzon	C	4	116	Can	Hull	QMJHL	57	21	47	68	36
Preston Mizzi	C	4	123	Can	Peterborough	OHL	67	21	21	42	74
Erik Leverstrom	D	6	168	Swe	Grums	Swe	29	3	9	12	42
Goran Bezina	D	8	234	Cro	Fribourg Jr	Swi	0	0	0	0	0
Alexei Litvinenko		9	262								

many of their players have down-side potential rather than upside potential.

If they make the playoffs, it will be in the seventh or eighth spot, but they're going to have to battle to get that far.

STAT SECTION

PLAYER	GP	G	A	PTS	+/-	PIM	PP	SH	GW	GT	S	PCTG
JEREMY ROENICK	78	24	48	72	7	130	4	0	3	0	203	11.8
ROBERT REICHEL	83	26	43	69	13-	54	8	1	4	1	236	11.0
KEITH TKACHUK	68	36	32	68	22	151	11	2	7	1	258	14.0
RICK TOCCHET	81	26	30	56	5	147	6	1	5	0	178	14.6
GREG ADAMS	75	19	24	43	1-	26	5	0	3	0	176	10.8
TEPPO NUMMINEN	82	10	30	40	3	30	1	0	0	2	156	6.4
DALLAS DRAKE	53	9	22	31	17	65	0	0	3	0	105	8.6
JYRKI LUMME	60	7	21	28	5	34	1	0	4	0	121	5.8
OLEG TVERDOVSKY	82	7	18	25	11	32	2	0	2	0	117	6.0
JUHA YLONEN	59	6	17	23	18	20	2	0	1	0	66	9.1
DANIEL BRIERE	64	8	14	22	3-	30	2	0	2	0	90	8.9
SHANE DOAN	79	6	16	22	5-	54	0	0	0	0	156	3.8
BOB CORKUM	77	9	10	19	9-	17	0	0	0	0	146	6.2
MIKE STAPLETON	76	9	9	18	6-	34	0	2	2	0	106	8.5
KEITH CARNEY	82	2	14	16	15	62	0	2	0	0	62	3.2
DERON QUINT	60	5	8	13	10-	20	2	0	0	0	94	5.3
J.J. DAIGNEAULT	70	2	9	11	12-	70	1	0	1	0	65	3.1
BRAD ISBISTER	32	4	4	8	1	46	0	0	2	0	48	8.3
JIM CUMMINS	55	1	7	8	3	190	0	0	0	0	26	3.8
MIKE SULLIVAN	63	2	4	6	11-	24	0	1	1	0	66	3.0
TREVOR LETOWSKI	14	2	2	4	1	2	0	0	0	0	8	25.0
STEPHEN LEACH	31	1	3	4	7-	43	0	0	0	0	27	3.7
TAVIS HANSEN	20	2	1	3	4-	12	0	0	0	0	14	14.3
ROB MURRAY	13	1	2	3	2	4	0	0	0	0	11	9.1
STAN NECKAR	32	0	3	3	1	18	0	0	0	0	16	.0
JAMIE HUSCROFT	37	0	2	2	4-	90	0	0	0	0	27	.0
GERALD DIDUCK	44	0	2	2	9	72	0	0	0	0	39	.0
JASON DOIG	9	0	1	1	2	10	0	0	0	0	0	.0
ANDREI VASILYEV	1	0	0	0	2-	0	0	0	0	0	0	.0
SCOTT LANGKOW	1	0	0	0	0	0	0	0	0	0	0	.0
JOE DZIEDZIC	2	0	0	0	2-	0	0	0	0	0	1	.0
SEAN GAGNON	2	0	0	0	2-	7	0	0	0	0	1	.0

ROBERT ESCHE	3	0	0	0	0	0	0	0	0	0	0	.0
BRIAN NOONAN	7	0	0	0	3-	0	0	0	0	0	1	.0
BRAD TILEY	8	0	0	0	1-	0	0	0	0	0	1	.0
LOUIE DEBRUSK	15	0	0	0	2-	34	0	0	0	0	6	.0
JIM WAITE	16	0	0	0	0	2	0	0	0	0	0	.0
M. SHTALENKOV	38	0	0	0	0	2	0	0	0	0	0	.0
N. KHABIBULIN	63	0	0	0	0	8	0	0	0	0	0	.0

TEAM RANKINGS

		Conference Rank	League Rank
Record	39-31-12	4	10
Home	23-13-5	3	8
Away	16-18-7	5	10
Versus Own Conference	28-21-7	5	9
Versus Other Conference	11-10-5	4	10
Team Plus\Minus	+12	6	12
Goals For	205	8	18
Goals Against	197	4	8
Average Shots For	29.0	3	6
Average Shots Against	27.1	6	12
Overtime	2-1-7	6	10
One Goal Games	12-10	4	10
Times outshooting opponent	42	5	9
Versus Teams Over .500	14-17-6	3	10
Versus Teams .500 or under	25-14-6	5	12
First Half Record	24-11-6	2	2
Second Half Record	15-20-6	10	19

MISCELLANEOUS STATS

FACEOFFS

Corkum	51.6%
Reichel	48.5%
Roenick	47.6%
Briere	47.5%

ICE TIME

Numminen	24:26
Carney	22:46
Tkachuk	20:59
Tverdovsky	20:47
Roenick	20:10

HITS

Doan	161
Roenick	154
Carney	133
Diduck	127
Tocchet	115
Drake	105
Daigneault	104
Tkachuk	102

PLAYOFFS

Results:

Lost in conference quarter-finals 4-3 to St. Louis

Record: 3-4

Home: 1-3

Away: 2-1

Goals For: 16 (2.3/game)

Goals Against: 19 (2.7/game)

Overtime: 1-2

Power play: 12.2% (11th)

Penalty Killing: 72.7% (15th)

PLAYER	GP	G	A	PTS	+/-	PIM	PP	SH	GW	OT	S	PCTG
DALLAS DRAKE	7	4	3	7	3	4	2	0	1	0	18	22.2
SHANE DOAN	7	2	2	4	4	6	0	0	2	1	17	11.8
ROBERT REICHEL	7	1	3	4	2-	2	0	0	0	0	16	6.3
KEITH TKACHUK	7	1	3	4	4-	13	1	0	0	0	22	4.5
TEPPO NUMMINEN	7	2	1	3	5-	4	2	0	0	0	18	11.1
KEITH CARNEY	7	1	2	3	5	10	0	0	0	0	5	20.0
RICK TOCCHET	7	0	3	3	3-	8	0	0	0	0	14	.0
LOUIE DEBRUSK	6	2	0	2	1-	6	0	0	0	0	5	40.0
STEPHEN LEACH	7	1	1	2	0	2	0	0	0	0	4	25.0
JUHA YLONEN	2	0	2	2	2	2	0	0	0	0	2	.0
BRIAN NOONAN	5	0	2	2	2	4	0	0	0	0	10	.0
OLEG TVERDOVSKY	6	0	2	2	3	6	0	0	0	0	6	.0
GREG ADAMS	3	1	0	1	1	0	0	0	0	0	9	11.1
MIKE STAPLETON	7	1	0	1	1-	0	0	0	0	0	3	33.3
JIM CUMMINS	3	0	1	1	1	0	0	0	0	0	0	.0
STAN NECKAR	6	0	1	1	3	4	0	0	0	0	0	.0
BOB CORKUM	7	0	1	1	1	4	0	0	0	0	6	.0
JYRKI LUMME	7	0	1	1	2-	6	0	0	0	0	8	.0
JEREMY ROENICK	1	0	0	0	1-	0	0	0	0	0	2	.0
BRAD TILEY	1	0	0	0	0	0	0	0	0	0	0	.0
TAVIS HANSEN	2	0	0	0	1	0	0	0	0	0	1	.0
GERALD DIDUCK	3	0	0	0	1-	2	0	0	0	0	4	.0
MIKE SULLIVAN	5	0	0	0	0	2	0	0	0	0	2	.0
J.J. DAIGNEAULT	6	0	0	0	1-	8	0	0	0	0	4	.0
N. KHABIBULIN	7	0	0	0	0	2	0	0	0	0	0	.0

GOALTENDER	GPI	MINS	AVG	W	L	T	EN	SO	GA	SA	SV %
N. KHABIBULI	7	449	2.41	3	4	1	0	0	18	236	.924
PHX TOTALS	7	453	2.52	3	4	1	0	0	19	237	.920

San Jose Sharks

The Sharks are close. So close they can smell the blood.

It's not easy stepping up to the next level, and precious few teams are actually in that territory. Many teams have flashes of brilliance before dying out, and some are built to win during the regular season, but few have the ability to be contenders and know with certainty that they will be the next year and the next.

In fact, there's probably only two franchises that know they'll be contenders in three years, no matter what happens in the interim. One of them is New Jersey, and the other is probably Colorado.

That's not to say the Sharks are in that category, but they're getting close. Here's why.

Smart Drafting. After the previous regime lost control of their senses and drafted half of Finland among other players who had no chance of making it to the NHL, the Sharks have a host of players from their last three drafts who are either on the team or ready to move up. That includes Patrick Marleau, Andrei Zyuzin, Marco Sturm, Scott Hannan and Brad Stuart.

Youth. The Sharks have some of the best young players in the game, with Jeff Friesen and Alexander Korolyuk in addition to those mentioned above.

Character. Too many teams don't realize the difference between skill and character. They think because a player can skate that's good enough in itself. It takes more to be successful. With players such as Mike Ricci, Owen Nolan, Stephane Matteau, and others, dedication, leadership and commitment make the team better as a whole, rather than depending on a couple individuals to go out and score all the goals.

Coaching. Coaches change frequently, of course, and each one has his own style of play he prefers. But, a disciplined team approach ensures they won't fold when the going gets tough. A good example of that was in the playoffs last year, after losing the first two games to Colorado. They came back to make it a six-game series, and if they had scored in overtime in that sixth game, they would have gone to a seventh game, where anything can happen.

Defense. The Sharks have some of the better up and coming defensemen in the game, which is probably the toughest and most important position to have stability in.

STUFF

The start of games have been delayed for various reasons, but few as strange as when the team mascot, S. J. Sharkie, was stranded above the ice surface before a game with Detroit, due to equipment malfunction.

The Sharks had a 10-game uninterrupted road trip, which is the longest in NHL history.

Nine shots in a game versus Dallas were the fewest in team history. They still won the game 4-0.

TEAM PREVIEW

GOAL: The Sharks can't complain about their goaltending, especially when Steve Shields stepped up and performed so well, after being considered just a backup at the start of last season. Few teams are as solid with their two goalies.

As well, the Sharks don't give up a lot of shots, so it's necessary for their goalies to stay focused, which is more difficult than you might think.

DEFENSE: The Sharks have one of the best young defense corps in the league. Brad Stuart is the next Chris Pronger, or maybe the first Brad Stuart. He's a future all-star who can be a major force at both ends of the rink. They also have Scott Hannan and Shawn Heins, both of whom are sure-fire NHLers. Andy Sutton is in the mix, too, as an enforcer.

Their other talented young defenseman is Andrei Zyuzin and while he obviously has the skills, he doesn't appear to have the commitment or the all-round game, yet. He spent time in the minors last season, and then left the team and returned late in the season.

The Sharks are in good shape anyway, with Marcus Ragnarsson and Mike Rathje both developing into solid NHLers.

Bill Houlder and Gary Suter, who missed almost all but one game of last season with injuries, should man the power play points. Brian Marchment suffered through injuries last year but should be better this year. Bob Rouse gives a veteran presence on the blueline, but his ice-time is diminishing and he will have to sit out or move on so some of the younger players can get into the lineup.

You'd have to look hard to find a better all round defense corps in the league. Nobody else has the overall balance, quality, and potential.

FORWARD: The Sharks aren't going to score a lot of goals in their current system, but they're not going to give up many either.

Vincent Damphousse added a spark to the offense late in the season after being acquired from Montreal, but it should be noted that players traded in-season often do the same thing before returning to the level they were at before they arrived with their new team.

In any event, it's not going to hurt the Sharks to have an offensive centre on board. At centre,

GOALTENDER	GPI	MINS	AVG	W	L	T	EN	SO	GA	SA	SV %
SEAN GAUTHIER	1	3	.00	0	0	0	0	0	0	2	1.000
STEVE SHIELDS	37	2,162	2.22	15	11	8	1	4	80	1,011	.921
MIKE VERNON	49	2,831	2.27	16	22	10	3	4	107	1,200	.911
S.J TOTALS	82	5,016	2.28	31	33	18	4	8	191	2,217	.914

they're in great shape with Damphousse, Patick Marleau, Mike Ricci and fourth-liner Ron Sutter.

The left side is in good shape, as well, topped by Jeff Friesen, Marco Sturm and Stephane Matteau.

On the right side is Owen Nolan, up-and-comer Alexander Korolyuk, and above-average scoring enforcer Ronnie Stern.

Rounding out the case of characters are Murray Craven, Jarrod Skalde, Tony Granato, Steve Guolla, Brantt Myhres, and perhaps even Mike Craig.

Gone to free agency is Joe Murphy, who led the team in goal scoring, but was inconsistent.

SPECIAL TEAMS: The power play was pathetic last year, but should be instantly better with Suter on board for the full season. Damphousse should help, too, especially if he can get the puck to Nolan, a natural sniper who hasn't been sniping enough.

Power Play	G	ATT	PCT
Overall	53	394	13.5% (T-20th NHL)
Home	23	194	11.9% (25th NHL)
Road	30	200	15.0% (T-13th NHL)
4 SHORT HANDED GOALS ALLOWED (T-1st NHL)			

Penalty Killing	G	TSH	PCT
Overall	59	400	85.3% (T-12th NHL)
Home	25	208	88.0% (T-3rd NHL)
Road	34	192	82.3% (T-18th NHL)
8 SHORT HANDED GOALS SCORED (T-8th NHL)			

Penalties	GP	MIN	AVG
SHARKS	81	1392	17.2 (21st NHL)

SHARKS SPECIAL TEAMS SCORING

Power play	G	A	PTS
FRIESEN	10	14	24

	G	A	PTS
DAMPHOUSSE	6	14	20
HOULDER	7	12	19
MURPHY	7	8	15
NOLAN	6	8	14
NORTON	2	10	12
STURM	3	8	11
MARLEAU	4	6	10
RICCI	2	5	7
KOROLYUK	2	5	7
RATHJE	2	2	4
LOWRY	2	1	3
RAGNARSSON	0	3	3
CRAVEN	0	3	3
ZYUZIN	2	0	2
ROUSE	0	2	2
NICHOLLS	0	2	2
GRANATO	0	2	2
STERN	1	0	1
SUTTON	0	1	1
MATTEAU	0	1	1
HANNAN	0	1	1
BURR	0	1	1

Short handed	G	A	PTS
STURM	2	2	4
DAMPHOUSSE	2	1	3
FRIESEN	1	2	3
NOLAN	2	0	2
RATHJE	0	2	2
RICCI	1	0	1
GRANATO	1	0	1
CRAVEN	1	0	1
RAGNARSSON	0	1	1
NORTON	0	1	1
MATTEAU	0	1	1

COACHING AND MANAGEMENT: Coach Darryl Sutter is a disciplinarian, demanding type, and rubs some players the wrong way. It doesn't matter how they feel about him personally, as long as they play. And they do.

Dean Lombardi continues to earn respect as a general manager. He's not too active in the trade area, preferring to build the team from within, which has been done nicely.

DRAFT: (see chart) Curious draft strategy by the Sharks, after being so successful in recent years. They drafted U.S. college or college bound players with their first four picks. Part of that strategy may be financial, because unlike junior players, they can't go back into the draft after two years if they're unsigned. Their two years starts from when they leave college.

With only one pick in the first two rounds, it probably doesn't matter what strategy they were using, anyway. First pick Jeff Jilson fits the team Sharks mold of character-type team players. He's an offensive talent, and a bruiser, which is somewhat rare for college hockey.

PROGNOSIS: This should be a good season for the Sharks, who should move up a level and earn their first ever winning season. The fact that so many teams around the league are switching to a more wide open offensive style is good for the Sharks, too, because those teams leave themselves open to more goals being scored against. The tradeoff doesn't usually work in their favor, as defense continues to rule success.

The Sharks aren't Stanley Cup contenders, but they are contenders and may even reach the top four in the Western Conference.

DRAFT

Player	Pos	Rnd	Sel.	Cntry	Team	Lge	Gms	G	A	P	PIM
Jeff Jilson	D	1	14	USA	U. Michigan CCHA		32	5	16	21	59
Mark Concannon	LW	3	82	USA	Winchendon US HS		26	23	28	51	11
Willie Levesque	RW	4	111	USA	Northeastern H.E.		34	12	10	22	38
N.s Dimitrakos	RW	5	155	USA	Maine	H.E.	29	5	16	21	28
Eric Betournay	C	8	229	Can	A-Bathurst	QMJHL	70	16	29	45	57
Doug Murray	D	8	241	Apple	Core	EJHL	60	17	47	64	62
Hannes Hyvonen	D	9	257	Espoo	Fin						

STAT SECTION

PLAYER	GP	G	A	PTS	+/-	PIM	PP	SH	GW	GT	S	PCTG
JEFF FRIESEN	78	22	35	57	3	42	10	1	3	1	215	10.2
V. DAMPHOUSSE	77	19	30	49	4-	50	6	2	3	0	190	10.0
JOE MURPHY	76	25	23	48	10	73	7	0	2	1	176	14.2
PATRICK MARLEAU	81	21	24	45	10	24	4	0	4	1	134	15.7
OWEN NOLAN	78	19	26	45	16	129	6	2	3	1	207	9.2
MIKE RICCI	82	13	26	39	1	68	2	1	2	1	98	13.3
MARCO STURM	78	16	22	38	7	52	3	2	3	2	140	11.4
BILL HOULDER	76	9	23	32	8	40	7	0	5	0	115	7.8
A. KOROLYUK	55	12	18	30	3	26	2	0	0	1	96	12.5
S. MATTEAU	68	8	15	23	2	73	0	0	0	0	72	11.1
JEFF NORTON	72	4	18	22	2	44	2	0	1	0	70	5.7
RONNIE STERN	78	7	9	16	3-	158	1	0	2	0	94	7.4
DAVE LOWRY	61	6	9	15	5-	24	2	0	0	1	58	10.3
MIKE RATHJE	82	5	9	14	15	36	2	0	1	0	67	7.5
MURRAY CRAVEN	43	4	10	14	3-	18	0	1	1	0	55	7.3
M. RAGNARSSON	74	0	13	13	7	66	0	0	0	0	87	.0
TONY GRANATO	35	6	6	12	4	54	0	1	1	1	65	9.2
BOB ROUSE	70	0	11	11	0	44	0	0	0	0	75	.0
RON SUTTER	59	3	6	9	8-	40	0	0	1	0	67	4.5
BRYAN MARCHMENT	59	2	6	8	7-	101	0	0	0	0	49	4.1
ANDREI ZYUZIN	25	3	1	4	5	38	2	0	0	0	44	6.8
STEPHEN GUOLLA	14	2	2	4	3	6	0	0	1	0	22	9.1
ANDY SUTTON	31	0	3	3	4-	65	0	0	0	0	24	.0
JARROD SKALDE	17	1	1	2	6-	4	0	0	0	1	17	5.9
SCOTT HANNAN	5	0	2	2	0	6	0	0	0	0	4	.0
BERNIE NICHOLLS	10	0	2	2	4-	4	0	0	0	0	11	.0
BRANTT MYHRES	30	1	0	1	2-	116	0	0	0	0	7	14.3
JAMIE BAKER	1	0	1	1	1	0	0	0	0	0	1	.0
SHAWN BURR	18	0	1	1	3-	29	0	0	0	0	22	.0
STEVE SHIELDS	37	0	1	1	0	6	0	0	0	0	0	.0
MIKE CRAIG	1	0	0	0	1-	0	0	0	0	0	1	.0
GARY SUTER	1	0	0	0	0	0	0	0	0	0	1	.0
SEAN GAUTHIER	1	0	0	0	0	0	0	0	0	0	0	.0
SHAWN HEINS	5	0	0	0	0	13	0	0	0	0	4	.0
MIKE VERNON	49	0	0	0	0	8	0	0	0	0	0	.0

TEAM RANKINGS

		Conference Rank	League Rank
Record	31-33-18	7	15
Home	17-15-9	7	16
Away	14-18-9	7	15
Versus Own Conference	21-26-10	9	18
Versus Other Conference	10-7-8	3	8
Team Plus\Minus	+13	5	11
Goals For	196	10	21
Goals Against	191	2	5
Average Shots For	25.8	11	21
Average Shots Against	26.7	3	9
Overtime	1-2-18	8	15
One Goal Games	10-11	7	15
Times outshooting opponent	36	7	14
Versus Teams Over .500	14-20-10	4	11
Versus Teams .500 or under	16-13-8	8	19
First Half Record	13-18-10	8	19
Second Half Record	18-15-8	5	9

MISCELLANEOUS STAT LEADERS

FACEOFFS

Damphousse	51.3%
Ricci	49.6%
Sutter	49.0%
Marleau	43.4%

ICE TIME

Houlder	22:08
Ragnarsson	21:56
Norton	20:46
Damphousse	20:17
Rathje	20:07

HITS

Nolan	174
Stern	153
Marchment	108
Rathje	100

PLAYOFFS

Results:

Lost 4-2 to Colorado in Conference quarterfinals

Record: 2-4
Home: 0-3
Away: 2-1
Goals For: 17 (2.8/game)
Goals Against: 19 (3.2/game)
Overtime: 0-2
Power play: 17.1% (7th)
Penalty Killing: 85.3% (6th)

PLAYER	GP	G	A	PTS	+/-	PIM	PP	SH	GW	OT	S	PCTG
JEFF NORTON	6	0	7	7	5	10	0	0	0	0	3	.0
V. DAMPHOUSSE	6	3	2	5	1	6	0	2	0	0	22	13.6
MIKE RICCI	6	2	3	5	1	10	1	0	0	0	9	22.2
JEFF FRIESEN	6	2	2	4	1-	14	1	0	0	0	20	10.0
MARCO STURM	6	2	2	4	1	4	0	0	1	0	15	13.3
A. KOROLYUK	6	1	3	4	3-	2	0	0	1	0	7	14.3
BILL HOULDER	6	3	0	3	2	4	3	0	0	0	8	37.5
PATRICK MARLEAU	6	2	1	3	1-	4	2	0	0	0	7	28.6
JOE MURPHY	6	0	3	3	0	4	0	0	0	0	21	.0
TONY GRANATO	6	1	1	2	1-	2	0	0	0	0	5	20.0
OWEN NOLAN	6	1	1	2	0	6	0	0	0	0	26	3.8
MIKE VERNON	5	0	1	1	0	0	0	0	0	0	0	.0
M. RAGNARSSON	6	0	1	1	4-	6	0	0	0	0	9	.0
DAVE LOWRY	1	0	0	0	0	0	0	0	0	0	0	.0
STEVE SHIELDS	1	0	0	0	0	0	0	0	0	0	0	.0
STEPHANE MATTEAU	5	0	0	0	3-	6	0	0	0	0	4	.0
BRYAN MARCHMENT	6	0	0	0	0	4	0	0	0	0	7	.0
BOB ROUSE	6	0	0	0	1-	6	0	0	0	0	4	.0
RONNIE STERN	6	0	0	0	1-	6	0	0	0	0	10	.0
RON SUTTER	6	0	0	0	1-	4	0	0	0	0	10	.0
MIKE RATHJE	6	0	0	0	6-	4	0	0	0	0	4	.0

GOALTENDER	GPI	MINS	AVG	W	L	T	EN	SO	GA	SA	SV %
MIKE VERNON	5	321	2.43	2	3	0	0	0	13	172	.924
STEVE SHIELDS	1	60	6.00	0	1	0	0	0	6	36	.833
S.J TOTALS	6	381	2.99	2	4	0	0	0	19	208	.909

St. Louis Blues

Somehow the Blues always manage to find a way. At least to get into the playoffs.

Last season was their 20th consecutive year in the playoffs, which is moving them up among the best of all-time

Most Consecutive Playoff Appearances — All Time

29	Boston	1968-1996
28	Chicago	1979-1997
24	Montreal	1971-1994
21	Montreal	1949-1969
20	ST. LOUIS	1980-1999
20	Detroit	1939-1958

Current Streaks:

20 St. Louis
9 Detroit
9 Pittsburgh
5 Philadelphia

The bad news is that they rarely do anything in the playoffs. Oh, they often get by the first round, but they've only been to the finals in their first three seasons, when one of the expansion teams had to be there.

The best they've done over the 20 years is get to the conference championship, just once.

It's not as if they have a great farm system. Their draft selections are routinely terrible, and a good portion of the time they've already traded away their first round pick.

Larry Pleau's predecessor's Mike Keenan and Ron Caron never believed in patience and lived for that particular year. That meant lots of trades and it meant giving up top draft picks.

But, it worked. At least to some extent. It's got them into the playoffs, where at least they have a chance.

A lot of years, the Blues had no right being in the playoffs, though. For some reason, they're a team where players come out of nowhere to be successful.

This past season, they were at it again. Who told Scott Pellerin he could score 20 goals? Who told Pavol Demitra he could be a star after beating the bushes for most of his six-year pro career? Where did Lubos Bartecko come from? And so on and so on.

Life could be worse in St. Louis. It could be like the Islanders, which have missed the playoffs for five straight seasons and are guaranteed a sixth.

STUFF

The Blues allowed just nine shots in a game against Toronto on March 4, and still lost 4-0.

TEAM PREVIEW

GOAL: Look for newcomer Roman Turek to get the bulk of the work this season. He's only been a backup so far in the NHL, and only a backup on the best defensive team in the league, so his stats look especially good.

The incumbent Blues goalies had the fewest shots in the league and were not consistent. Jamie McLellan was a disappointment and Grant Fuhr wasn't much better.

Nobody, however, could have looked as bad as Jim Carey, former star turned sieve. He was a disaster and the Blues couldn't get rid of him fast enough.

DEFENSE: It was finally the year for Al MacInnis to win the Norris Trophy as the league's best defenseman. It was the 18th season the 35-year-old had played in the NHL.

It shouldn't take Chris Pronger quite as long. In fact, he was fourth in the voting last season.

With the first and the fourth best defensemen in the league, it was no wonder the two of them were on the ice constantly. Pronger averaged over 30 minutes a game to lead the league, and MacInnis was right behind him at just over 29 minutes.

The supporting cast on defense should be able to play their roles, but they're not integral parts, and can be interchanged. Ideally, you just don't want them to hurt you. To that end, a couple journeymen seemed to do fairly well. Jeff Finley when he joined the team late in the season, and Marc Bergevin when he wasn't hurt. Ricard Persson didn't embarrass himself, either.

A couple young players were disappointments — Chris McAlpine and Jamie Rivers — but the Blues won't give up on them quite yet.

The Blues don't have any serious prospects yet at this position, so if they need help they'll just fill with veterans, like they did last year, such as Brad Shaw.

Not that it matters too much, because the with two defensemen playing half the game, the other four don't get a lot of ice time.

FORWARD: Pavol Demitra had a breakout season, and receives this year's Hockey Annual award for the most improved player. There is no actual award, apart from the prestige, which, well — isn't that much of an award either.

The first winner was Jason Allison of the Bruins last year, and if we ever get an actual trophy, we'll engrave their names on it.

Scott Pellerin could have been a candidate for the award, as well. He stepped in for injured Geoff Courtnall and started scoring goals like never before.

GOALTENDER	GPI	MINS	AVG	W	L	T	EN	SO	GA	SA	SV %
*BRENT JOHNSON	6	286	2.10	3	2	0	0	0	10	127	.921
JAMIE MCLENNAN	33	1,763	2.38	13	14	4	3	3	70	640	.891
GRANT FUHR	39	2,193	2.44	16	11	8	1	2	89	827	.892
RICH PARENT	10	519	2.54	4	3	1	1	1	22	193	.886
JIM CAREY	4	202	3.86	1	2	0	0	0	13	76	.829
STL TOTALS	82	4,989	2.51	37	32	13	5	6	209	1,868	.888

Scott Young also had an outstanding season for the Blues, and that was unexpected, too. Typical of the Blues.

The Blues would like to get some of their younger players to play more regularly.

Michal Handzus, Lubor Bartecko, Marty Reasoner, Jochen Hecht and Jamal Mayers all fit into that category after auditions last season. Look for all four to show some improvement, although there's a big difference between looking as if you can produce, and actually doing it.

Craig Conroy and Mike Eastwood give the Blues two of the better role players in the league at centre. They can even score some, too. Eastwood is a master at faceoffs and if the puck is on the boards and he's in the vicinity, it ends up on his stick. He has always been one of the more underrated players in the league.

Jim Campbell should be back to try and play for real this year. No telling what he was up to last season.

Pierre Turgeon re-signed and could be a 40-40 man if he stays healthy, which isn't that frequently.

On paper, this group doesn't look like anything special, but they didn't last year, either, or the year before, or the year before that.

SPECIAL TEAMS: With the best point man in the league on the point, naturally they're going to be among the best on the power play. They were good at penalty-killing as well, giving them the best combined special teams in the league.

Power Play	G	ATT	PCT
Overall	61	301	20.3% (3rd NHL)
Home	33	155	21.3% (T-3rd NHL)
Road	28	146	19.2% (3rd NHL)

4 SHORT HANDED GOALS ALLOWED (T-1st NHL)

Penalty Killing	G	TSH	PCT
Overall	47	387	87.9% (2nd NHL)
Home	24	194	87.6% (T-5th NHL)
Road	23	193	88.1% (2nd NHL)

7 SHORT HANDED GOALS SCORED (T-15th NHL)

Penalties	GP	MIN	AVG
BLUES	82	1308	16.0 (T-13th NHL)

BLUES SPECIAL TEAMS SCORING

Power play	G	A	PTS
MACINNIS	11	26	37
DEMITRA	14	15	29
PRONGER	8	17	25
TURGEON	10	9	19
YOUNG	8	11	19
YAKE	3	11	14
CAMPBELL	1	8	9
REASONER	1	4	5
BARTECKO	0	4	4
RIVERS	1	2	3
COURTNALL	1	2	3
RHEAUME	2	0	2
ATCHEYNUM	2	0	2
PELLERIN	0	2	2
PICARD	0	1	1
PERSSON	0	1	1
HANDZUS	0	1	1
CHASE	0	1	1

Short handed	G	A	PTS
PELLERIN	5	1	6
MACINNIS	1	2	3
CONROY	1	2	3
ATCHEYNUM	0	2	2
PRONGER	0	1	1

COACHING AND MANAGEMENT: Joel Quenneville doesn't get a lot of recognition, but considering the Blues were not expected to do well last year, he did a great job.

Larry Pleau is still learning in the role of GM, but he seems to pick up the players when he needs them, and stole Roman Turek with an insiginificant draft pick.

DRAFT: (see chart) Barrett Jackman is considered a two-way player with a lot of character. His 259 minutes shows his toughness, and his offensive stats are going to improve. He's not Chris Pronger, but Chris Pronger wasn't Chris Pronger when he was drafted.

PROGNOSIS: The Blues should make the playoffs, because they always do, but going far in them would be a stretch.

They expect to have a lot of young players up front, so that's an iffy situation. Oddly enough, their best success has come from career minor-leaguers which they've been so masterful at uncovering.

The team should hover around the .500 mark because they're not too good and not too bad.

DRAFT

Player	Pos	Rnd	Sel.	Cntry	Team	Lge	Gms	G	A	P	PIM
Barret Jackman	D	1	17	Can	Regina	WHL	70	8	36	44	259
Peter Smrek	D	3	85	Slo	Des Moines	USHL	52	6	26	32	59
Chad Starling	D	4	114	Can	Kamloops	WHL	65	4	13	17	96
Trevor Byrne	D	5	143	USA	Deerfield	US HS	25	9	19	28	22
Roe Vikingstad	W	6	180	Nor	Farjestad	Swe	49	9	11	20	18
Phil Osaer	G	7	203	USA	Ferris St.	CCHA	1.66	.936			
Colin Hemingway	W	8	221	Can	Burnaby	BCJHL					
A. Khavanov	D	8	232	Rus	Dynamo	Rus	40	2	7	9	14
Brian McMeekin	D	9	260	Can	Cornell	ECAC	26	0	1	1	12
James Desmariais	C	9	270	Can	R-Noranda	QMJHL	66	62	73	135	127

STAT SECTION

PLAYER	GP	G	A	PTS	+/-	PIM	PP	SH	GW	GT	S	PCTG
PAVOL DEMITRA	82	37	52	89	13	16	14	0	10	1	259	14.3
PIERRE TURGEON	67	31	34	65	4	36	10	0	5	2	193	16.1
AL MACINNIS	82	20	42	62	33	70	11	1	2	2	314	6.4
SCOTT YOUNG	75	24	28	52	8	27	8	0	4	0	205	11.7
CHRIS PRONGER	67	13	33	46	3	113	8	0	0	0	172	7.6
SCOTT PELLERIN	80	20	21	41	1	42	0	5	4	0	138	14.5
CRAIG CONROY	69	14	25	39	14	38	0	1	1	0	134	10.4
MIKE EASTWOOD	82	9	21	30	6	36	0	0	0	0	76	11.8

TERRY YAKE	60	9	18	27	9-	34	3	0	4	0	59	15.3
PASCAL RHEAUME	60	9	18	27	10	24	2	0	0	0	85	10.6
JIM CAMPBELL	55	4	21	25	8-	41	1	0	0	0	99	4.0
MICHEL PICARD	45	11	11	22	5	16	0	0	2	0	69	15.9
BLAIR ATCHEYNUM	65	10	8	18	8-	18	2	0	2	0	93	10.8
LUBOS BARTECKO	32	5	11	16	4	6	0	0	1	0	37	13.5
MICHAL HANDZUS	66	4	12	16	9-	30	0	0	0	0	78	5.1
RICARD PERSSON	54	1	12	13	4	94	0	0	0	0	52	1.9
GEOFF COURTNALL	24	5	7	12	2	28	1	0	2	0	60	8.3
MARTY REASONER	22	3	7	10	2	8	1	0	0	0	33	9.1
KELLY CHASE	45	3	7	10	2	143	0	0	1	0	25	12.0
JAMAL MAYERS	34	4	5	9	3-	40	0	0	0	0	48	8.3
TONY TWIST	63	2	6	8	0	149	0	0	0	0	23	8.7
JAMIE RIVERS	76	2	5	7	3-	47	1	0	0	0	78	2.6
BRYAN HELMER	40	0	4	4	5	42	0	0	0	0	49	.0
JEFF FINLEY	32	1	2	3	11	20	0	0	0	0	16	6.3
CHRIS MCALPINE	51	1	1	2	10-	50	0	0	0	0	56	1.8
MARC BERGEVIN	52	1	1	2	14-	99	0	0	0	0	40	2.5
RORY FITZPATRICK	1	0	0	0	3-	2	0	0	0	0	0	.0
TYSON NASH	2	0	0	0	1-	5	0	0	0	0	1	.0
JOCHEN HECHT	3	0	0	0	2-	0	0	0	0	0	4	.0
JIM CAREY	4	0	0	0	0	0	0	0	0	0	0	.0
BRENT JOHNSON	6	0	0	0	0	0	0	0	0	0	0	.0
RICH PARENT	10	0	0	0	0	2	0	0	0	0	0	.0
RUDY POESCHEK	16	0	0	0	0	33	0	0	0	0	8	.0
BRAD SHAW	16	0	0	0	0	8	0	0	0	0	15	.0
JAMIE MCLENNAN	33	0	0	0	0	0	0	0	0	0	0	.0
GRANT FUHR	39	0	0	0	0	12	0	0	0	0	0	.0

TEAM RANKINGS

		Conference Rank	League Rank
Record	37-32-13	5	12
Home	18-17-6	8	17
Away	19-15-7	3	6
Versus Own Conference	27-20-8	4	8
Versus Other Conference	10-12-5	8	16
Team Plus\Minus	14	5	10
Goals For	237	3	7
Goals Against	209	7	13
Average Shots For	30.1	2	3
Average Shots Against	22.8	1	1
Overtime	1-1-13	7	13
One Goal Games	8-13	12	24
Times outshooting opponent	62	1	1
Versus Teams Over .500	11-18-9	6	13
Versus Teams .500 or under	26-14-4	4	8
First Half Record	16-16-9	4	14
Second Half Record	21-16-4	4	7

MISCELLANEOUS STAT LEADERS
FACEOFFS

Eastwood	56.6%
Conroy	54.6%
Turgeon	50.0%
Demitra	44.0%

ICE TIME

Pronger	30:37
MacInnis	29:07
Demitra	20:10

HITS

Pronger	132
Rivers	131
Rheaume	105
Pellerin	90
Bergevin	90

PLAYOFFS

Results:

Defeated Phoenix 4-3 in conference quarter-finals

Lost to Dallas 4-2 in conference semi-finals

Record: 6-7

Home: 3-3

Away: 3-4

Goals For: 31 (2.4/game)

Goals Against: 33 (2.5/game)

Overtime: 4-3

Power play: 18.0% (5th)

Penalty Killing: 88.7% (3rd)

PLAYER	GP	G	A	PTS	+/-	PIM	PP	SH	GW	OT	S	PCTG
PIERRE TURGEON	13	4	9	13	3	6	0	0	2	2	42	9.5
AL MACINNIS	13	4	8	12	2-	20	2	0	0	0	66	6.1
SCOTT YOUNG	13	4	7	11	2	10	1	0	1	1	40	10.0
PAVOL DEMITRA	13	5	4	9	5-	4	3	0	1	1	31	16.1
GEOFF COURTNALL	13	2	4	6	4-	10	2	0	0	0	18	11.1
CHRIS PRONGER	13	1	4	5	2-	28	1	0	0	0	43	2.3
BLAIR ATCHEYNUM	13	1	3	4	2	6	0	0	0	0	19	5.3
CRAIG CONROY	13	2	1	3	3-	6	0	0	0	0	20	10.0
JEFF FINLEY	13	1	2	3	4-	8	0	0	1	0	5	20.0
TERRY YAKE	13	1	2	3	3-	14	1	0	0	0	13	7.7
RICARD PERSSON	13	0	3	3	1-	17	0	0	0	0	12	.0
JOCHEN HECHT	5	2	0	2	4	0	0	0	0	0	20	10.0
JAMIE RIVERS	9	1	1	2	2-	2	1	0	1	0	4	25.0
MIKE EASTWOOD	13	1	1	2	2	6	0	0	0	0	8	12.5
MICHAL HANDZUS	11	0	2	2	0	8	0	0	0	0	16	.0
PASCAL RHEAUME	5	1	0	1	1	4	0	0	0	0	10	10.0
SCOTT PELLERIN	8	1	0	1	2-	4	0	0	0	0	11	9.1
JAMAL MAYERS	11	0	1	1	2-	8	0	0	0	0	9	.0
GRANT FUHR	13	0	1	1	0	2	0	0	0	0	0	.0
TONY TWIST	1	0	0	0	1-	0	0	0	0	0	0	.0
JAMIE MCLENNAN	1	0	0	0	0	6	0	0	0	0	0	.0
TYSON NASH	1	0	0	0	3-	2	0	0	0	0	0	.0
BRAD SHAW	4	0	0	0	2	0	0	0	0	0	3	.0
MICHEL PICARD	5	0	0	0	3-	2	0	0	0	0	7	.0
LUBOS BARTECKO	5	0	0	0	3-	2	0	0	0	0	8	.0
CHRIS MCALPINE	13	0	0	0	0	2	0	0	0	0	7	.0

GOALTENDER	GPI	MINS	AVG	W	L	T	EN	SO	GA	SA	SV %
JAMIE MCLENNAN	1	37	.00	0	1	1	0	0	0	7	1.000
GRANT FUHR	13	790	2.35	6	6	1	1	31	0	305	.898
STL TOTALS	13	832	2.38	6	7	2	1	33	0	314	.895

Vancouver Canucks

The drafting of the Sedin brothers has taken the heat off the dismal Canucks performance and given the fans some hope.

But, you know, there's something about this franchise and hope. They always have lots of it, hope that is, but it so rarely pans out for them and invariably it ends in disappointment. In fact, it's almost a yearly thing. Consider:

Mike Keenan — was supposed to bring this franchise back to their winning ways. Didn't work out.

Marc Crawford — was supposed to create an instant turnaround. The Canucks record under him was 8-23-6.

Alexander Mogilny — a perennial hope. He scored 14 goals last season. Somebody named Bill Muckhalt had 16.

Mark Messier — they hoped he could bring leadership to the team. Too late.

Draft Day 1970 — Wouldn't so much be different had they got Gilbert Perreault instead of Dale Tallon?

A good number one draft choice they still had when he became good. Oh, there was Trevor Linden in 1988. The rest had to be traded before becoming stars. Cam Neely and Rick Vaive are good examples, although Petr Nedved had one good season before becoming a holdout. The rest of their top draft picks either became useful journeymen for other teams, or had names such as Dan Woodley, Jason Herter, Alek Stoyanov, and Libor Polasek. The latest draft hopes are pinned to Mattias Ohlund, who has looked good so far.

Pavel Bure — Just the way he left that was the disappointment.

Canucks fans might have hoped that their team would at least be better than the expansion Nashville team. No such luck there, either.

It's just awfully frustrating to be a Canucks fan because they always look so much better before they get onto the ice. Why shouldn't a team that had Bure, Messier and Mogilny for starters, be successful? Why should a team that had some of the best young defensemen in the league allow the third most goals?

Why does nothing ever seem to work out for this team?

STUFF

Mark Messier became the 10th player to score 600 NHL goals.

192 goals were the fewest in franchise history.

47 losses were the most since the 1972-73 season.

58 points were the fewest since the 1973-74 season.

TEAM PREVIEW

GOAL: Yes, Kevin Weekes stunk in his Canucks debut last season, but there are some mitigating circumstances. For one, it was late in the season and the team had already given up. In five of his eight starts, the Canucks scored exactly one goal. It should be noted, also, that while Weekes was in Vancouver, Snow was playing terribly too, and had to be pulled three times. As well, Weekes was a holdout as a free agent, so he was rusty.

In any event, the Canucks protected Weekes in the expansion draft and left Snow available, so you can see they weren't going to judge Weekes on 12 games.

Snow managed to perform a minor miracle last year, however, earning six shutouts.

DEFENSE: Even with McCabe traded to Chicago in the Sedin deal, they still have an excellent stable of young talent.

Mattias Ohlund may have slumped some during the season, but he's already put his abundant talent on display, and needs to only develop consistency.

Ed Jovanovski, the first overall pick in the 1994 draft, just turned 23 over the summer.

Adrian Aucoin took a while to make it to the NHL as a regular, but he's only 26, and led all league defensemen in goals scored.

Jason Strudwick, just 24, has a chance to be a consistent NHL perfomer.

And Bryan Allen, the fourth pick in the 1998 draft, looks very much like he's going to be a star.

They've also got dependable veteran Murray Baron, so again, on paper these guys look as if they'd be a good group. And remember they had another good young defenseman in Bryan McCabe last year.

Tough to figure.

Aucoin came out of nowhere to score 23 goals. There's nothing in his history to suggest such an outbreak was imminent. In 155 previous games with the Canucks he had just 13 goals.

These are the top goal scoring defensemen in the league last season.

Adrian Aucoin	Van.	23
Sergei Gonchar	Wsh	21
Al MacInnis	StL	20
Fredrik Olausson	Ana	16
Eric Desjardins	Phi	15

FORWARD: If it hadn't been a breakout season for Markus Naslund the Canucks would have been in an even deeper hole, if that's possible. He had 36 goals, more than double the next top scoring forward, Bill Muckhalt with 16.

Mark Messier and Alexander Mogilny both missed over 20 games, but neither one was making much of an impact anyway. Messier is 38-years-old, and as good as he's been, can't go on

GOALTENDER	GPI	MINS	AVG	W	L	T	EN	SO	GA	SA	SV %
GARTH SNOW	65	3,501	2.93	20	31	8	5	6	171	1,715	.900
COREY HIRSCH	20	919	3.13	3	8	3	0	1	48	435	.890
KEVIN WEEKES	11	532	3.83	0	8	1	0	0	34	257	.868
VAN TOTALS	82	4,981	3.11	23	47	12	5	7	258	2,412	.893

forever. With Mogilny, the Canucks would desperately like him to start showing something again, so at least he has some trade value.

It's not even a surety that Naslund will even duplicate his results from last season, so where does that leave them for goal scoring? In rough shape.

It did look, however that Todd Bertuzzi was going to have a breakout season, until he broke his leg, causing him to miss most of the season.

If Bertuzzi is on the top line with Messier and Naslund, it leaves free agent acquisition Andrew Cassels and Mogilny looking for a left winger. Maybe Brad May.
Cassels got a hefty contract with the Canucks, which is kind of surprising after a couple miserable seasons in Calgary.

Remember we're assuming at this point that the Sedin twins won't be coming over this year, as was the indication late in July.

Dave Scatchard and Josh Holden should hold down the other two centre spots, leaving Bill Muckhalt, Trent Klatt, Darby Hendricksson, Harry York, enforcer Donald Brashear, Peter Scheaffer, Matt Cooke and Mike Brown. Brown was obtained from Florida in the Bure deal and is an enforcer who puts the puck in the net.

Brashear sometimes forgets his enforcer role and fancies himself a goal scorer. That's not such a bad thing, because teams are having less use for one-dimensional enforcers. If they can fight and score at the same time it makes them that much more valuable.

Forward is one area in which the Canucks don't even look good on paper. There isn't even one sure thing for goal scoring in the whole bunch.

SPECIAL TEAMS: The Canucks were the second most penalized team in the league last year, so they had better find a way to be better at penalty killing besides getting a lot of practise at it.

On the power play, Aucoin had 18 goals, which placed him third best in the league. That falls into the bizarre category. He also had almost one-third of all Vancouver's power play goals. That's bizarre, too.

Another oddity is that Naslund was fifth in the league with 15 power play goals, giving Vancouver two of the top five. If he and Aucoin hadn't had breakout seasons, who knows how much worse

Power Play	G	ATT	PCT
Overall	57	358	15.9% (12th NHL)
Home	28	183	15.3% (T-14th NHL)
Road	29	175	16.6% (9th NHL)

9 SHORT HANDED GOALS ALLOWED (T-15th NHL)

Penalty Killing	G	TSH	PCT
Overall	77	450	82.9% (19th NHL)
Home	30	210	85.7% (14th NHL)
Road	47	240	80.4% (24th NHL)

17 SHORT HANDED GOALS SCORED (1st NHL)

Penalties	GP	MIN	AVG
CANUCKS	82	1764	21.5 (26th NHL)

CANUCKS SPECIAL TEAMS SCORING

Power play	G	A	PTS
NASLUND	15	13	28
MESSIER	4	18	22
AUCOIN	18	3	21
OHLUND	2	15	17
MOGILNY	3	12	15
GAGNER	2	10	12
MUCKALT	4	7	11
MCCABE	1	6	7

JOVANOVSKI	1	6	7
MAY	1	4	5
BERTUZZI	1	3	4
BRASHEAR	2	1	3
YORK	1	2	3
ZEZEL	1	1	2
SCHAEFER	1	1	2
SOPEL	1	0	1
HOLDEN	1	0	1
HENDRICKSON	1	0	1
SCATCHARD	0	1	1

Short handed	G	A	PTS
MESSIER	2	5	7
SCATCHARD	2	3	5
MOGILNY	2	3	5
NASLUND	2	1	3
MCCABE	2	1	3
MUCKALT	2	0	2
AUCOIN	2	0	2
OHLUND	1	0	1
STRUDWICK	0	1	1
MAY	0	1	1
KLATT	0	1	1
JOVANOVSKI	0	1	1

COACHING AND MANAGEMENT: Mike Keenan didn't work out, but he usually takes a year before his act starts to pay dividends. He may be a dinosaur anyway, with his style. He's coached almost every team in the league, now, and nobody appears anxious to give him another try, especially with the wake of destruction he leaves in his path.

Marc Crawford didn't exactly make an immediate impact with just a 8-23-6 mark after Keenan was ousted. He does have a Stanley Cup win to his credit though, so we can assume he knows what he's doing.

Brian Burke is doing his best to try and turn this team around. Getting the Sedin twins was a stroke of genius in itself. Plus, he's brought in some good players, but nothing has worked yet.

DRAFT: (see chart) Some incredible draft day maneuvering by Burke meant the Swedish phenom twins could stay together. The key now is getting them to come to North America together. So far, it doesn't appear likely for this year.

PROGNOSIS: The Canucks could bring in the Sedin quintuplets and they wouldn't make the Canucks a winner this year. Fewer injuries to

DRAFT

Player	Pos	Rnd	Sel.	Cntry	Team	Lge	Gms	G	A	P	PIM
Daniel Sedin	LW	1	2	Swe	Modo	Swe	50	21	21	42	20
Henrik Sedin	C	1	3	Swe	Modo	Swe	49	12	22	34	32
Rene Vydareny	D	3	69	Slo	Bratislava	Slo	42	4	7	11	65
Ryan Thorpe	LW	5	129	Can	Spokane	WHL	41	12	4	16	89
Josh Reed	D	6	172	Can	Vernon	BCJHL	54	16	38	54	110
Kevin Swanson	G	7	189	Can	Kelowna	WHL	3.45				
M. Kankaanpera	D	8	218	Swe	Jyvaskyla	Fin	50	0	2	2	85
Darrell Hay	D	9	271	Can	Tri-City	WHL	72	13	49	62	87

key players would probably help a little bit, plus if the defense matures together.

But, they still need to score goals and that's clearly a problem. Plus, they're still iffy in net.

Another long season for the Canucks, but at least when it's over they'll have the Sedin twins at the end of the rainbow.

STAT SECTION

PLAYER	GP	G	A	PTS	+/-	PIM	PP	SH	GW	GT	S	PCTG
MARKUS NASLUND	80	36	30	66	13-	74	15	2	3	1	205	17.6
MARK MESSIER	59	13	35	48	12-	33	4	2	2	0	97	13.4
A. MOGILNY	59	14	31	45	0	58	3	2	1	1	110	12.7
BILL MUCKALT	73	16	20	36	9-	98	4	2	1	0	119	13.4
MATTIAS OHLUND	74	9	26	35	19-	83	2	1	1	0	129	7.0
ADRIAN AUCOIN	82	23	11	34	14-	77	18	2	3	1	174	13.2
DAVE GAGNER	69	6	22	28	16-	63	2	0	1	1	100	6.0
ED JOVANOVSKI	72	5	22	27	9-	126	1	0	1	0	109	4.6
DAVE SCATCHARD	82	13	13	26	12-	140	0	2	2	0	130	10.0
BRYAN MCCABE	69	7	14	21	11-	120	1	2	0	0	98	7.1
D. BRASHEAR	82	8	10	18	25-	209	2	0	1	0	112	7.1
BRAD MAY	66	6	11	17	14-	102	1	0	1	0	91	6.6
TODD BERTUZZI	32	8	8	16	6-	44	1	0	3	0	72	11.1
HARRY YORK	56	7	9	16	3-	24	1	0	0	1	60	11.7
PETER ZEZEL	41	6	8	14	5	16	1	0	2	0	45	13.3
TRENT KLATT	75	4	10	14	3-	12	0	0	0	0	60	6.7
D. HENDRICKSON	62	4	5	9	19-	52	1	0	0	0	70	5.7
PETER SCHAEFER	25	4	4	8	1-	8	1	0	1	0	24	16.7
MURRAY BARON	81	2	6	8	23-	115	0	0	0	0	53	3.8
JOSH HOLDEN	30	2	4	6	10-	10	1	0	0	0	44	4.5
BERT ROBERTSSON	39	2	2	4	7-	13	0	0	0	0	13	15.4
JASON STRUDWICK	65	0	3	3	19-	114	0	0	0	0	25	.0
DANA MURZYN	12	0	2	2	1	21	0	0	0	0	7	.0
MATT COOKE	30	0	2	2	12-	27	0	0	0	0	22	.0
STEVE STAIOS	57	0	2	2	12-	54	0	0	0	0	33	.0
BRENT SOPEL	5	1	0	1	1-	4	1	0	0	0	5	20.0
GARTH SNOW	65	0	1	1	0	34	0	0	0	0	0	.0
ROBB GORDON	4	0	0	0	0	2	0	0	0	0	1	.0
KEVIN WEEKES	11	0	0	0	0	0	0	0	0	0	0	.0
STEVE WASHBURN	12	0	0	0	1-	6	0	0	0	0	6	.0
COREY HIRSCH	20	0	0	0	0	0	0	0	0	0	0	.0

TEAM RANKINGS

		Conference Rank	League Rank
Record	23-47-12	13	26
Home	14-21-6	13	25
Away	9-26-6	13	26
Versus Own Conference	15-32-8	13	25
Versus Other Conference	8-15-4	12	24
Team Plus\Minus	-46	13	26
Goals For	192	11	23
Goals Against	258	12	25
Average Shots For	23.7	13	27
Average Shots Against	29.4	10	21
Overtime	0-1-12	10	19
One Goal Games	7-15	13	26
Times outshooting opponent	23	13	25
Versus Teams Over .500	12-23-7	9	19
Versus Teams .500 or under	9-25-7	13	26
First Half Record	14-22-5	10	22
Second Half Record	9-25-7	13	27

MISCELLANEOUS STAT LEADERS

FACEOFFS

Scatchard	56.3%
Messier	53.9%
Gagner	49.1%

ICE TIME

McCabe	24:13
Aucoin	23:52
Messier	22:36
Jovanovski	22:01
Mogilny	20:35

HITS

Aucoin	208
Jovanovski	156
Scatchard	147
Ohlund	133
York	131
Brashear	126

PLAYOFFS

- Did not make the playoffs

Stat Section

TEAM STANDINGS

(PCTG) PERCENTAGE OF ACTUAL POINTS VERSUS POSSIBLE POINTS

EASTERN CONFERENCE
Northeast Division

	GP	W	L	T	GF	GA	PTS	PCTG
OTTAWA (2)	82	44	23	15	239	179	103	.628
TORONTO (4)	82	45	30	7	268	231	97	.591
BOSTON (6)	82	39	30	13	214	181	91	.555
BUFFALO (7)	82	37	28	17	207	175	91	.555
MONTREAL (11)	82	32	39	11	184	209	75	.457

Atlantic Division

	GP	W	L	T	GF	GA	PTS	PCTG
NEW JERSEY (1)	82	47	24	11	248	196	105	.640
PHILADELPHIA(5)	82	37	26	19	231	196	93	.567
PITTSBURGH (8)	82	38	30	14	242	225	90	.549
NY RANGERS (10)	82	33	38	11	217	227	77	.470
NY ISLANDERS (13)	82	24	48	10	194	244	58	.354

Southeast Division

	GP	W	L	T	GF	GA	PTS	PCTG
CAROLINA (3)	82	34	30	18	210	202	86	.524
FLORIDA (9)	82	30	34	18	210	228	78	.476
WASHINGTON (12)	82	31	45	6	200	218	68	.415
TAMPA BAY (14)	82	19	54	9	179	292	47	.287

WESTERN CONFERENCE
Central Division

	GP	W	L	T	GF	GA	PTS	PCTG
DETROIT (3)	82	43	32	7	245	202	93	.567
ST LOUIS (5)	82	37	32	13	237	209	87	.530
CHICAGO (10)	82	29	41	12	202	248	70	.427
NASHVILLE (12)	82	28	47	7	190	261	63	.384

Pacific Division

	GP	W	L	T	GF	GA	PTS	PCTG
DALLAS (1)	82	51	19	12	236	168	114	.695
PHOENIX (4)	82	39	31	12	205	197	90	.549
ANAHEIM (6)	82	35	34	13	215	206	83	.506
SAN JOSE (7)	82	31	33	18	196	191	80	.488
LOS ANGELES (11)	82	32	45	5	189	222	69	.421

Northwest Division

	GP	W	L	T	GF	GA	PTS	PCTG
COLORADO (2)	82	44	28	10	239	205	98	.598
EDMONTON (8)	82	33	37	12	230	226	78	.476
CALGARY (9)	82	30	40	12	211	234	72	.439
VANCOUVER (13)	82	23	47	12	192	258	58	.354

TEAMS' DIVISIONAL RECORD
AGAINST OWN DIVISION
Northeast Division

	GP	W	L	T	GF	GA	PTS	PCTG
OTTAWA (3)	20	8	8	4	42	42	20	.500
TORONTO (4)	20	8	11	1	43	55	17	.425
BOSTON (1)	20	11	7	2	57	40	24	.600
BUFFALO (2)	20	10	6	4	54	37	24	.600
MONTREAL (5)	20	7	12	1	40	62	15	.375
DIVISION TOTAL	100	44	44	12	236	236	100	.500

Atlantic Division

	GP	W	L	T	GF	GA	PTS	PCTG
NEW JERSEY (1)	20	15	4	1	71	55	31	.775
PHILADELPHIA (3)	20	7	8	5	58	54	19	.475

	GP	W	L	T	GF	GA	PTS	PCTG
PITTSBURGH (5)	20	5	11	4	46	64	14	.350
NY RANGERS (2)	20	8	8	4	52	52	20	.500
NY ISLANDERS (4)	20	7	11	2	57	59	16	.400
DIVISION TOTAL	100	42	42	16	284	284	100	.500

Southeast Division

	GP	W	L	T	GF	GA	PTS	PCTG
CAROLINA (2)	15	5	2	8	41	38	18	.600
FLORIDA (3)	15	6	4	5	36	34	17	.567
WASHINGTON (1)	15	8	5	2	53	31	18	.600
TAMPA BAY (4)	15	2	10	3	32	59	7	.233
DIVISION TOTAL	60	21	21	18	162	162	60	.500

Central Division

	GP	W	L	T	GF	GA	PTS	PCTG
DETROIT (1)	18	12	4	2	62	40	26	.722
ST LOUIS (2)	18	10	6	2	59	46	22	.611
CHICAGO (3)	18	7	10	1	47	56	15	.417
NASHVILLE (4)	18	4	13	1	44	70	9	.250
DIVISION TOTAL	72	33	33	6	212	212	72	.500

Pacific Division

	GP	W	L	T	GF	GA	PTS	PCTG
DALLAS (1)	24	18	4	2	62	43	38	.792
PHOENIX (3)	24	11	11	2	47	46	24	.500
ANAHEIM (2)	24	12	7	5	62	48	29	.604
SAN JOSE (4)	24	7	14	3	47	55	17	.354
LOS ANGELES (5)	24	6	18	0	41	67	12	.250
DIVISION TOTAL	120	54	54	12	259	259	120	.500

Northwest Division

	GP	W	L	T	GF	GA	PTS	PCTG
COLORADO (2)	18	8	8	2	48	52	18	.500
EDMONTON (1)	18	12	4	2	57	40	26	.722
CALGARY (3)	18	6	10	2	45	50	14	.389
VANCOUVER (4)	18	6	10	2	46	54	14	.389
DIVISION TOTAL	72	32	32	8	196	196	72	.500

AGAINST OTHER DIVISIONS

Northeast Division

	GP	W	L	T	GF	GA	PTS	PCTG
OTTAWA (1)	62	36	15	11	197	137	83	.669
TORONTO (2)	62	37	19	6	225	176	80	.645
BOSTON (3)	62	28	23	11	157	141	67	.540
BUFFALO (4)	62	27	22	13	153	138	67	.540
MONTREAL (5)	62	25	27	10	144	147	60	.484
DIVISION TOTAL	310	153	106	51	876	739	357	.576

Atlantic Division

	GP	W	L	T	GF	GA	PTS	PCTG
NEW JERSEY (2)	62	32	20	10	177	141	74	.597
PHILADELPHIA (3)	62	30	18	14	173	142	74	.597
PITTSBURGH (1)	62	33	19	10	196	161	76	.613
NY RANGERS (4)	62	25	30	7	165	175	57	.460
NY ISLANDERS (5)	62	17	37	8	137	185	42	.339
DIVISION TOTAL	310	137	124	49	848	804	323	.521

Southeast Division

	GP	W	L	T	GF	GA	PTS	PCTG
CAROLINA (1)	67	29	28	10	169	164	68	.507
FLORIDA (2)	67	24	30	13	174	194	61	.455
WASHINGTON (3)	67	23	40	4	147	187	50	.373
TAMPA BAY (4)	67	17	44	6	147	233	40	.299
DIVISION TOTAL	268	93	142	33	637	778	219	.409

Central Division

	GP	W	L	T	GF	GA	PTS	PCTG
DETROIT (1)	64	31	28	5	183	162	67	.523
ST LOUIS (2)	64	27	26	11	178	163	65	.508
CHICAGO (3)	64	22	31	11	155	192	55	.430
NASHVILLE (4)	64	24	34	6	146	191	54	.422
DIVISION TOTAL	256	104	119	33	662	708	241	.471

Pacific Division

	GP	W	L	T	GF	GA	PTS	PCTG
DALLAS (1)	58	33	15	10	174	125	76	.655

	GP	W	L	T	GF	GA	PTS	PCTG
PHOENIX (2)	58	28	20	10	158	151	66	.569
ANAHEIM (5)	58	23	27	8	153	158	54	.466
SAN JOSE (3)	58	24	19	15	149	136	63	.543
LOS ANGELES (4)	58	26	27	5	148	155	57	.491
DIVISION TOTAL	290	134	108	48	782	725	316	.545

Northwest Division

	GP	W	L	T	GF	GA	PTS	PCTG
COLORADO (1)	64	36	20	8	191	153	80	.625
EDMONTON (3)	64	21	33	10	173	186	52	.406
CALGARY (2)	64	24	30	10	166	184	58	.453
VANCOUVER (4)	64	17	37	10	146	204	44	.344
DIVISION TOTAL	256	98	120	38	676	727	234	.457

**TEAM STANDINGS
BY CONFERENCE**
Eastern Conference

	GP	W	L	T	GF	GA	PTS	PCTG
NEW JERSEY	82	47	24	11	248	196	105	.640
OTTAWA	82	44	23	15	239	179	103	.628
TORONTO	82	45	30	7	268	231	97	.591
PHILADELPHIA	82	37	26	19	231	196	93	.567
BOSTON	82	39	30	13	214	181	91	.555
BUFFALO	82	37	28	17	207	175	91	.555
PITTSBURGH	82	38	30	14	242	225	90	.549
CAROLINA	82	34	30	18	210	202	86	.524
FLORIDA	82	30	34	18	210	228	78	.476
NY RANGERS	82	33	38	11	217	227	77	.470
MONTREAL	82	32	39	11	184	209	75	.457
WASHINGTON	82	31	45	6	200	218	68	.415
NY ISLANDERS	82	24	48	10	194	244	58	.354
TAMPA BAY	82	19	54	9	179	292	47	.287

Western Conference

	GP	W	L	T	GF	GA	PTS	PCTG
DALLAS	82	51	19	12	236	168	114	.695
COLORADO	82	44	28	10	239	205	98	.598
DETROIT	82	43	32	7	245	202	93	.567

PHOENIX	82	39	31	12	205	197	90	.549
ST LOUIS	82	37	32	13	237	209	87	.530
ANAHEIM	82	35	34	13	215	206	83	.506
SAN JOSE	82	31	33	18	196	191	80	.488
EDMONTON	82	33	37	12	230	226	78	.476
CALGARY	82	30	40	12	211	234	72	.439
CHICAGO	82	29	41	12	202	248	70	.427
LOS ANGELES	82	32	45	5	189	222	69	.421
NASHVILLE	82	28	47	7	190	261	63	.384
VANCOUVER	82	23	47	12	192	258	58	.354

TEAMS' HOME-AND-ROAD RECORD BY CONFERENCE

HOME
Eastern Conference

	GP	W	L	T	GF	GA	PTS	PCTG
BOSTON (1)	41	22	10	9	112	79	53	.646
PHILADELPHIA (2)	41	21	9	11	128	90	53	.646
BUFFALO (3)	41	23	12	6	117	88	52	.634
OTTAWA (4)	41	22	11	8	120	79	52	.634
PITTSBURGH (5)	41	21	10	10	132	103	52	.634
TORONTO (6)	41	23	13	5	135	111	51	.622
CAROLINA (7)	41	20	12	9	110	96	49	.598
MONTREAL (8)	41	21	15	5	105	97	47	.573
NEW JERSEY (9)	41	19	14	8	123	102	46	.561
FLORIDA (10)	41	17	17	7	115	114	41	.500
NY RANGERS (11)	41	17	19	5	105	102	39	.476
WASHINGTON (12)	41	16	23	2	107	111	34	.415
NY ISLANDERS (13)	41	11	23	7	104	122	29	.354
TAMPA BAY (14)	41	12	25	4	90	127	28	.341
CONFERENCE TOTAL	574	265	213	96	1,603	1,421	626	.545

Western Conference

	GP	W	L	T	GF	GA	PTS	PCTG
DALLAS (1)	41	29	8	4	134	86	62	.756
DETROIT (2)	41	27	12	2	137	96	56	.683
PHOENIX 3)	41	23	13	5	106	97	51	.622

	GP	W	L	T	GF	GA	PTS	PCTG
COLORADO (4)	41	21	14	6	127	100	48	.585
ANAHEIM (5)	41	21	14	6	121	96	48	.585
CHICAGO (6)	41	20	17	4	109	112	44	.537
SAN JOSE (7)	41	17	15	9	96	86	43	.524
ST LOUIS (8)	41	18	17	6	118	99	42	.512
LOS ANGELES (9)	41	18	20	3	105	107	39	.476
EDMONTON (10)	41	17	19	5	113	112	39	.476
CALGARY (11)	41	15	20	6	103	110	36	.439
NASHVILLE (12)	41	15	22	4	104	126	34	.415
VANCOUVER (13)	41	14	21	6	95	111	34	.415
CONFERENCE TOTAL	533	255	212	66	1,468	1,338	576	.540
HOME TOTAL	**1,107**	**520**	**425**	**162**	**3,071**	**2,759**	**1,202**	**.543**

ROAD

Eastern Conference

	GP	W	L	T	GF	GA	PTS	PCTG
NEW JERSEY (1)	41	28	10	3	125	94	59	.720
OTTAWA (2)	41	22	12	7	119	100	51	.622
TORONTO (3)	41	22	17	2	133	120	46	.561
PHILADELPHIA (4)	41	16	17	8	103	106	40	.488
BUFFALO (5)	41	14	16	11	90	87	39	.476
BOSTON (6)	41	17	20	4	102	102	38	.463
PITTSBURGH (7)	41	17	20	4	110	122	38	.463
NY RANGERS (8)	41	16	19	6	112	125	38	.463
CAROLINA (9)	41	14	18	9	100	106	37	.451
FLORIDA (10)	41	13	17	11	95	114	37	.451
WASHINGTON (11)	41	15	22	4	93	107	34	.415
NY ISLANDERS (12)	41	13	25	3	90	122	29	.354
MONTREAL (13)	41	11	24	6	79	112	28	.341
TAMPA BAY (14)	41	7	29	5	89	165	19	.232
CONFERENCE TOTAL	574	225	266	83	1,440	1,582	533	.464

Western Conference

	GP	W	L	T	GF	GA	PTS	PCTG
DALLAS (1)	41	22	11	8	102	82	52	.634
COLORADO (2)	41	23	14	4	112	105	50	.610
ST LOUIS (3)	41	19	15	7	119	110	45	.549

EDMONTON (4)	41	16	18	7	117	114	39	.476
PHOENIX (5)	41	16	18	7	99	100	39	.476
DETROIT (6)	41	16	20	5	108	106	37	.451
SAN JOSE (7)	41	14	18	9	100	105	37	.451
CALGARY (8)	41	15	20	6	108	124	36	.439
ANAHEIM (9)	41	14	20	7	94	110	35	.427
LOS ANGELES (10)	41	14	25	2	84	115	30	.366
NASHVILLE (11)	41	13	25	3	86	135	29	.354
CHICAGO (12)	41	9	24	8	93	136	26	.317
VANCOUVER (13)	41	9	26	6	97	147	24	.293
CONFERENCE TOTAL	533	200	254	79	1,319	1,489	479	.449

ROAD TOTAL	**1,107**	**425**	**520**	**162**	**2,759**	**3,071**	**1,012**	**.457**

TEAMS' INTER-CONFERENCE RECORD
AGAINST OWN CONFERENCE

Eastern Conference

	GP	W	L	T	GF	GA	PTS	PCTG
NEW JERSEY (1)	58	35	15	8	178	137	78	.672
OTTAWA (2)	57	30	18	9	177	134	69	.605
BUFFALO (3)	57	28	17	12	142	111	68	.596
BOSTON (4)	58	29	20	9	150	127	67	.578
CAROLINA (5)	59	25	19	15	155	151	65	.551
PITTSBURGH 6)	58	26	23	9	170	164	61	.526
PHILADELPHIA (7)	57	23	21	13	145	137	59	.518
WASHINGTON (8)	57	26	26	5	157	145	57	.500
TORONTO (9)	56	25	26	5	165	166	55	.491
FLORIDA (10)	58	22	25	11	145	162	55	.474
NY RANGERS (11)	58	21	28	9	147	162	51	.440
MONTREAL (12)	56	21	28	7	133	152	49	.438
NY ISLANDERS (13)	58	17	37	4	142	184	38	.328
TAMPA BAY (14)	57	12	37	8	126	200	32	.281
CONFERENCE TOTAL	804	340	340	124	2,132	2,132	804	.500

Western Conference

	GP	W	L	T	GF	GA	PTS	PCTG
DALLAS (1)	56	35	14	7	154	115	77	.688
COLORADO (2)	56	29	19	8	160	136	66	.589

	GP	W	L	T	GF	GA	PTS	PCTG
DETROIT (3)	54	30	20	4	163	131	64	.593
PHOENIX (4)	56	28	21	7	143	126	63	.563
ST LOUIS (5)	55	27	20	8	171	143	62	.564
ANAHEIM (6)	57	25	24	8	148	139	58	.509
EDMONTON (7)	55	25	24	6	163	158	56	.509
SAN JOSE (8)	57	21	26	10	136	138	52	.456
CALGARY (9)	55	21	25	9	148	150	51	.464
NASHVILLE (10)	55	21	30	4	140	174	46	.418
LOS ANGELES (11)	57	21	32	4	131	158	46	.404
CHICAGO (12)	54	18	29	7	131	164	43	.398
VANCOUVER (13)	55	15	32	8	128	184	38	.345
CONFERENCE TOTAL	722	316	316	90	1,916	1,916	722	.500

VS. OWN CONFERENCE	**1,526**	**656**	**656**	**214**	**4,048**	**4,048**	**1,526**	**.500**

AGAINST OTHER CONFERENCE
Eastern Conference

	GP	W	L	T	GF	GA	PTS	PCTG
TORONTO (1)	26	20	4	2	103	65	42	.808
PHILADELPHIA (2)	25	14	5	6	86	59	34	.680
OTTAWA (3)	25	14	5	6	62	45	34	.680
PITTSBURGH (4)	24	12	7	5	72	61	29	.604
NEW JERSEY (5)	24	12	9	3	70	59	27	.563
NY RANGERS (6)	24	12	10	2	70	65	26	.542
MONTREAL (7)	26	11	11	4	51	57	26	.500
BOSTON (8)	24	10	10	4	64	54	24	.500
FLORIDA (9)	24	8	9	7	65	66	23	.479
BUFFALO (10)	25	9	11	5	65	64	23	.460
CAROLINA (11)	23	9	11	3	55	51	21	.457
NY ISLANDERS (12)	24	7	11	6	52	60	20	.417
TAMPA BAY (13)	25	7	17	1	53	92	15	.300
WASHINGTON (14)	25	5	19	1	43	73	11	.220
CONFERENCE TOTAL	344	150	139	55	911	871	355	.516

Western Conference

	GP	W	L	T	GF	GA	PTS	PCTG
DALLAS (1)	26	16	5	5	82	53	37	.712
COLORADO (2)	26	15	9	2	79	69	32	.615

DETROIT (3)	28	13	12	3	82	71	29	.518
SAN JOSE (4)	25	10	7	8	60	53	28	.560
PHOENIX (5)	26	11	10	5	62	71	27	.519
CHICAGO (6)	28	11	12	5	71	84	27	.482
ANAHEIM (7)	25	10	10	5	67	67	25	.500
ST LOUIS (8)	27	10	12	5	66	66	25	.463
LOS ANGELES (9)	25	11	13	1	58	64	23	.460
EDMONTON (10)	27	8	13	6	67	68	22	.407
CALGARY (11)	27	9	15	3	63	84	21	.389
VANCOUVER (12)	27	8	15	4	64	74	20	.370
NASHVILLE (13)	27	7	17	3	50	87	17	.315
CONFERENCE TOTAL	344	139	150	55	871	911	333	.484
VS. OTHER CONF.	**688**	**289**	**289**	**110**	**1,782**	**1,782**	**688**	**.500**

OVERALL STANDINGS

	GP	W	L	T	GF	GA	PTS	PCTG
DALLAS	82	51	19	12	236	168	114	.695
NEW JERSEY	82	47	24	11	248	196	105	.640
OTTAWA	82	44	23	15	239	179	103	.628
COLORADO	82	44	28	10	239	205	98	.598
TORONTO	82	45	30	7	268	231	97	.591
DETROIT	82	43	32	7	245	202	93	.567
PHILADELPHIA	82	37	26	19	231	196	93	.567
BOSTON	82	39	30	13	214	181	91	.555
BUFFALO	82	37	28	17	207	175	91	.555
PHOENIX	82	39	31	12	205	197	90	.549
PITTSBURGH	82	38	30	14	242	225	90	.549
ST LOUIS	82	37	32	13	237	209	87	.530
CAROLINA	82	34	30	18	210	202	86	.524
ANAHEIM	82	35	34	13	215	206	83	.506
SAN JOSE	82	31	33	18	196	191	80	.488
EDMONTON	82	33	37	12	230	226	78	.476
FLORIDA	82	30	34	18	210	228	78	.476
NY RANGERS	82	33	38	11	217	227	77	.470
MONTREAL	82	32	39	11	184	209	75	.457
CALGARY	82	30	40	12	211	234	72	.439
CHICAGO	82	29	41	12	202	248	70	.427

	GP	W	L	T	GF	GA	PTS	PCTG
LOS ANGELES	82	32	45	5	189	222	69	.421
WASHINGTON	82	31	45	6	200	218	68	.415
NASHVILLE	82	28	47	7	190	261	63	.384
NY ISLANDERS	82	24	48	10	194	244	58	.354
VANCOUVER	82	23	47	12	192	258	58	.354
TAMPA BAY	82	19	54	9	179	292	47	.287

TEAMS' HOME-AND-ROAD RECORD
OVERALL
Home

	GP	W	L	T	GF	GA	PTS	PCTG
DALLAS (1)	41	29	8	4	134	86	62	.756
DETROIT (2)	41	27	12	2	137	96	56	.683
BOSTON (3)	41	22	10	9	112	79	53	.646
PHILADELPHIA (4)	41	21	9	11	128	90	53	.646
BUFFALO (5)	41	23	12	6	117	88	52	.634
OTTAWA (6)	41	22	11	8	120	79	52	.634
PITTSBURGH (7)	41	21	10	10	132	103	52	.634
TORONTO (8)	41	23	13	5	135	111	51	.622
PHOENIX (9)	41	23	13	5	106	97	51	.622
CAROLINA (10)	41	20	12	9	110	96	49	.598
COLORADO (11)	41	21	14	6	127	100	48	.585
ANAHEIM (12)	41	21	14	6	121	96	48	.585
MONTREAL (13)	41	21	15	5	105	97	47	.573
NEW JERSEY (14)	41	19	14	8	123	102	46	.561
CHICAGO (15)	41	20	17	4	109	112	44	.537
SAN JOSE (16)	41	17	15	9	96	86	43	.524
ST LOUIS (17)	41	18	17	6	118	99	42	.512
FLORIDA (18)	41	17	17	7	115	114	41	.500
LOS ANGELES (19)	41	18	20	3	105	107	39	.476
NY RANGERS (20)	41	17	19	5	105	102	39	.476
EDMONTON (21)	41	17	19	5	113	112	39	.476
CALGARY (22)	41	15	20	6	103	110	36	.439
WASHINGTON (23)	41	16	23	2	107	111	34	.415
NASHVILLE (24)	41	15	22	4	104	126	34	.415
VANCOUVER (25)	41	14	21	6	95	111	34	.415
NY ISLANDERS (26)	41	11	23	7	104	122	29	.354
TAMPA BAY (27)	41	12	25	4	90	127	28	.341

Road

	GP	W	L	T	GF	GA	PTS	PCTG
NEW JERSEY (1)	41	28	10	3	125	94	59	.720
DALLAS (2)	41	22	11	8	102	82	52	.634
OTTAWA (3)	41	22	12	7	119	100	51	.622
COLORADO (4)	41	23	14	4	112	105	50	.610
TORONTO (5)	41	22	17	2	133	120	46	.561
ST LOUIS (6)	41	19	15	7	119	110	45	.549
PHILADELPHIA (7)	41	16	17	8	103	106	40	.488
EDMONTON (8)	41	16	18	7	117	114	39	.476
PHOENIX (9)	41	16	18	7	99	100	39	.476
BUFFALO (10)	41	14	16	11	90	87	39	.476
BOSTON (11)	41	17	20	4	102	102	38	.463
PITTSBURGH (12)	41	17	20	4	110	122	38	.463
NY RANGERS (13)	41	16	19	6	112	125	38	.463
DETROIT (14)	41	16	20	5	108	106	37	.451
SAN JOSE (15)	41	14	18	9	100	105	37	.451
CAROLINA (16)	41	14	18	9	100	106	37	.451
FLORIDA (17)	41	13	17	11	95	114	37	.451
CALGARY (18)	41	15	20	6	108	124	36	.439
ANAHEIM (19)	41	14	20	7	94	110	35	.427
WASHINGTON (20)	41	15	22	4	93	107	34	.415
LOS ANGELES (21)	41	14	25	2	84	115	30	.366
NY ISLANDERS (22)	41	13	25	3	90	122	29	.354
NASHVILLE (23)	41	13	25	3	86	135	29	.354
MONTREAL (24)	41	11	24	6	79	112	28	.341
CHICAGO (25)	41	9	24	8	93	136	26	.317
VANCOUVER (26)	41	9	26	6	97	147	24	.293
TAMPA BAY (27)	41	7	29	5	89	165	19	.232

INDIVIDUAL SCORING LEADERS

PLAYER	TEAM	GP	G	A	PTS	+/-	PIM	PP	SH	GW	GT	S	PCTG
JAROMIR JAGR	PITTSBURGH	81	44	83	127	17	66	10	1	7	2	343	12.8
TEEMU SELANNE	ANAHEIM	75	47	60	107	18	30	25	0	7	1	281	16.7
PAUL KARIYA	ANAHEIM	82	39	62	101	17	40	11	2	4	0	429	9.1
PETER FORSBERG	COLORADO	78	30	67	97	27	108	9	2	7	0	217	13.8
JOE SAKIC	COLORADO	73	41	55	96	23	29	12	5	6	1	255	16.1
ALEXEI YASHIN	OTTAWA	82	44	50	94	16	54	19	0	5	1	337	13.1

ERIC LINDROS	PHILADELPHIA	71	40	53	93	35	120	10	1	2	3	242	16.5
THEOREN FLEURY	CGY-COL	75	40	53	93	26	86	8	3	5	2	301	13.3
JOHN LECLAIR	PHILADELPHIA	76	43	47	90	36	30	16	0	7	3	246	17.5
PAVOL DEMITRA	ST LOUIS	82	37	52	89	13	16	14	0	10	1	259	14.3
MARTIN STRAKA	PITTSBURGH	80	35	48	83	12	26	5	4	4	1	177	19.8
MATS SUNDIN	TORONTO	82	31	52	83	22	58	4	0	6	0	209	14.8
MIKE MODANO	DALLAS	77	34	47	81	29	44	6	4	7	1	224	15.2
JASON ALLISON	BOSTON	82	23	53	76	5	68	5	1	3	0	158	14.6
TONY AMONTE	CHICAGO	82	44	31	75	0	60	14	3	8	0	256	17.2
LUC ROBITAILLE	LOS ANGELES	82	39	35	74	1-	54	11	0	7	0	292	13.4
STEVE YZERMAN	DETROIT	80	29	45	74	8	42	13	2	4	0	231	12.6
R. BRIND'AMOUR	PHILADELPHIA	82	24	50	74	3	47	10	0	3	2	191	12.6
STEVE THOMAS	TORONTO	78	28	45	73	26	33	11	0	7	0	209	13.4
PETR SYKORA	NEW JERSEY	80	29	43	72	16	22	15	0	7	0	222	13.1
JEREMY ROENICK	PHOENIX	78	24	48	72	7	130	4	0	3	0	203	11.8
DMITRI KHRISTICH	BOSTON	79	29	42	71	11	48	13	1	6	1	144	20.1
ROBERT REICHEL	NYI-PHX	83	26	43	69	13-	54	8	1	4	1	236	11.0
KEITH TKACHUK	PHOENIX	68	36	32	68	22	151	11	2	7	1	258	14.0
MIROSLAV SATAN	BUFFALO	81	40	26	66	24	44	13	3	6	1	208	19.2
MARKUS NASLUND	VANCOUVER	80	36	30	66	13-	74	15	2	3	1	205	17.6

DEFENCEMEN SCORING LEADERS

PLAYER	TEAM	GP	G	A	PTS	+/-	PIM	PP	SH	GW	GT	S	PCTG
AL MACINNIS	ST LOUIS	82	20	42	62	33	70	11	1	2	2	314	6.4
N. LIDSTROM	DETROIT	81	14	43	57	14	14	6	2	3	0	205	6.8
RAY BOURQUE	BOSTON	81	10	47	57	7-	34	8	0	3	0	262	3.8
F. OLAUSSON	ANAHEIM	74	16	40	56	17	30	10	0	2	0	121	13.2
BRIAN LEETCH	NY RANGERS	82	13	42	55	7-	42	4	0	1	0	184	7.1
PHIL HOUSLEY	CALGARY	79	11	43	54	14	52	4	0	1	0	193	5.7
LARRY MURPHY	DETROIT	80	10	42	52	21	42	5	1	2	0	168	6.0
ERIC DESJARDINS	PHILADELPHIA	68	15	36	51	18	38	6	0	2	0	190	7.9
SERGEI ZUBOV	DALLAS	81	10	41	51	9	20	5	0	3	0	155	6.5
BORIS MIRONOV	EDM-CHI	75	11	38	49	13	131	5	0	4	1	173	6.4

INDIVIDUAL LEADERS

GOAL SCORING

NAME	TEAM	GP	G
TEEMU SELANNE	ANAHEIM	75	47
JAROMIR JAGR	PITTSBURGH	81	44

ASSISTS

NAME	TEAM	GP	A
JAROMIR JAGR	PITTSBURGH	81	83
PETER FORSBERG	COLORADO	78	67

NAME	TEAM	GP	G		NAME	TEAM	GP	PTS
TONY AMONTE	CHICAGO	82	44		PAUL KARIYA	ANAHEIM	82	62
ALEXEI YASHIN	OTTAWA	82	44		TEEMU SELANNE	ANAHEIM	75	60
JOHN LECLAIR	PHILADELPHIA	76	43		JOE SAKIC	COLORADO	73	55
JOE SAKIC	COLORADO	73	41		WAYNE GRETZKY	NY RANGERS	70	53
ERIC LINDROS	PHILADELPHIA	71	40		ERIC LINDROS	PHILADELPHIA	71	53
THEOREN FLEURY	CGY-COL	75	40		THEOREN FLEURY	CGY-COL	75	53
MIROSLAV SATAN	BUFFALO	81	40		JASON ALLISON	BOSTON	82	53
LUC ROBITAILLE	LOS ANGELES	82	39		MATS SUNDIN	TORONTO	82	52
PAUL KARIYA	ANAHEIM	82	39		PAVOL DEMITRA	ST LOUIS	82	52
ADAM GRAVES	NY RANGERS	82	38		ROD BRIND'AMOUR	PHILADELPHIA	82	50
SERGEI BEREZIN	TORONTO	76	37		ALEXEI YASHIN	OTTAWA	82	50
PAVOL DEMITRA	ST LOUIS	82	37		IGOR LARIONOV	DETROIT	75	49
KEITH TKACHUK	PHOENIX	68	36		JEREMY ROENICK	PHOENIX	78	48
MARKUS NASLUND	VANCOUVER	80	36		MARTIN STRAKA	PITTSBURGH	80	48
MARTIN STRAKA	PITTSBURGH	80	35		JOHN LECLAIR	PHILADELPHIA	76	47
MIKE MODANO	DALLAS	77	34		MIKE MODANO	DALLAS	77	47
					RAY BOURQUE	BOSTON	81	47

POWER PLAY GOALS

NAME	TEAM	GP	PP
TEEMU SELANNE	ANAHEIM	75	25
ALEXEI YASHIN	OTTAWA	82	19
ADRIAN AUCOIN	VANCOUVER	82	18
JOHN LECLAIR	PHILADELPHIA	76	16
BRETT HULL	DALLAS	60	15
MARKUS NASLUND	VANCOUVER	80	15
PETR SYKORA	NEW JERSEY	80	15

SHORT HAND GOALS

NAME	TEAM	GP	SH
JOE SAKIC	COLORADO	73	5
SCOTT PELLERIN	ST LOUIS	80	5
BRIAN ROLSTON	NEW JERSEY	82	5
MIKE MODANO	DALLAS	77	4
MARTIN STRAKA	PITTSBURGH	80	4
MAGNUS ARVEDSON	OTTAWA	80	4
RADEK DVORAK	FLORIDA	82	4

POWER PLAY ASSISTS

NAME	TEAM	GP	PPA
JAROMIR JAGR	PITTSBURGH	81	34
FREDRIK OLAUSSON	ANAHEIM	74	33
PAUL KARIYA	ANAHEIM	82	32
RAY BOURQUE	BOSTON	81	31
TEEMU SELANNE	ANAHEIM	75	29
PETER FORSBERG	COLORADO	78	28
WAYNE GRETZKY	NY RANGERS	70	27
DARRYL SYDOR	DALLAS	74	26
AL MACINNIS	ST LOUIS	82	26

SHORT HAND ASSISTS

NAME	TEAM	GP	SHA
MARK MESSIER	VANCOUVER	59	5
PETER FORSBERG	COLORADO	78	4
A. MOGILNY	VANCOUVER	59	3
ADAM OATES	WASHINGTON	59	3
ANDREW CASSELS	CALGARY	70	3
BENOIT HOGUE	T.B-DAL	74	3
SCOTT STEVENS	NEW JERSEY	75	3
KRIS DRAPER	DETROIT	80	3
ROBERT SVEHLA	FLORIDA	80	3

| BRIAN LEETCH | NY RANGERS | 82 | 25 |
| JASON ALLISON | BOSTON | 82 | 25 |

| DAVE SCATCHARD | VANCOUVER | 82 | 3 |

POWER PLAY POINTS

NAME	TEAM	GP	PPP
TEEMU SELANNE	ANAHEIM	75	54
JAROMIR JAGR	PITTSBURGH	81	44
FREDRIK OLAUSSON	ANAHEIM	74	43
PAUL KARIYA	ANAHEIM	82	43
ALEXEI YASHIN	OTTAWA	82	42
RAY BOURQUE	BOSTON	81	39
PETER FORSBERG	COLORADO	78	37
AL MACINNIS	ST LOUIS	82	37
DARRYL SYDOR	DALLAS	74	35
JOE SAKIC	COLORADO	73	34
ROD BRIND'AMOUR	PHILADELPHIA	82	32
ROBERT REICHEL	NYI-PHX	83	31

SHORT HAND POINTS

NAME	TEAM	GP	SHP
MARK MESSIER	VANCOUVER	59	7
JOE SAKIC	COLORADO	73	6
PETER FORSBERG	COLORADO	78	6
SCOTT PELLERIN	ST LOUIS	80	6
MARTIN STRAKA	PITTSBURGH	80	6
A. MOGILNY	VANCOUVER	59	5
THEOREN FLEURY	CGY-COL	75	5
YANIC PERREAULT	L.A-TOR	76	5
MIKE MODANO	DALLAS	77	5
MAGNUS ARVEDSON	OTTAWA	80	5
BRIAN ROLSTON	NEW JERSEY	82	5
DAVE SCATCHARD	VANCOUVER	82	5

GAME WINNING GOALS

NAME	TEAM	GP	GW
BRETT HULL	DALLAS	60	11
PAVOL DEMITRA	ST LOUIS	82	10
JOE NIEUWENDYK	DALLAS	67	8
BOBBY HOLIK	NEW JERSEY	78	8
SERGEI SAMSONOV	BOSTON	79	8
CLAUDE LEMIEUX	COLORADO	82	8
TONY AMONTE	CHICAGO	82	8
MICHAEL PECA	BUFFALO	82	8

GAME TYING GOALS

NAME	TEAM	GP	GT
SCOTT MELLANBY	FLORIDA	67	3
ERIC LINDROS	PHILADELPHIA	71	3
ROBERT LANG	PITTSBURGH	72	3
ERIC DAZE	CHICAGO	72	3
JOHN LECLAIR	PHILADELPHIA	76	3
CURTIS BROWN	BUFFALO	78	3

SHOTS

NAME	TEAM	GP	S
PAUL KARIYA	ANAHEIM	82	429
JAROMIR JAGR	PITTSBURGH	81	343
ALEXEI YASHIN	OTTAWA	82	337
AL MACINNIS	ST LOUIS	82	314
THEOREN FLEURY	CGY-COL	75	301

SHOOTING PERCENTAGE (MIN 82 SHOTS)

NAME	TEAM	GP	G	S	PCTG
DMITRI KHRISTICH	BOSTON	79	29	144	20.1
MARTIN STRAKA	PITTSBURGH	80	35	177	19.8
DIXON WARD	BUFFALO	78	20	101	19.8
ANSON CARTER	BOSTON	55	24	123	19.5
MIROSLAV SATAN	BUFFALO	81	40	208	19.2

PLUS/MINUS

NAME	TEAM	GP	+/-
ALEXANDER KARPOVTS	NYR-TOR	58	39
JOHN LECLAIR	PHILADELPHIA	76	36
ERIC LINDROS	PHILADELPHIA	71	35
MAGNUS ARVEDSON	OTTAWA	80	33
AL MACINNIS	ST LOUIS	82	33

CONSECUTIVE SCORING STREAKS

Goals scored in consecutive games

GM	PLAYER	TEAM	FROM	TO	G
8	MIROSLAV SATAN	BUFFALO	Dec 19	Jan 02	11
8	TEEMU SELANNE	ANAHEIM	Feb 17	Mar 05	10
7	ERIC LINDROS	PHILADELPHIA	Jan 07	Jan 21	7
6	BOBBY HOLIK	NEW JERSEY	Dec 05	Dec 18	7
6	RAY SHEPPARD	CAROLINA	Nov 14	Nov 25	7
6	TONY AMONTE	CHICAGO	Mar 10	Mar 21	7
6	ROB BROWN	PITTSBURGH	Mar 28	Apr 08	6
6	KIP MILLER	PITTSBURGH	Feb 07	Feb 17	6
6	MIROSLAV SATAN	BUFFALO	Feb 11	Feb 21	6

Assists awarded in consecutive games

GM	PLAYER	TEAM	FROM	TO	A
9	JOHN LECLAIR	PHILADELPHIA	Dec 31	Jan 21	11
8	JAROMIR JAGR	PITTSBURGH	Mar 10	Mar 25	11
7	ERIC LINDROS	PHILADELPHIA	Nov 14	Nov 29	15
7	PETER FORSBERG	COLORADO	Oct 15	Nov 02	11
7	PAUL KARIYA	ANAHEIM	Dec 06	Dec 21	11
7	TEEMU SELANNE	ANAHEIM	Mar 26	Apr 07	9
7	ALEXEI YASHIN	OTTAWA	Dec 28	Jan 08	9

7	PETER FORSBERG	COLORADO	Dec 26	Jan 06	8
7	ROD BRIND'AMOUR	PHILADELPHIA	Mar 14	Mar 30	7
7	ANDREI KOVALENKO	EDMONTON	Oct 14	Oct 31	7

Points gained in consecutive games

GM	PLAYER	TEAM	FROM	TO	G	A	PTS
18	ERIC LINDROS	PHILADELPHIA	Jan 07	Feb 18	14	21	35
17	TEEMU SELANNE	ANAHEIM	Feb 03	Mar 10	15	14	29
13	JAROMIR JAGR	PITTSBURGH	Dec 26	Jan 28	8	17	25
11	SERGEI FEDOROV	DETROIT	Mar 19	Apr 09	7	10	17
11	ALEXEI YASHIN	OTTAWA	Dec 28	Jan 16	7	9	16
11	PAUL KARIYA	ANAHEIM	Nov 06	Nov 27	7	9	16
10	KIP MILLER	PITTSBURGH	Jan 31	Feb 19	9	8	17
10	KEITH TKACHUK	PHOENIX	Oct 25	Nov 20	9	6	15
10	PETER FORSBERG	COLORADO	Dec 26	Jan 12	3	11	14
10	STEVE THOMAS	TORONTO	Feb 03	Feb 25	3	10	13
10	ALEXEI KOVALEV	NYR-PIT	Jan 28	Feb 15	6	6	12

INDIVIDUAL ROOKIE SCORING LEADERS

PLAYER	TEAM	GP	G	A	PTS	+/-	PIM	PP	SH	GW	GT	S	PCTG
MILAN HEJDUK	COLORADO	82	14	34	48	8	26	4	0	5	0	178	7.9
B. MORRISON	NEW JERSEY	76	13	33	46	4-	18	5	0	2	0	111	11.7
CHRIS DRURY	COLORADO	79	20	24	44	9	62	6	0	3	1	138	14.5
JAN HRDINA	PITTSBURGH	82	13	29	42	2-	40	3	0	2	0	94	13.8
MARK PARRISH	FLORIDA	73	24	13	37	6-	25	5	0	5	1	129	18.6
BILL MUCKALT	VANCOUVER	73	16	20	36	9-	98	4	2	1	0	119	13.4
MARIAN HOSSA	OTTAWA	60	15	15	30	18	37	1	0	2	2	124	12.1
A. KOROLYUK	SAN JOSE	55	12	18	30	3	26	2	0	0	1	96	12.5
V. LECAVALIER	TAMPA BAY	82	13	15	28	19-	23	2	0	2	1	125	10.4
V. SHARIFIJANOV	NEW JERSEY	53	11	16	27	11	28	1	0	2	0	71	15.5

RECORD OF GOALTENDERS

All goals aginst a team in any game are charged to the goaltender of that game for purposes of awarding the Bill Jennings trophy.

Won-Lost-Tied record is based upon which goaltender was playing when the winning or tying goal was scored.

Overall ranking is based on goals against average, (minimum of 1,140 minutes played)

Empty-net goals are not counted in personal averages but are included in the team total.

(GPI) games played in | (MINS) minutes played | (AVG) 60 minute average
(ENG) empty-net goals against | (SO) shutouts | (GA) goals against
(SA) shots against | (SV %) save percentage | (RNK) overall ranking

RNK	SW#	GOALTENDER	GPI	MINS	AVG	W	L	T	EN	SO	GA	SA	SV %	G	A	PIM
4	20	ED BELFOUR	61	3,536	1.99	35	15	9	0	5	117	1,373	.915	0	0	26
	30	*E. FERNANDE	1	60	2.00	0	1	0	0	0	2	29	.931	0	0	0
5	1	ROMAN TUREK	26	1,382	2.08	16	3	3	1	1	48	562	.915	0	0	0
DALLAS TOTALS			82	4,986	2.02	51	19	12	1	6	168	1,965	.915			
2	39	DOMINIK HASEK	64	3,817	1.87	30	18	14	2	9	119	1,877	.937	0	0	14
	43	*MARTIN BIRON	6	281	2.14	1	2	1	1	0	10	120	.917	0	0	0
	30	D. ROLOSON	18	911	2.77	6	8	2	1	1	42	460	.909	0	0	4
BUFFALO TOTALS			82	5,020	2.09	37	28	17	4	10	175	2,461	.929			
1	31	RON TUGNUTT	43	2,508	1.79	22	10	8	2	3	75	1,005	.925	0	0	0
17	1	D. RHODES	45	2,480	2.44	22	13	7	1	3	101	1,060	.905	1	1	4
OTTAWA TOTALS			82	4,999	2.15	44	23	15	3	6	179	2,068	.913			
3	34	BYRON DAFOE	68	4,001	1.99	32	23	11	3	10	133	1,800	.926	0	2	25
	35	ROBBIE TALLAS	17	987	2.61	7	7	2	2	1	43	421	.898	0	0	0
BOSTON TOTALS			82	5,001	2.17	39	30	13	5	11	181	2,226	.919			
	30	SEAN GAUTHIER	1	3	.00	0	0	0	0	0	0	2	1.000	0	0	0
9	31	STEVE SHIELDS	37	2,162	2.22	15	11	8	1	4	80	1,011	.921	0	1	6
10	29	MIKE VERNON	49	2,831	2.27	16	22	10	3	4	107	1,200	.911	0	0	8
SAN JOSE TOTALS			82	5,016	2.28	31	33	18	4	8	191	2,217	.914			

7	34	J. VANBIESBROUC	62	3,712	2.18	27	18	15	4	6	135	1,380	.902	0	1	12
23	27	RON HEXTALL	23	1,235	2.53	10	7	4	0	0	52	464	.888	0	2	2
	49	*J-M. PELLETI	1	60	5.00	0	1	0	0	0	5	29	.828	0	0	0
PHILIDELPHIA TOTALS			82	5025	2.34	37	26	19	4	7	196	1877	.896			

RON HEXTALL and JOHN VANBIESBROUCK shared a shutout vs CAR on Jan 9, 1999

11	30	M. BRODEUR	70	4,239	2.29	39	21	10	4	4	162	1,728	.906	0	4	4
	31	CHRIS TERRERI	12	726	2.48	8	3	1	0	1	30	294	.898	0	1	0
NEW JERSEY TOTALS			82	4,986	2.36	47	24	11	4	5	196	2,026	.903			

6	35	N. KHABIBULI	63	3,657	2.13	32	23	7	6	8	130	1,681	.923	0	0	8
29	30	M. SHTALENKO	4	243	2.22	1	2	1	1	0	9	104	.913	0	0	0
	28	JIM WAITE	16	898	2.74	6	5	4	0	1	41	390	.895	0	0	2
	42	*ROBERT ESCHE	3	130	3.23	0	1	0	0	0	7	50	.860	0	0	0
	31	*SCOTT LANGKOW	1	35	5.14	0	0	0	0	0	3	17	.824	0	0	0
PHOENIX TOTALS			82	4,985	2.37	39	31	12	7	9	197	2,249	.912			

8	1	ARTURS IRBE	62	3,643	2.22	27	20	12	3	6	135	1,753	.923	0	0	10
33	37	TREVOR KIDD	25	1,358	2.70	7	10	6	3	2	61	640	.905	0	0	0
CAROLINA TOTALS			82	5,022	2.41	34	30	18	6	8	202	2,399	.916			

42	40	BILL RANFORD	4	244	1.97	3	0	1	0	0	8	98	.918	0	0	0
	38	*N. MARACLE	16	821	2.27	6	5	2	1	0	31	379	.918	0	0	0
16	30	CHRIS OSGOOD	63	3,691	2.42	34	25	4	4	3	149	1,654	.910	0	3	8
	31	KEVIN HODSON	4	175	3.09	0	2	0	0	0	9	79	.886	0	0	0
DETROIT TOTALS			82	4,962	2.44	43	32	7	5	3	202	2,215	.909			

12	33	PATRICK ROY	61	3,648	2.29	32	19	8	4	5	139	1,673	.917	0	2	28
	30	*MARC DENIS	4	217	2.49	1	1	1	0	0	9	110	.918	0	0	0
	1	C. BILLINGTON	21	1,086	2.87	11	8	1	1	0	52	492	.894	0	0	2
COLORADO TOTALS			82	4,974	2.47	44	28	10	5	5	205	2,280	.910			

15	31	GUY HEBERT	69	4,083	2.42	31	29	9	3	6	165	2,114	.922	0	1	0
	30	D. ROUSSEL	18	884	2.51	4	5	4	1	1	37	478	.923	0	0	0
ANAHEIM TOTALS			82	4,990	2.48	35	34	13	4	7	206	2,596	.921			

	39	F. CHABOT	11	430	2.23	1	3	0	0	0	16	188	.915	0	0	2
20	31	JEFF HACKETT	53	3,091	2.27	24	20	9	2	5	117	1,360	.914	0	1	6
32	41	J. THIBAULT	10	529	2.61	3	4	2	0	1	23	250	.908	0	0	0
	60	*J. THEODORE	18	913	3.29	4	12	0	1	1	50	406	.877	0	0	0
MONTREAL TOTALS			82	4,988	2.51	32	39	11	3	7	209	2,207	.905			
	1	*B. JOHNSON	6	286	2.10	3	2	0	0	0	10	127	.921	0	0	0
13	29	J. MCLENNAN	33	1,763	2.38	13	14	4	3	3	70	640	.891	0	0	0
18	31	GRANT FUHR	39	2,193	2.44	16	11	8	1	2	89	827	.892	0	0	12
	30	*RICH PARENT	10	519	2.54	4	3	1	1	1	22	193	.886	0	0	2
	35	JIM CAREY	4	202	3.86	1	2	0	0	0	13	76	.829	0	0	0
ST. LOUIS TOTALS			82	4,989	2.51	37	32	13	5	6	209	1,868	.888			
	40	MIKE ROSATI	1	28	.00	1	0	0	0	0	0	12	1.000	0	0	0
21	31	R. TABARACCI	23	1,193	2.51	4	12	3	3	2	50	530	.906	0	0	2
27	37	OLAF KOLZIG	64	3,586	2.58	26	31	3	5	4	154	1,538	.900	0	2	19
	1	*MARTIN BROCHU	2	120	3.00	0	2	0	0	0	6	55	.891	0	0	2
WASHINGTON TOTALS			82	4,959	2.64	31	45	6	8	6	218	2,143	.898			
14	1	*JAMIE STORR	28	1,525	2.40	12	12	2	3	4	61	724	.916	0	1	6
	32	*M. LEGACE	17	899	2.60	2	9	2	5	0	39	439	.911	0	1	0
28	35	STEPHANE FISET	42	2,403	2.60	18	21	1	2	3	104	1,217	.915	0	0	2
	31	*RYAN BACH	3	108	4.44	0	3	0	0	0	8	66	.879	0	0	0
LOS ANGELES TOTALS			82	4,960	2.69	32	45	5	10	8	222	2,456	.910			

STEPHANE FISET and MANNY LEGACE shared a shutout vs N.J on Oct 28, 1998

	30	*J-S. AUBIN	17	756	2.22	4	3	6	0	2	28	304	.908	0	0	0
24	35	TOM BARRASSO	43	2,306	2.55	19	16	3	4	4	98	993	.901	0	3	20
37	1	*PETER SKUDRA	37	1,914	2.79	15	11	5	6	3	89	822	.892	0	0	2
PITTSBURGH TOTALS			82	5,011	2.69	38	30	14	10	9	225	2,129	.894			
26	35	TOMMY SALO	13	700	2.31	8	2	2	0	0	27	279	.903	0	0	0
29	30	M. SHTALENKO	34	1,819	2.67	12	17	3	2	3	81	782	.896	0	0	2
36	30	BOB ESSENSA	39	2,091	2.75	12	14	6	2	0	96	974	.901	0	1	0
	29	*S. PASSMORE	6	362	2.82	1	4	1	1	0	17	183	.907	0	1	2
EDMONTON TOTALS			82	4,997	2.71	33	37	12	5	3	226	2,223	.898			

			GP	MIN	GAA	W	L	T	EN	SO	GA	SA	SV%			
31	31	SEAN BURKE	59	3,402	2.66	21	24	14	3	3	151	1,624	.907	0	4	27
34	1	KIRK MCLEAN	30	1,597	2.74	9	10	4	1	2	73	727	.900	0	0	2
FLORIDA TOTALS			82	5,017	2.73	30	34	18	4	5	228	2,355	.903			
30	35	MIKE RICHTER	68	3,878	2.63	27	30	8	6	4	170	1,898	.910	0	0	0
	39	*DAN CLOUTIER	22	1,097	2.68	6	8	3	2	0	49	570	.914	0	0	2
NY RANGERS TOTALS			82	4,996	2.73	33	38	11	8	4	227	2,476	.908			
25	31	CURTIS JOSEPH	67	4,001	2.56	35	24	7	4	3	171	1,903	.910	0	5	6
	30	GLENN HEALY	9	546	2.97	6	3	0	1	0	27	257	.895	0	0	0
	28	FELIX POTVIN	5	299	3.81	3	2	0	1	0	19	142	.866	0	0	0
	35	JEFF REESE	2	106	4.53	1	1	0	0	0	8	51	.843	0	0	0
TORONTO TOTALS			82	4,972	2.79	45	30	7	6	3	231	2,359	.902			
19	40	F. BRATHWAITE	28	1,663	2.45	11	9	7	3	1	68	796	.915	0	2	2
	30	*TYLER MOSS	11	550	2.51	3	7	0	0	0	23	295	.922	0	1	0
22	31	KEN WREGGET	27	1,590	2.53	10	12	4	2	1	67	712	.906	0	1	8
	47	*J GIGUERE	15	860	3.21	6	7	1	2	0	46	447	.897	0	1	4
	35	A. TREFILOV	4	162	4.07	0	3	0	0	0	11	84	.869	0	0	0
	1	*T. GARNER	3	139	5.18	0	2	0	0	0	12	74	.838	0	0	0
CALGARY TOTALS			82	4,990	2.81	30	40	12	7	2	234	2,415	.903			
26	35	TOMMY SALO	51	3,018	2.62	17	26	7	5	5	132	1,368	.904	0	0	12
	1	*M. COUSINEAU	6	293	2.87	0	4	0	0	0	14	119	.882	0	0	0
	30	WADE FLAHERTY	20	1,048	3.03	5	11	2	3	0	53	491	.892	0	0	4
	28	FELIX POTVIN	11	606	3.66	2	7	1	0	0	37	345	.893	0	0	0
NY ISLANDERS TOTALS			82	4,990	2.93	24	48	10	8	5	244	2,331	.895			
32	41	J. THIBAULT	52	3,014	2.71	21	26	5	6	4	136	1,435	.905	0	1	2
35	30	M. FITZPATRICK	27	1,403	2.74	6	8	6	2	0	64	682	.906	0	1	8
20	31	JEFF HACKETT	10	524	3.78	2	6	1	3	0	33	256	.871	0	0	6
	35	ANDREI TREFILOV	1	25	9.60	0	1	0	0	0	4	20	.800	0	0	0
CHICAGO TOTALS			82	4,989	2.98	29	41	12	11	4	248	2,404	.897			
38	30	GARTH SNOW	65	3,501	2.93	20	31	8	5	6	171	1,715	.900	0	1	34
	31	COREY HIRSCH	20	919	3.13	3	8	3	0	1	48	435	.890	0	0	0
	35	*KEVIN WEEKES	11	532	3.83	0	8	1	0	0	34	257	.868	0	0	0
VANCOUVER TOTALS			82	4,981	3.11	23	47	12	5	7	258	2,412	.893			

39	29	*T. VOKOUN	37	1,954	2.95	12	18	4	4	1	96	1,041	.908	0	1	6
40	1	MIKE DUNHAM	44	2,472	3.08	16	23	3	3	1	127	1,387	.908	0	0	4
	35	ERIC FICHAUD	9	447	3.22	0	6	0	1	0	24	229	.895	0	0	0
	30	*CHRIS MASON	3	69	5.22	0	0	0	0	0	6	44	.864	0	0	0
NASHVILLE TOTALS			82	4,964	3.15	28	47	7	8	2	261	2,709	.904			
	1	*ZAC BIERK	1	59	2.03	0	1	0	0	0	2	21	.905	0	0	0
	31	KEVIN HODSON	5	238	2.77	2	1	1	0	0	11	118	.907	0	0	0
	93	DAREN PUPPA	13	691	2.87	5	6	1	1	2	33	350	.906	0	1	0
	35	*D. WILKINSON	5	253	3.08	1	3	1	0	0	13	128	.898	0	0	0
41	32	COREY SCHWAB	40	2,146	3.52	8	25	3	2	0	126	1,153	.891	0	4	4
42	40	BILL RANFORD	32	1,568	3.90	3	18	3	2	1	102	858	.881	0	0	2
TAMPA BAY TOTALS			82	4,974	3.52	1,9	54	9	5	4	292	2,633	.889			

COREY SCHWAB and KEVIN HODSON shared a shutout vs BOS on Apr 8, 1999

GOALTENDING LEADERS (MIN. 25 GPI)

Goals Against Average

GOALTENDER	TEAM	GPI	MINS	GA	AVG
RON TUGNUTT	OTTAWA	43	2508	75	1.79
DOMINIK HASEK	BUFFALO	64	3817	119	1.87
BYRON DAFOE	BOSTON	68	4001	133	1.99
ED BELFOUR	DALLAS	61	3536	117	1.99
ROMAN TUREK	DALLAS	26	1382	48	2.08

Wins

GOALTENDER	TEAM	GPI	MINS	W	L	T
MARTIN BRODEUR	NEW JERSEY	70	4,239	39	21	10
ED BELFOUR	DALLAS	61	3,536	35	15	9
CURTIS JOSEPH	TORONTO	67	4,001	35	24	7
CHRIS OSGOOD	DETROIT	63	3,691	34	25	4
PATRICK ROY	COLORADO	61	3,648	32	19	8
NIKOLAI KHABIBULIN	PHOENIX	63	3,657	32	23	7
BYRON DAFOE	BOSTON	68	4,001	32	23	11

Save Percentage

GOALTENDER	TEAM	GPI	MINS	GA	SA	SPCTG	W	L	T
DOMINIK HASEK	BUFFALO	64	3,817	119	1,877	.937	30	18	14
BYRON DAFOE	BOSTON	68	4,001	133	1,800	.926	32	23	11

RON TUGNUTT	OTTAWA	43	2508	75	1005	.925	22	10	8
NIKOLAI KHABIBULIN	PHOENIX	63	3657	130	1681	.923	32	23	7
ARTURS IRBE	CAROLINA	62	3643	135	1753	.923	27	20	12

Shutouts

GOALTENDER	TEAM	GPI	MINS	SO	W	L	T
BYRON DAFOE	BOSTON	68	4001	10	32	23	11
DOMINIK HASEK	BUFFALO	64	3817	9	30	18	14
NIKOLAI KHABIBULIN	PHOENIX	63	3657	8	32	23	7
GARTH SNOW	VANCOUVER	65	3501	6	20	31	8
ARTURS IRBE	CAROLINA	62	3643	6	27	20	12
JOHN VANBIESBROUCK	PHILADELPHIA	62	3712	6	27	18	15
GUY HEBERT	ANAHEIM	69	4083	6	31	29	9

TEAMS' POWER PLAY RECORD

(ADV) Total advantages (PPGF) Power-play goals for
(PCTG) Arrived by dividing number of power-play goals by total advantages

	HOME					ROAD					OVER ALL				
	TEAM	GP	ADV	PPGF	PCTG	TEAM	GP	ADV	PPGF	PCTG	TEAM	GP	ADV	PPGF	PCTG
1	ANA	41	192	49	25.5	NYR	41	153	35	22.9	ANA	82	378	83	22.0
2	DAL	41	213	47	22.1	PIT	41	174	36	20.7	NYR	82	348	71	20.4
3	COL	41	207	44	21.3	STL	41	146	28	19.2	STL	82	301	61	20.3
4	STL	41	155	33	21.3	WSH	41	150	28	18.7	N.J	82	304	60	19.7
5	N.J	41	152	32	21.1	N.J	41	152	28	18.4	COL	82	375	71	18.9
6	PHI	41	189	39	20.6	ANA	41	186	34	18.3	DAL	82	393	74	18.8
7	MTL	41	175	34	19.4	BOS	41	187	34	18.2	PIT	82	363	65	17.9
8	NYI	41	176	34	19.3	VAN	41	175	29	16.6	BOS	82	368	65	17.7
9	NYR	41	195	36	18.5	COL	41	168	27	16.1	WSH	82	301	52	17.3
10	DET	41	211	38	18.0	CGY	41	188	30	16.0	PHI	82	386	65	16.8
11	BOS	41	181	31	17.1	CHI	41	147	23	15.6	DET	82	415	67	16.1
12	WSH	41	151	24	15.9	S.J	41	200	30	15.0	VAN	82	358	57	15.9
13	FLA	41	185	29	15.7	DAL	41	180	27	15.0	NYI	82	341	54	15.8
14	VAN	41	183	28	15.3	TOR	41	193	28	14.5	CHI	82	335	50	14.9
15	PIT	41	189	29	15.3	OTT	41	174	25	14.4	OTT	82	397	59	14.9
16	OTT	41	223	34	15.2	DET	41	204	29	14.2	MTL	82	344	50	14.5
17	EDM	41	207	31	15.0	EDM	41	231	32	13.9	TOR	82	367	53	14.4
18	T.B	41	160	24	15.0	BUF	41	182	25	13.7	EDM	82	438	63	14.4

19	L.A	41	177	26	14.7	PHI	41	197	26	13.2	CGY	82	357	51	14.3
20	TOR	41	174	25	14.4	T.B	41	150	19	12.7	T.B	82	310	43	13.9
21	CHI	41	188	27	14.4	PHX	41	165	21	12.7	BUF	82	363	49	13.5
22	BUF	41	181	24	13.3	NYI	41	165	20	12.1	FLA	82	380	51	13.4
23	NSH	41	183	24	13.1	FLA	41	195	22	11.3	S.J	82	399	53	13.3
24	CGY	41	169	21	12.4	L.A	41	150	17	11.3	L.A	82	327	43	13.1
25	S.J	41	199	23	11.6	NSH	41	141	16	11.3	NSH	82	324	40	12.3
26	PHX	41	177	20	11.3	CAR	41	192	21	10.9	PHX	82	342	41	12.0
27	CAR	41	190	21	11.1	MTL	41	169	16	9.5	CAR	82	382	42	11.0
		1,107	4,982	827	16.6		1,107	4,714	706	15.0		1,107	9,696	1,533	15.8

TEAMS' PENALTY KILLING RECORD

(TSH) Total times short-handed (PPGA) Power-play goals against

(PCTG) Arrived by dividing (times short minus power-play goals against) by (times short)

HOME						ROAD						OVER ALL				
	TEAM	GP	TSH	PPGA	PCTG	TEAM	GP	TSH	PPGA	PCTG	TEAM	GP	TSH	PPGA	PCTG
1	BOS	41	145	11	92.4	MTL	41	169	20	88.2	BOS	82	305	33	89.2
2	NYR	41	180	19	89.4	STL	41	193	23	88.1	STL	82	387	47	87.9
3	OTT	41	166	20	88.0	DET	41	185	24	87.0	DET	82	355	45	87.3
4	PHX	41	174	21	87.9	BUF	41	204	27	86.8	MTL	82	344	44	87.2
5	DET	41	170	21	87.6	BOS	41	160	22	86.3	PHX	82	348	45	87.1
6	STL	41	194	24	87.6	DAL	41	153	21	86.3	DAL	82	319	43	86.5
7	S.J	41	215	27	87.4	PHX	41	174	24	86.2	BUF	82	399	55	86.2
8	DAL	41	166	22	86.7	L.A	41	155	22	85.8	OTT	82	317	44	86.1
9	CAR	41	156	21	86.5	COL	41	189	27	85.7	L.A	82	330	47	85.8
10	MTL	41	175	24	86.3	N.J	41	173	25	85.5	NYR	82	336	48	85.7
11	ANA	41	194	27	86.1	CAR	41	190	30	84.2	N.J	82	325	47	85.5
12	WSH	41	163	23	85.9	EDM	41	202	32	84.2	CAR	82	346	51	85.3
13	VAN	41	210	30	85.7	OTT	41	151	24	84.1	S.J	82	407	61	85.0
14	L.A	41	175	25	85.7	PHI	41	185	31	83.2	ANA	82	387	60	84.5
15	BUF	41	195	28	85.6	FLA	41	202	34	83.2	WSH	82	353	55	84.4
16	N.J	41	152	22	85.5	WSH	41	190	32	83.2	PHI	82	333	53	84.1
17	PIT	41	149	22	85.2	ANA	41	193	33	82.9	COL	82	386	63	83.7
18	NYI	41	168	25	85.1	S.J	41	192	34	82.3	NYI	82	363	60	83.5
19	PHI	41	148	22	85.1	NYI	41	195	35	82.1	VAN	82	450	77	82.9
20	T.B	41	183	29	84.2	TOR	41	167	30	82.0	T.B	82	387	68	82.4
21	NSH	41	175	31	82.3	NYR	41	156	29	81.4	EDM	82	374	67	82.1
22	COL	41	197	36	81.7	T.B	41	204	39	80.9	FLA	82	370	67	81.9

23	CHI	41	191	37	80.6	CGY	41	211	41	80.6	PIT	82	302	56	81.5
24	FLA	41	168	33	80.4	VAN	41	240	47	80.4	TOR	82	325	64	80.3
25	EDM	41	172	35	79.7	CHI	41	214	43	79.9	CHI	82	405	80	80.2
26	CGY	41	175	37	78.9	PIT	41	153	34	77.8	CGY	82	386	78	79.8
27	TOR	41	158	34	78.5	NSH	41	182	44	75.8	NSH	82	357	75	79.0
		1,107	4714	706	85.0		1,107	4,982	827	83.4		1,107	9,696	1,533	84.2

SHORT HAND GOALS FOR

	HOME			ROAD			OVER ALL		
	TEAM	GP	SHGF	TEAM	GP	SHGF	TEAM	GP	SHGF
1	EDM	41	7	VAN	41	11	VAN	82	17
2	PIT	41	7	DET	41	9	DET	82	14
3	VAN	41	6	CGY	41	9	CGY	82	12
4	L.A	41	6	T.B	41	7	L.A	82	12
5	FLA	41	5	L.A	41	6	T.B	82	11
6	TOR	41	5	FLA	41	5	FLA	82	10
7	MTL	41	5	NYI	41	5	PIT	82	10
8	CHI	41	5	WSH	41	5	S.J	82	8
9	DET	41	5	S.J	41	4	MTL	82	8
10	NSH	41	4	NYR	41	4	NYI	82	8
11	COL	41	4	N.J	41	4	WSH	82	8
12	S.J	41	4	PHX	41	4	CHI	82	8
13	PHX	41	4	PHI	41	3	EDM	82	8
14	T.B	41	4	STL	41	3	PHX	82	8
15	BUF	41	4	PIT	41	3	NYR	82	7
16	STL	41	4	ANA	41	3	STL	82	7
17	NYR	41	3	OTT	41	3	TOR	82	7
18	CGY	41	3	CAR	41	3	N.J	82	7
19	BOS	41	3	CHI	41	3	NSH	82	7
20	NYI	41	3	DAL	41	3	COL	82	7
21	WSH	41	3	COL	41	3	ANA	82	6
22	DAL	41	3	MTL	41	3	OTT	82	6
23	N.J	41	3	NSH	41	3	DAL	82	6
24	OTT	41	3	BUF	41	2	BUF	82	6
25	ANA	41	3	TOR	41	2	CAR	82	5
26	CAR	41	2	EDM	41	1	PHI	82	4
27	PHI	41	1	BOS	41	0	BOS	82	3
		1,107	109		1,107	111		1,107	220

SHORT HAND GOALS AGAINST

	HOME			ROAD			OVER ALL		
	TEAM	GP	SHGA	TEAM	GP	SHGA	TEAM	GP	SHGA
1	CAR	41	1	PHI	41	0	S.J	82	4
2	PHX	41	1	STL	41	1	STL	82	4
3	N.J	41	1	DAL	41	1	DAL	82	4
4	DET	41	1	S.J	41	2	N.J	82	5
5	S.J	41	2	CGY	41	2	PHX	82	5
6	ANA	41	2	BUF	41	3	CGY	82	6
7	BOS	41	3	TOR	41	3	TOR	82	6
8	TOR	41	3	CHI	41	3	CAR	82	6
9	NYI	41	3	T.B	41	4	PHI	82	7
10	WSH	41	3	NYR	41	4	DET	82	7
11	DAL	41	3	N.J	41	4	NYI	82	7
12	STL	41	3	NYI	41	4	WSH	82	7
13	CGY	41	4	COL	41	4	ANA	82	7
14	MTL	41	4	WSH	41	4	BUF	82	7
15	NSH	41	4	VAN	41	4	NYR	82	9
16	BUF	41	4	PHX	41	4	BOS	82	9
17	NYR	41	5	PIT	41	5	VAN	82	9
18	FLA	41	5	ANA	41	5	T.B	82	10
19	EDM	41	5	L.A	41	5	MTL	82	10
20	VAN	41	5	CAR	41	5	CHI	82	10
21	T.B	41	6	EDM	41	5	NSH	82	10
22	L.A	41	6	DET	41	6	EDM	82	10
23	OTT	41	6	FLA	41	6	FLA	82	11
24	CHI	41	7	BOS	41	6	L.A	82	11
25	PHI	41	7	MTL	41	6	COL	82	12
26	COL	41	8	NSH	41	6	OTT	82	13
27	PIT	41	9	OTT	41	7	PIT	82	14
		1,107	111		1,107	109		1,107	220

TEAM STREAKS
Consecutive Wins

GM	TEAM	FROM	TO
12	COLORADO	JAN. 10	FEB. 7
10	PITTSBURGH	JAN. 28	FEB. 15

8	PHOENIX	NOV. 11	NOV. 28
8	DETROIT	MAR. 24	APR. 7
7	ANAHEIM	FEB. 20	MAR. 7

Consecutive Undefeated

GM	TEAM	W	T	FROM	TO
15	DALLAS	12	3	DEC. 6	JAN. 6
15	PHILADELPHIA	10	5	DEC. 12	JAN. 13
14	PHOENIX	12	2	OCT. 25	NOV. 28
12	COLORADO	12	0	JAN. 10	FEB. 7
11	OTTAWA	8	3	DEC. 28	JAN. 16
10	PITTSBURGH	10	0	JAN. 28	FEB. 15

Consecutive Home Wins

GM	TEAM	FROM	TO
9	PITTSBURGH	JAN. 28	FEB. 22
9	CHICAGO	MAR. 17	APR. 17
7	TORONTO	NOV. 11	DEC. 2
7	BUFFALO	NOV. 14	DEC. 18
7	PHOENIX	NOV. 14	DEC. 20
7	OTTAWA	FEB. 13	MAR. 8
7	DETROIT	MAR. 24	APR. 7

Consecutive Home Ties - Minimum 3 games

GM	TEAM	FROM	TO
3	CAROLINA	OCT. 10	OCT. 17
3	NEW JERSEY	NOV. 21	DEC. 8
3	MONTREAL	DEC. 14	DEC. 21

Consecutive Home Undefeated - Minimum 5 games

GM	TEAM	W	T	FROM	TO
11	PHOENIX	10	1	OCT. 15	DEC. 20
11	PITTSBURGH	9	2	JAN. 28	MAR. 5
10	BUFFALO	9	1	OCT. 30	DEC. 18

10	NEW JERSEY	7	3	OCT. 31	DEC. 16
10	COLORADO	8	2	MAR. 18	APR. 18
9	CHICAGO	9	0	MAR. 17	APR. 17
8	MONTREAL	4	4	DEC. 14	JAN. 18

Consecutive Road Wins - Minimum 3 games

GM	TEAM	FROM	TO
7	COLORADO	JAN. 10	FEB. 7
7	DALLAS	JAN. 13	FEB. 23
6	PHOENIX	OCT. 26	NOV. 28
6	ST LOUIS	FEB. 1	MAR. 2
5	NEW JERSEY	JAN. 20	FEB. 4
5	NEW JERSEY	MAR. 3	MAR. 17
5	OTTAWA	MAR. 19	APR. 3

Consecutive Road Undefeated - Minimum 5 games

GM	TEAM	W	T	FROM	TO
10	PHILADELPHIA	7	3	DEC. 8	JAN. 18
10	COLORADO	8	2	JAN. 10	MAR. 3
10	DALLAS	8	2	JAN. 12	MAR. 4
9	DALLAS	7	2	DEC. 6	JAN. 1

TEAM PENALTY INFORMATION

(GP) Games played
(PEN) Total penalty minutes including bench minutes
(BMI) Total Bench minor minutes
(AVG) Average penalty minutes/game arrived by dividing total penalty minutes by games played

MINUTES

TEAM	GP	PEN	BMI	AVG
OTT	82	892	12	10.9
PIT	82	977	12	11.9
PHI	82	1075	12	13.1
NYR	82	1087	14	13.3
TOR	82	1095	16	13.4

DAL	82	1108	8	13.5
NYI	82	1111	22	13.5
CAR	82	1158	10	14.1
BOS	82	1182	6	14.4
DET	82	1202	10	14.7
WSH	82	1281	6	15.6
MTL	82	1299	14	15.8
STL	82	1308	6	16.0
T.B	82	1316	10	16.0
ANA	82	1323	14	16.1
N.J	82	1355	14	16.5
EDM	82	1373	12	16.7
CGY	82	1389	8	16.9
L.A	82	1383	14	16.9
PHX	82	1412	12	17.2
NSH	82	1420	14	17.3
S.J	82	1423	10	17.4
FLA	82	1522	18	18.6
BUF	82	1561	16	19.0
COL	82	1619	14	19.7
VAN	82	1764	16	21.5
CHI	82	1807	8	22.0
TOT	1107	35442	328	32.0

TEAMS' OVERTIME RECORDS

	HOME						ROAD						OVERALL					
	GP	W	L	T	PTS	PCTG	GP	W	L	T	PTS	PCTG	GP	W	L	T	PTS	PCTG
TOR	9	4	0	5	13	.722	5	2	1	2	6	.600	14	6	1	7	19	.679
PIT	14	4	0	10	18	.643	8	3	1	4	10	.625	22	7	1	14	28	.636
L.A	6	2	1	3	7	.583	6	3	1	2	8	.667	12	5	2	5	15	.625
COL	6	0	0	6	6	.500	6	2	0	4	8	.667	12	2	0	10	14	.583
N.J	11	2	1	8	12	.545	4	1	0	3	5	.625	15	3	1	11	17	.567
CGY	9	2	1	6	10	.556	7	1	0	6	8	.571	16	3	1	12	18	.563
DAL	5	1	0	4	6	.600	11	2	1	8	12	.545	16	3	1	12	18	.563
NYR	10	3	2	5	11	.550	9	2	1	6	10	.556	19	5	3	11	21	.553
DET	5	2	1	2	6	.600	5	0	0	5	5	.500	10	2	1	7	11	.550
PHX	7	1	1	5	7	.500	8	1	0	7	9	.563	15	2	1	12	16	.533

BUF	9	1	2	6	8	.444	14	2	1	11	15	.536	23	3	3	17	23	.500
BOS	12	2	1	9	13	.542	5	0	1	4	4	.400	17	2	2	13	17	.500
STL	6	0	0	6	6	.500	9	1	1	7	9	.500	15	1	1	13	15	.500
PHI	12	0	1	11	11	.458	12	2	2	8	12	.500	24	2	3	19	23	.479
S.J	11	0	2	9	9	.409	10	1	0	9	11	.550	21	1	2	18	20	.476
FLA	9	1	1	7	9	.500	12	0	1	11	11	.458	21	1	2	18	20	.476
OTT	8	0	0	8	8	.500	10	1	2	7	9	.450	18	1	2	15	17	.472
CHI	6	0	2	4	4	.333	9	1	0	8	10	.556	15	1	2	12	14	.467
VAN	6	0	0	6	6	.500	7	0	1	6	6	.429	13	0	1	12	12	.462
T.B	4	0	0	4	4	.500	8	1	2	5	7	.438	12	1	2	9	11	.458
WSH	5	1	2	2	4	.400	6	1	1	4	6	.500	11	2	3	6	10	.455
EDM	9	0	4	5	5	.278	11	3	1	7	13	.591	20	3	5	12	18	.450
NSH	5	0	1	4	4	.400	5	1	1	3	5	.500	10	1	2	7	9	.450
ANA	9	1	2	6	8	.444	8	0	1	7	7	.438	17	1	3	13	15	.441
CAR	12	1	2	9	11	.458	12	0	3	9	9	.375	24	1	5	18	20	.417
MTL	6	0	1	5	5	.417	9	0	3	6	6	.333	15	0	4	11	11	.367
NYI	11	0	4	7	7	.318	6	1	2	3	5	.417	17	1	6	10	12	.353
TOT	222	28	32	162	218	.491	222	32	28	162	226	.509	222	60	60	162	444	1.000

TEAM PLAYOFF RECORDS

	GP	W	L	GF	GA	PCTG
DALLAS	23	16	7	64	44	.696
BUFFALO	21	14	7	59	49	.667
COLORADO	19	11	8	56	54	.579
TORONTO	17	9	8	43	46	.529
DETROIT	10	6	4	31	27	.600
BOSTON	12	6	6	30	27	.500
PITTSBURGH	13	6	7	35	36	.462
ST LOUIS	13	6	7	31	33	.462
NEW JERSEY	7	3	4	18	21	.429
PHOENIX	7	3	4	16	19	.429
PHILADELPHIA	6	2	4	11	9	.333
SAN JOSE	6	2	4	17	19	.333
CAROLINA	6	2	4	10	16	.333
EDMONTON	4	0	4	7	11	.000
OTTAWA	4	0	4	6	12	.000
ANAHEIM	4	0	4	6	17	.000

TEAMS' PLAYOFF HOME/ROAD RECORD
Home

	GP	W	L	GF	GA	PCTG
DALLAS	12	9	3	38	25	.750
BUFFALO	10	8	2	29	16	.800
COLORADO	9	3	6	20	29	.333
TORONTO	9	5	4	24	22	.556
DETROIT	5	2	3	17	20	.400
BOSTON	6	4	2	18	12	.667
PITTSBURGH	6	3	3	18	18	.500
ST LOUIS	6	3	3	17	16	.500
NEW JERSEY	4	2	2	10	12	.500
PHOENIX	4	1	3	6	9	.250
PHILADELPHIA	3	1	2	6	5	.333
SAN JOSE	3	0	3	4	8	.000
CAROLINA	3	1	2	6	8	.333
EDMONTON	2	0	2	4	6	.000
OTTAWA	2	0	2	3	5	.000
ANAHEIM	2	0	2	2	7	.000
TOTALS	86	42	44	222	218	.488

Road

	GP	W	L	GF	GA	PCTG
DALLAS	11	7	4	26	19	.636
BUFFALO	11	6	5	30	33	.545
COLORADO	10	8	2	36	25	.800
TORONTO	8	4	4	19	24	.500
DETROIT	5	4	1	14	7	.800
BOSTON	6	2	4	12	15	.333
PITTSBURGH	7	3	4	17	18	.429
ST LOUIS	7	3	4	14	17	.429
NEW JERSEY	3	1	2	8	9	.333
PHOENIX	3	2	1	10	10	.667
PHILADELPHIA	3	1	2	5	4	.333
SAN JOSE	3	2	1	13	11	.667
CAROLINA	3	1	2	4	8	.333

EDMONTON	2	0	2	3	5	.000					
OTTAWA	2	0	2	3	7	.000					
ANAHEIM	2	0	2	4	10	.000					
TOTALS	86	44	42	218	222	.512					

PLAYOFF SCORING LEADERS

PLAYER	TEAM	GP	G	A	PTS	+/-	PIM	PP	SH	GW	OT	S	PCTG
PETER FORSBERG	COLORADO	19	8	16	24	7	31	1	1	0	0	54	14.8
MIKE MODANO	DALLAS	23	5	18	23	6	16	1	1	1	1	83	6.0
J. NIEUWENDYK	DALLAS	23	11	10	21	7	19	3	0	6	2	72	15.3
JOE SAKIC	COLORADO	19	6	13	19	2-	8	1	1	1	0	56	10.7
J. LANGENBRUNNE	DALLAS	23	10	7	17	7	16	4	0	3	0	46	21.7
T. FLEURY	COLORADO	18	5	12	17	2-	20	2	0	0	0	56	8.9
MATS SUNDIN	TORONTO	17	8	8	16	2	16	3	0	2	0	44	18.2
BRETT HULL	DALLAS	22	8	7	15	3	4	3	0	2	1	86	9.3
MARTIN STRAKA	PITTSBURGH	13	6	9	15	0	6	1	0	0	0	27	22.2
JASON WOOLLEY	BUFFALO	21	4	11	15	0	10	2	0	1	1	43	9.3
ALEXEI ZHITNIK	BUFFALO	21	4	11	15	6-	52	4	0	2	0	58	6.9
C. LEMIEUX	COLORADO	19	3	11	14	5	26	1	0	0	0	69	4.3
JERE LEHTINEN	DALLAS	23	10	3	13	8	2	1	1	0	0	55	18.2
STEVE YZERMAN	DETROIT	10	9	4	13	2	0	4	0	2	0	41	22.0
CURTIS BROWN	BUFFALO	21	7	6	13	3	10	3	0	3	0	34	20.6
MICHAEL PECA	BUFFALO	21	5	8	13	1	18	2	1	0	0	37	13.5
PIERRE TURGEON	ST LOUIS	13	4	9	13	3	6	0	0	2	2	42	9.5
SERGEI ZUBOV	DALLAS	23	1	12	13	13	4	0	0	0	0	46	2.2

STANLEY CUP PLAYOFF RESULTS

Conference Quarterfinals (best-of-seven series)
Eastern Conference

SERIES 'A'

Thu, Apr 22	PITTSBURGH	1	AT	NEW JERSEY	3
Sat, Apr 24	PITTSBURGH	4	AT	NEW JERSEY	1
Sun, Apr 25	NEW JERSEY	2	AT	PITTSBURGH	4
Tue, Apr 27	NEW JERSEY	4	AT	PITTSBURGH	2
Fri, Apr 30	PITTSBURGH	3	AT	NEW JERSEY	4

Sun, May 2	NEW JERSEY	2	AT	PITTSBURGH	3 *
Tue, May 4	PITTSBURGH	4	AT	NEW JERSEY	2

* JAROMIR JAGR SCORED AT 8:59 OF OVERTIME

(PITTSBURGH WON SERIES 4-3)

SERIES 'B'

Wed, Apr 21	BUFFALO	2	AT	OTTAWA	1
Fri, Apr 23	BUFFALO	3	AT	OTTAWA	2 *
Sun, Apr 25	OTTAWA	0	AT	BUFFALO	3
Tue, Apr 27	OTTAWA	3	AT	BUFFALO	4

* MIROSLAV SATAN SCORED AT 30:35 OF OVERTIME

(BUFFALO WON SERIES 4-0)

SERIES 'C'

Thu, Apr 22	BOSTON	2	AT	CAROLINA	0
Sat, Apr 24	BOSTON	2	AT	CAROLINA	3 *
Mon, Apr 26	CAROLINA	3	AT	BOSTON	2
Wed, Apr 28	CAROLINA	1	AT	BOSTON	4
Fri, Apr 30	BOSTON	4	AT	CAROLINA	3 **
Sun, May 2	CAROLINA	0	AT	BOSTON	2

* RAY SHEPPARD SCORED AT 17:05 OF OVERTIME

** ANSON CARTER SCORED AT 34:45 OF OVERTIME

(BOSTON WON SERIES 4-2)

SERIES 'D'

Thu, Apr 22	PHILADELPHIA	3	AT	TORONTO	0
Sat, Apr 24	PHILADELPHIA	1	AT	TORONTO	2
Mon, Apr 26	TORONTO	2	AT	PHILADELPHIA	1
Wed, Apr 28	TORONTO	2	AT	PHILADELPHIA	5
Fri, Apr 30	PHILADELPHIA	1	AT	TORONTO	2 *
Sun, May 2	TORONTO	1	AT	PHILADELPHIA	0

* YANIC PERREAULT SCORED AT 11:51 OF OVERTIME

(TORONTO WON SERIES 4-2)

Western Conference

SERIES 'E'

Wed, Apr 21	EDMONTON	1	AT	DALLAS	2
Fri, Apr 23	EDMONTON	2	AT	DALLAS	3
Sun, Apr 25	DALLAS	3	AT	EDMONTON	2
Tue, Apr 27	DALLAS	3	AT	EDMONTON	2 *

* JOE NIEUWENDYK SCORED AT 57:34 OF OVERTIME

(DALLAS WON SERIES 4-0)

SERIES 'F'

Sat, Apr 24	COLORADO	3	AT	SAN JOSE	1
Mon, Apr 26	COLORADO	2	AT	SAN JOSE	1 *
Wed, Apr 28	SAN JOSE	4	AT	COLORADO	2
Fri, Apr 30	SAN JOSE	7	AT	COLORADO	3
Sat, May 1	SAN JOSE	2	AT	COLORADO	6
Mon, May 3	COLORADO	3	AT	SAN JOSE	2 **

* MILAN HEJDUK SCORED AT 7:53 OF OVERTIME

** MILAN HEJDUK SCORED AT 13:12 OF OVERTIME

(COLORADO WON SERIES 4-2)

SERIES 'G'

Wed, Apr 21	ANAHEIM	3	AT	DETROIT	5
Fri, Apr 23	ANAHEIM	1	AT	DETROIT	5
Sun, Apr 25	DETROIT	4	AT	ANAHEIM	2
Tue, Apr 27	DETROIT	3	AT	ANAHEIM	0

(DETROIT WON SERIES 4-0)

SERIES 'H'

Thu, Apr 22	ST LOUIS	3	AT	PHOENIX	1
Sat, Apr 24	ST LOUIS	3	AT	PHOENIX	4 *
Sun, Apr 25	PHOENIX	5	AT	ST LOUIS	4
Tue, Apr 27	PHOENIX	2	AT	ST LOUIS	1
Fri, Apr 30	ST LOUIS	2	AT	PHOENIX	1 **
Sun, May 2	PHOENIX	3	AT	ST LOUIS	5
Tue, May 4	ST LOUIS	1	AT	PHOENIX	0 ***

* SHANE DOAN SCORED AT 8:58 OF OVERTIME

** SCOTT YOUNG SCORED AT 5:43 OF OVERTIME

*** PIERRE TURGEON SCORED AT 17:59 OF OVERTIME

(ST LOUIS WON SERIES 4-3)

Conference Semifinals (best-of-seven series)
Eastern Conference

SERIES 'I'

Fri, May 7	PITTSBURGH	2	AT	TORONTO	0
Sun, May 9	PITTSBURGH	2	AT	TORONTO	4
Tue, May 11	TORONTO	3	AT	PITTSBURGH	4
Thu, May 13	TORONTO	3	AT	PITTSBURGH	2 *
Sat, May 15	PITTSBURGH	1	AT	TORONTO	4
Mon ,May 17	TORONTO	4	AT	PITTSBURGH	3 **

* SERGEI BEREZIN SCORED AT 2:18 OF OVERTIME
** GARRY VALK SCORED AT 1:57 OF OVERTIME
(TORONTO WON SERIES 4-2)

SERIES 'J'

Thu, May 6	BUFFALO	2	AT	BOSTON	4
Sun, May 9	BUFFALO	3	AT	BOSTON	1
Wed, May 12	BOSTON	2	AT	BUFFALO	3
Fri, May 14	BOSTON	0	AT	BUFFALO	3
Sun, May 16	BUFFALO	3	AT	BOSTON	5
Tue, May 18	BOSTON	2	AT	BUFFALO	3

(BUFFALO WON SERIES 4-2)

Western Conference

SERIES 'K'

Thu, May 6	ST LOUIS	0	AT	DALLAS	3
Sat, May 8	ST LOUIS	4	AT	DALLAS	5 *
Mon, May 10	DALLAS	2	AT	ST LOUIS	3 **
Wed, May 12	DALLAS	2	AT	ST LOUIS	3 ***
Sat, May 15	ST LOUIS	1	AT	DALLAS	3
Mon, May 17	DALLAS	2	AT	ST LOUIS	1 ****

* JOE NIEUWENDYK SCORED AT 8:22 OF OVERTIME
** PAVOL DEMITRA SCORED AT 2:43 OF OVERTIME
*** PIERRE TURGEON SCORED AT 5:52 OF OVERTIME
**** MIKE MODANO SCORED AT 2:21 OF OVERTIME
(DALLAS WON SERIES 4-2)

SERIES 'L'

Fri, May 7	DETROIT	3	AT	COLORADO	2 *
Sun, May 9	DETROIT	4	AT	COLORADO	0
Tue, May 11	COLORADO	5	AT	DETROIT	3
Thu, May 13	COLORADO	6	AT	DETROIT	2
Sun, May 16	DETROIT	0	AT	COLORADO	3
Tue, May 18	COLORADO	5	AT	DETROIT	2

* KIRK MALTBY SCORED AT 4:18 OF OVERTIME
(COLORADO WON SERIES 4-2)

Conference Finals (best-of-seven series)
Eastern Conference

SERIES 'M'

Sun, May 23	BUFFALO	5	AT	TORONTO	4
Tue, May 25	BUFFALO	3	AT	TORONTO	6
Thu, May 27	TORONTO	2	AT	BUFFALO	4
Sat, May 29	TORONTO	2	AT	BUFFALO	5
Mon, May 31	BUFFALO	4	AT	TORONTO	2

(BUFFALO WON SERIES 4-1)

Western Conference

SERIES 'N'

Sat, May 22	COLORADO	2	AT	DALLAS	1
Mon, May 24	COLORADO	2	AT	DALLAS	4
Wed, May 26	DALLAS	3	AT	COLORADO	0
Fri, May 28	DALLAS	2	AT	COLORADO	3 *
Sun, May 30	COLORADO	7	AT	DALLAS	5
Tue, June 1	DALLAS	4	AT	COLORADO	1
Fri, June 4	COLORADO	1	AT	DALLAS	4

* CHRIS DRURY SCORED AT 19:29 OF OVERTIME
(DALLAS WON SERIES 4-3)

Stanley Cup Finals (best-of-seven series)

SERIES 'O'

Tue, June 8	BUFFALO	3	AT	DALLAS	2 *
Thu, June10	BUFFALO	2	AT	DALLAS	4
Sat, June12	DALLAS	2	AT	BUFFALO	1
Tue, June15	DALLAS	1	AT	BUFFALO	2
Thu, June17	BUFFALO	0	AT	DALLAS	2
Sat, June19	DALLAS	2	AT	BUFFALO	1 **

* JASON WOOLLEY SCORED AT 15:30 OF OVERTIME
** BRETT HULL SCORED AT 54:51 OF OVERTIME
(DALLAS WON SERIES 4-2)

Pool Notes

The book that never ends. As long as you have a computer and you're hooked up to the internet.

Need help with your hockey pool? Wondering if you should trade so and so for so and so? Draft coming up and you have some questions? Wondering about an injury?

Any time you have a question feel free to email me at mtownsend@mail.interhop.net. I usually reply the same day unless I'm swamped. Last year I received thousands of questions both from readers of this book and from my online column for *The Hockey News* at http://www.thn.com

The player ratings include last year's stats and a comment. The comments will point out anything you need to know, and in some cases things you don't need to know. If you're going by the list, the comments might help you pick between players who are close.

I've also done a team-by-team recap section with a number of different categories if they fit that particular team.

Good luck with your pool.

ANAHEIM
Probable Top Line: Kariya-Cullen-Selanne.
Top Power Play Unit: Kariya, McInnis, Selanne, Tverdovsky, Olausson.
Breakout Possibilities: Cullen, Banham.
Newcomers: Donato, Tverdovsky
Possible Rookies: LW - Balmochnykh, D - Havelid, D - Vishnevsky.
Going Up: Tverdovsky
Going Down: McInnis
Goalies: Hebert will play 60-65 games; Roussel is the backup.
Enforcer: Stu Grimsom
Notes: The key, obviously, is the get the centre man between Kariya and Selanne. McInnis should see less power play time with two legitimate pointmen.

ATLANTA
Probable Top Line: Brunette-Stefan-Emerson
Top Power Play Unit: Watch during training camp.
Breakout Possibilities: Too many to mention.
Newcomers: All of them
Possible Rookies: Stefan, Kallio, and Robitaille head the class.
Going Up: Impossible to tell.
Going Down: Impossible to do.
Goalies: Rhodes, Maracle
Enforcer: Matt Johnson
Notes: Everything is up for grabs with an expansion team. It's important to pay closer attention to them than any other team during training camp.

BOSTON
Probable Top Line: Samsonov, Allison, Khristich
Top Power Play Unit: Top line with Bourque on point and McLaren, Van Impe or Nick Boynton on the other.
Breakout Possibilities: Thornton
Newcomers: None
Possible Rookies: Boynton, Zultek.
Going Up: Joe Thornton
Going Down: Khristich
Goalies: Dafoe, with Tallas as backup
Enforcer: Belanger
Notes: Khristich is on thin ice and on the trading block. Thornton could take over the number one centre job.

BUFFALO
Probable Top Line: Kind of mix and match, but it could be Grosek-Brown-Varada or Ward-Peca-Varada.
Top Power Play Unit: Wooley and Zhitnik on the points, with specialist Barnes up front with Peca and Satan. But only the points consistent.
Breakout Possibilities: Rasmussen, Primeau.
Newcomers: none
Possible Rookies: none.
Going Up: Sanderson
Going Down: Grosek and Satan
Goalies: Hasek, with Roloson as backup
Enforcer: Rob Ray.

CALGARY
Probable Top Line: Corbet-Stillman-Iginla
Top Power Play Unit: Housely and Morris on the points, take your pick up front.
Breakout Possibilities: Dominichelli
Newcomers: Savard
Possible Rookies: Tkachuk, Fata
Going Up: Morris
Going Down: Stillman a possibility with Savard on board

Goalies: Braithwaite, Giguere
Enforcer: Wiemer, though not a pure goon.
Notes: The Flames are more likely to have two second lines as opposed to one big first line. Addition of Savard means he and Stillman are battling for ice time as top centre.

CAROLINA

Probable Top Line: Gelinas-Primeau-Kapanan, but far from a certainty.
Top Power Play Unit: Looking for a power play point man, Francis, Kapanan, Primeau up front.
Breakout Possibilities: O'Neill
Newcomers: None
Possible Rookies: Willis, MacDonald, Ritchie
Going Up: O'Neill
Going Down: Kovalenko
Goalies: Irbe with Fichaud as backup
Enforcer: Don't have one
Notes: Primeau was a restricted free agent during the summer and there was considerable talk about trading him rather than trying to meet his demands.

CHICAGO

Probable Top Line: Gilmour-Zhamnov-Amonte
Top Power Play Unit: Top line with Mironov and Eriksson or McCabe on point.
Breakout Possibilities: Dumont
Newcomers: None
Possible Rookies: Dumont, Bell
Going Up: Everybody, with the new offensive style
Going Down: Nobody
Goalies: Hackett, with Passmore as backup
Enforcer: Probert, Brown
Notes: There's talk of either trading Gilmour or moving him to left wing on top line. New coach Molleken has a more offensive style which the Hawks showed late in the season will dramatically increase point totals.

COLORADO

Probable Top Line: Deadmarsh-Sakic-Hejduk (at least until return of Forsberg)
Top Power Play Unit: Ozolinsh on the point with four forwards.
Breakout Possibilities: None
Newcomers: None
Possible Rookies: Tanguay
Going Up: Deadmarsh, Ozolinsh
Going Down: Forsberg (will miss first month with injury)
Goalies: Roy and future number one Denis.
Enforcer: deVries
Notes: Forsberg is expected to be recovering from injuries for the first month of the season.

DALLAS

Probable Top Line: Lehtinen-Modano-Hull
Top Power Play Unit: Sydor and Zubov on the points with Modano, Hull and Nieuwendyk.
Breakout Possibilities: Langenbrunner
Newcomers: Lind returns from Europe
Possible Rookies: Sim, Luhning
Going Up: Langenbrunner
Going Down: None
Goalies: Belfour, with Turco or Fernandez as backup
Enforcer: none

DETROIT

Probable Top Line: Changes constantly
Top Power Play Unit: Changes constantly, but Lidstrom and Chelios on the point is a good get, with Murphy reduced to second unit duty.

Breakout Possibilities: Holmstrom
Newcomers: None
Possible Rookies: None
Going Up: Too iffy to predict
Going Down: Murphy
Goalies: Osgood, with Wregget as new backup.
Enforcer: Kocur (maybe)
Notes: The Wings are more of a balanced team as opposed to one with a top line, although Shanahan, Yzerman and McCarty formed an effective unit early last year and stayed together for some time.

EDMONTON
Probable Top Line: Smyth-Weight-Gueren
Top Power Play Unit: Top line with Harlik, Niinimaa and Poti sharing the points
Breakout Possibilities: Moreau, Poti, Kilger
Newcomers: None
Possible Rookies: None
Going Up: WeightSmyth
Going Down: Beranek
Goalies: Salo
Enforcer: Brown

FLORIDA
Probable Top Line: Bure with any number of possibilities
Top Power Play Unit: Bure with Svehla, with Spacek or Boyle on point
Breakout Possibilities: Kozlov (again) Dvorak (again).
Newcomers:
Possible Rookies: Novoseltsev, Dopita, Boyle, Shvidki
Going Up: Spacek, Kozlov, Parrish
Going Down: Whitney, Mellanby
Goalies: Kidd and Burke

Enforcer: Worrell
Notes: A lot depends on whether or not the Panthers can convince Dopita to join the fold and whether Novoseltsev is as good as they hope.

LOS ANGELES
Probable Top Line: Robitaille-Stumpel-Palffy
Top Power Play Unit: Top line with Blake on one point and the other to be determined.
Breakout Possibilities: Rosa
Newcomers: Palffy, Smolinski, Tuomainen
Possible Rookies: Jason Blake, Barney
Going Up: Stumpel, Murray, Blake, Murray
Going Down: Robitaille
Goalies: Fiset and Storr
Enforcer: None
Notes: Stumpel was bothered by injuries last year and didn't have a chance to show what he can do. Should be able to with Palffy as his linemate.

MONTREAL
Probable Top Line: Don't have one, but Koivu should be on there somewhere
Top Power Play Unit: Don't have one, but Koivu and Corson should be on there somewhere with Malakhov on the point.
Breakout Possibilities: Zubrus
Newcomers: Linden, Petrov
Possible Rookies: None
Going Up: Everybody could go up because they were down so low last year
Going Down: Unlikely possibility
Goalies: Hackett and Theodore
Enforcer: Cummins

NASHVILLE
Probable Top Line: Peltonen-Ronning-Krivokrasov

Top Power Play Unit: Top line, but it's a crap-shoot for the points.
Breakout Possibilities: Peltonen
Newcomers: None
Possible Rookies: Legwand
Going Up: None
Going Down: A number of players could see a slight to moderate decrease
Goalies: Dunham, Vokoun
Enforcer: Cote, Lambert, Boughner

NEW JERSEY
Probable Top Line: Elias-Arnott-Sykora
Top Power Play Unit: Lots of possibilities for that duty up front, with Niedermay on one of the points.
Breakout Possibilities: Morrison, Brylin
Newcomers: None
Possible Rookies: Madden, White
Going Up: Brylin
Going Down: Holik
Goalies: Brodeur, Terreri
Enforcer: Oliwa

NY ISLANDERS
Probable Top Line: Good Luck
Top Power Play Unit: Good Luck
Breakout Possibilities: Much of that team is in that territory, so many possibilities.
Newcomers: Jokkinen, Green, Heward
Possible Rookies: Jorgen Jonsson, Krog, Connolly
Going Up: Anybody
Going Down: Czercawski, Lawrence.
Goalies: Potvin
Enforcer: Odjick

NY RANGERS
Probable Top Line: Kamensky-Nedved-Fleury
Top Power Play Unit: Lots of candidates, but Leetch and Schnieder on point
Breakout Possibilities: Harvey
Newcomers: Kamensky, Fleury, Quintal, Lefebvre, Taylor
Possible Rookies:Brendl, Hlavak
Going Up: None
Going Down: Graves, MacLean, Stevens
Goalies: Richter and new backup McLean
Enforcer: Ndur

OTTAWA
Probable Top Line: McEachern-Yashin-Alfredsson
Top Power Play Unit: Top line, with pointmen by committee
Breakout Possibilities: Hossa, Bonk
Newcomers: Zamuner
Possible Rookies:
Going Up: Alfredsson
Going Down: Dackell, Arvedsson
Goalies: Tugnutt with Lalime as backup
Enforcer: None
Notes: Yashin was yakking about being a hold-out again, despite having signed a contract.

PHILADELPHIA
Probable Top Line: LeClair-Lindros-Recchi
Top Power Play Unit: Top line, but Brind'Amour needs to get in there, too. Desjardins and McGillis on the points.
Breakout Possibilities: Langkow
Newcomers: None
Possible Rookies: Eaton, Chernov
Going Up: Recchi
Going Down: Jones

Goalies: Vanbiesbrouck, with Boucher as backup
Enforcer: McCarthy

PHOENIX
Probable Top Line: Tkachuk-Roenick-Drake
Top Power Play Unit: Tkachuk, Roenick, Reichel, with Numminen and Lumme on the points.
Breakout Possibilities: Briere
Newcomers: Green
Possible Rookies:
Going Up: Tkachuk
Going Down: Adams, Tocchet
Goalies: Khabibulin, with Shtalenkov as backup
Enforcer: none
Notes: Reichel was threatening to go back and play in Europe during the off-season.

PITTSBURGH
Probable Top Line: Jagr and two other guys
Top Power Play Unit: Jagr, Hatcher and three other guys
Breakout Possibilities: Morozov
Newcomers: None
Possible Rookies:
Going Up: Anybody who plays with Jagr
Going Down: Anybody who doesn't play with Jagr
Goalies: Barrasso, with injury backups Aubin and Skudra
Enforcer: Barnaby

SAN JOSE
Probable Top Line: Friesen-Damphousse-Nolan
Top Power Play Unit: Top line with Suter and Houlder on the points
Breakout Possibilities: Marleau, Korolyuk
Newcomers: None

Possible Rookies: Stuart, Heins, Hannan
Going Up: Nolan
Going Down: none
Goalies: Vernon and Shields, maybe equal duty
Enforcer: Stern

ST. LOUIS
Probable Top Line: Something puts Turgeon and Demitra out together
Top Power Play Unit: MacInnis and Pronger on the points, with Turgeon, Demitra and another forward up front.
Breakout Possibilities: Bartecko, Reasoner
Newcomers:
Possible Rookies:
Going Up: Bartecko, Mayers, Campbell
Going Down: Young, Pellerin
Goalies: Turek and Fuhr
Enforcer: Chase

TAMPA BAY
Probable Top Line: Nylander-LeCavalier-Sundstrom
Top Power Play Unit: To be determined
Breakout Possibilities: Daigle (just kidding) Nylander (just kidding) Petrovicky (just kidding) Forbes.
Newcomers: Sundstrom, Johansson, Gusev
Possible Rookies: Mara
Going Up: Gratton, Nylander
Going Down: Tucker
Goalies: Cloutier, with Puppa and/or Hodson as backup.
Enforcer: None

TORONTO
Probable Top Line: ?-Sundin-Thomas
Top Power Play Unit: Sundin, Thomas, Berezin,

Berard on one point and take your pick for the other
Breakout Possibilities: McCauley, Modin
Newcomers:
Possible Rookies: Mair
Going Up: Johnson
Going Down: Almost everybody has that possibility because they scored so much last year.
Goalies: Joseph, with Healy on the bench.
Enforcer: Domi, K. King

VANCOUVER

Probable Top Line: Bertuzzi-Messier-Naslund
Top Power Play Unit: Ohlund and Aucoin on the points, with the top line of Mogilny if he wakes up.
Breakout Possibilities: Bertuzzi
Newcomers: Cassels
Possible Rookies: Sedin twins

Going Up: Bertuzzi, Mogilny
Going Down: Naslund
Goalies: Weekes and Snow, with no clear number one yet
Enforcer: Brashear

WASHINGTON

Probable Top Line: Konowalchuk-Oates-Bondra
Top Power Play Unit: Gonchar, Mironov or Johansson on the points with Oates, Bondra and whoever's hot up front.
Breakout Possibilities: Svejkovsky, Zednik, Bulis
Newcomers:
Possible Rookies: Gratton
Going Up: Most everybody has that potential since they were so low last season.
Going Down:
Goalies: Kolzig with Billington as backup
Enforcer: Ciccone

	Team	1998-99 Stats				
		GP	G	A	P	
Jagr	Pit	81	44	83	127	A lock as the top scorer
Kariya	Ana	82	39	62	101	goal scoring should increase
Selanne	Ana	75	47	60	107	Only worry is fast cars during the off-season
Lindros	Phi	71	40	53	93	If he can only stay healthy
LeClair	Phi	76	43	47	90	Should be on top scoring line in league
Tkachuk	Pho	68	36	32	68	Big comeback season with different team offense
Palffy	LA	50	22	28	50	Renewed life with new team
Sundin	Tor	82	31	52	83	"If he gets better help on wings, will score more"
Allison	Bos	82	23	53	76	"Off-year, but still got 76 points"
Yashin	Ott	82	44	50	94	Possible holdout - again.
Sakic	Col	73	41	55	96	Won't have Forsberg around for a month
Fleury	NYR	75	40	53	93	Has big contract now - less motivation.
"Bure,P"	Fla	11	13	3	16	50 goal return a possibility
Amonte	Chi	82	44	31	75	could score 50
Demitra	StL	82	37	52	89	Has tough act to follow
Modano	Dal	77	34	47	81	Might suffer slight relapse from Stanley Cup season
Brind'Amour	Phi	82	24	50	74	power player on potent power play
Recchi	Phi	71	16	37	53	Back up to scoring elite on big Flyer line
Bondra	Wsh	66	31	24	55	Major comeback season in works
Sykora	NJ	80	29	43	72	"Coming off breakout season, could fall back slightly"
Turgeon	StL	67	31	34	65	Consistent performer but injury prone
Fedorov	Det	77	26	37	63	Should return to former self sooner or later
Weight	Edm	43	6	31	37	Missed much of last season
Roenick	Pho	78	24	48	72	Could score more with new style in Phoenix
Zhamnov	Chi	76	20	41	61	was great after coaching change
Stumpel	LA	64	13	21	34	Sleeper pick of the year gets to play with Palffy
Yzerman	Det	80	29	45	74	34-years-old
Oates	Wsh	59	12	42	54	37-years-old
Nedved	NYR	56	20	27	47	Top centre in New York now
Straka	Pit	80	30	48	78	Career marked by inconsistency
Langenbrunner	Dal	75	12	33	45	could break out with consistent scoring
Friesen	SJ	78	22	35	57	San Jose is a defensive team
Alfredsson	Ott	58	11	22	33	Could be comeback player of the year
Peca	Buf	82	27	29	56	May be best two-way player in the game.
Kozlov	Det	79	29	29	58	"Great 2nd half, but why poor 1st half?"
Forsberg	Col	78	30	67	97	Will miss first month with injury
Leetch	NYR	82	13	42	55	Lots of new friends to play with
Kovalev	Pit	77	23	30	53	Always looks like he could be better than he is
Reichel	Pho	83	26	43	69	Threatening to play in Europe
"Blake,Rob"	LA	62	12	23	35	coming off injury season - has Palffy now
Shanahan	Det	81	31	27	58	Subject of trade rumors
Primeau	Car	78	30	32	62	Restricted free agent - could be traded
Rolston	NJ	82	24	33	57	Seems to get better each year
Thornton	Bos	81	16	25	41	Will be break-out player of the year
Kozlov	Fla	65	16	35	51	Finally set for breakout season?
Kapanen	Car	81	24	35	59	solid first line winger
Brown	Buf	78	16	31	47	should build on breakout season
Ozolinish	Col	39	7	25	32	Missed half of last season in contract holdout
Daze	Chi	72	22	20	42	potential to score 40 goals

Name	Team	GP	G	A	Pts	Notes
"Hull, B"	Dal	60	32	26	58	on downslope of career
Stillman	Cgy	76	27	30	57	Has developed level of consistencey
Nieuwendyk	Dal	67	28	27	55	Injuries always a concern
Hossa	Ott	60	15	15	30	Talented scorer gets full season
Naslund	Van	80	36	30	66	Coming off breakout season - duplication tough
Koivu	Mtl	65	14	30	44	Has to put it together one of these years
Kamensky	NYR	65	14	30	44	"Was fading in Colorado, but has new life"
Niedermayer	NJ	76	13	33	46	Could lead defensemen in scoring
Iginla	Cgy	82	28	23	51	Still improving
Marleau	SJ	81	21	24	45	"Future star, but scoring tough on SJ"
Arnott	NJ	74	27	27	54	Earned top centre status later in season
Kvasha	Fla	68	12	13	25	Showed potential as a rookie
MacInnis	StL	82	20	42	62	Duplicating might be difficult
Francis	Car	82	21	31	52	Led the team in scoring in second half
"Mironov, B"	Chi	75	11	38	49	power play pointman
Morrison	NJ	76	13	33	46	Rookie got more comfortable as season went on
Satan	Buf	81	40	26	66	Not likely to score 40 goals again
Guerin	Edm	80	30	34	64	power forward could benefit with full year of Weight
Nolan	SJ	78	19	26	45	Potential to score more goals
Damphousse	SJ	77	19	30	49	Playmaker may find points tough to come by in SJ
Lidstrom	Det	81	14	43	57	"Possibility he will return to Europe, but not a big one"
Savard	Cgy	70	9	36	45	Playmaker will be bigger cheese in Calgary than NY
McEachern	Ott	77	31	25	56	"Great season, but dupicating won't be easy"
"Niedermayer,R"	Fla	82	18	33	51	Can do better than last year
Smolinski	LA	82	16	24	40	Should rebound after awful situation with NYI
Gilmour	Chi	72	16	40	56	"aging and injury-prone, but still good setup man"
Deadmarsh	Col	66	22	27	49	With Kamensky gone is top left winger
LeCavalier	TB	82	13	15	28	Shows flashes of brilliance
Hrdina	Pit	82	13	29	42	Depend who he plays with
Lehtinen	Dal	74	20	32	52	Selke Trophy winner can also score
Titov	Pit	72	11	45	56	Depends which line he's on
Elias	NJ	74	17	33	50	playing on top line
Robitaille	LA	82	39	35	74	Duplicating will be very tough
Korolyuk	SJ	55	12	18	30	Up and comer
Johnson	Tor	79	20	24	44	Suffered sophomore jinx
Gratton	TB	78	8	26	34	Will definitely be better than last year
Whitney	Fla	81	26	38	64	Depends on what line he's on
Svehla	Fla	80	8	29	37	Needs to rebound from poor season
Lemieux	Col	82	27	24	51	"power play sniper, but getting older"
Carter	Bos	55	24	16	40	Last year's goals project to 36 over 82 games
Harvey	NYR	37	11	17	28	Was on way to breakout season before injury
Holik	NJ	78	27	37	64	Pushed out as top centre
Khristich	Bos	79	29	42	71	Falling out of favor in Boston
Hejduk	Col	82	14	34	48	could be on top line
Numminen	Pho	82	10	30	40	PP could be better this year
Zubov	Dal	81	10	41	51	power play pointman
Berezin	Tor	76	37	22	59	More likely to fall back than move forward
Samsonov	Bos	79	25	26	51	Fell off big-time in second half
Bertuzzi	Van	32	8	8	16	breakout possibility
Ronning	Nsh	79	20	40	60	"Playmaker, but could see less ice-time because of age"
Heinze	Bos	73	22	18	40	injury prone

Player	Team	GP	G	A	Pts	Comment
Mogilny	Van	59	14	31	45	Worth a risk if you have a strong stomach
Peltonen	Nsh	14	5	5	10	"Injured most of last year, but great potential"
Thomas	Tor	78	28	45	73	Will be tough for aging vet to repeat
Stefan	Atl	0	0	0	0	First overall draft pick
Holzinger	Buf	81	17	17	34	Steady improvement should move him up a notch
O'Neill	Car	75	16	15	31	breakout possibility
"Bure,V"	Cgy	80	26	27	53	Top two lines in Calgary
Drury	Col	79	20	24	44	Last year's rookie of the year
Linden	Mtl	82	18	29	47	No longer a dependable scorer
Rucchin	Ana	69	23	49	72	Gets points even if not on top line
Tverdovsky	Ana	82	7	18	25	Bonanza on the power play point with new team
Pronger	StL	67	13	33	46	PP Point - 30 minutes a game
Rucinsky	Mtl	73	17	17	34	Streaky
Sullivan	Tor	63	20	20	40	Feisty little guy has to fight for ice time
Bourque	Bos	81	10	47	57	No signs of slowing down yet
Housley	Cgy	79	11	43	54	"Big comeback season, but is 35"
Ohlund	Van	74	9	26	35	Needs to show consistency
Verbeek	F/A	78	17	17	34	unsigned at press time
Holmstrom	Det	82	13	21	34	should increase scoring
Drake	Pho	53	9	22	31	Has been playing on top line
Hatcher.K	Pit	66	11	27	38	"Fading, but still on PP point"
Olausson	Ana	74	16	40	56	Less pressure to produce with Tverdovsky on board
Woolley	Buf	80	10	33	43	power play pointman
Larionov	Det	75	14	49	63	old but valuable playmaker
McGillis	Phi	78	8	37	45	pp point
Graves	NYR	82	38	15	53	pp sniper
Gelinas	Car	76	13	15	28	potential to be much better scorer
Dumont	Chi	25	9	6	15	Rookie of the Year
Cullen	Ana	75	11	14	25	Needs to be on top line to get points
Lumme	Pho	60	7	21	28	pp point
Smyth	Edm	71	13	18	31	return to form not out of question
Tocchet	Pho	81	26	30	56	Repeat tough at his age
Legwand	Nsh	1	0	0	0	Rookie of the year candidate
Juneau	F/A	72	15	28	43	unsigned at press time - needs a good fit
McCauley	Tor	39	9	15	24	Was on way to breakout season when got hurt
Cassels	Van	70	12	25	37	"Did little in Calgary, but they were more defensive"
Conroy	StL	69	14	25	39	two-way centre doesn't have to score so might not
Bulis	Wsh	38	7	16	23	High hopes but hasn't shown much yet
Desjardins	Phi	68	15	36	51	pp point
"Murphy,J"	F/A	76	25	23	48	unsigned at press time
Willis	Car	7	0	0	0	rookie candidate
Langkow	Phi	78	14	19	33	possible breakout season
Korolev	Tor	66	13	34	47	Soft player is injury prone
Morris	Cgy	71	7	27	34	Should get more power play time
Malakhov	Mtl	62	13	21	34	"Poor character player, injury prone, trade bait"
Nikolishin	Wsh	73	8	27	35	return to form a possibility
Jokinen	NYI	66	9	12	21	"Could be team's top centre, and that's no Jokinen."
Messier	Van	59	13	35	48	Just hanging in there
Sydor	Dal	74	14	34	48	pp pointman cooled down after fast start
Sanderson	Buf	75	12	18	30	Late round sleeper could return to form
Krivokrasov	Nsh	70	25	23	48	Will have a tough time equaling last year's totals

Hamrlik	Edm	75	8	24	32	counted on more for offense with Mironov gone
Corbet	Cgy	73	13	18	31	Counted on more for scoring than when in Colorado
Sharijanov	NJ	53	11	16	27	Showing some potential
"Robitaille,R"	Atl	4	0	2	2	Big scorer in minors
Dvorak	Fla	82	19	24	43	Possible breakout season
Sturm	SJ	78	16	22	38	showing good potential
Chelios	Det	75	9	27	36	pp pointman
Suter	SJ	1	0	0	0	PP Pointman missed almost all of last season
Savage	Mtl	54	16	10	26	could and should rebound
Falloon	Edm	82	17	23	40	Surprise contributors don't last long in Edmonton
Sheppard	F/A				0	unsigned at press time
Audette	LA	49	18	18	36	Was a holdout for part of last year with Buffalo
Morozov	Pit	67	9	10	19	possible breakout player
Green	Pho	79	13	17	30	Could score more with Phoenix than Anaheim
Konowalchuk	Wsh	45	12	12	24	Should be 20-20 man
Emerson	Atl	65	13	24	37	Should be right winger on first line
Grosek	Buf	76	20	30	50	Inconsistent - not guaranteed of top line status
Sundstrom	TB	81	13	30	43	could play on top line
Svejkovsky	Wsh	25	6	8	14	"Potential, but that's all so far"
MacLean	NYR	82	28	27	55	quality ice time reduced with Fleury on board
Barnes	Buf	81	20	16	36	Could be power play sniper
Nylander	TB	33	4	10	14	Even if healthy no sure thing
Varada	Buf	72	7	24	31	"Could break out, but inconsistent so far"
Zhitnik	Buf	81	7	26	33	Established level of between 35 and 45 points.
Clark	F/A				0	unsigned at press time
Murray	LA	61	16	15	31	Needs a rebound season
Renberg	Phi	66	15	23	38	needs to play on top line
Young	StL	75	24	28	52	will have tough time duplicating
"Courtnall, G"	StL	24	5	7	12	risky with concussion problems and age
Berard	Tor	69	9	25	34	Has a chance to come up big on PP point
Roberts	Car	77	14	28	42	Not the scorer he once was
Ferraro	F/A				0	unsigned at press time
McAmmond	Chi	77	10	20	30	should move up a notch or two
Richer	TB	64	12	21	33	"Going, going...."
Tuomainen	LA	0	0	0	0	Import expected to score
Adams	Pho	75	19	24	43	old and injury prone
"Johnson,G"	Nsh	68	16	34	50	second in scoring on Predators
Zamuner	Ott	58	8	11	19	career revived after debocle in Tampa Bay
Dackell	Ott	77	15	35	50	Could be on third line instead of first
Redden	Ott	72	8	21	29	showing more offense
Schneider	NYR	75	10	24	34	pp point
Arvedsson	Ott	80	21	26	47	Defensive specialist might concetrate more on role
Lawrence	NYI	82	14	23	37	"career minor-leaguer, could have been fluke season"
Bonk	Ott	81	16	16	32	Possibly getting better?
Bordeleau	Nsh	72	16	24	40	injury problems
Jones	Phi	78	20	33	53	knocked off top line
McInnis	Ana	81	19	35	54	Reduced pp time means reduced points
Briere	Pho	64	8	14	22	breakout possibility
McCarty	Det	69	14	26	40	Got most of points when on top line
Marchant	Edm	82	14	22	36	"Speed to burn, but not many points to show for it"
Brylin	NJ	47	5	10	15	"Risky, but could pay off"

Name	Team	GP	G	A	Pts	Comment
Berenek	Edm	66	19	30	49	Beware - got most of points when Weight injured
Rosa	LA	29	4	12	16	Pure scorer has been bothered with injuries
Poti	Edm	73	5	16	21	Up and comer should get more PP time
Duchesne	F/A				0	unsigned at press time
Murphy	Det	80	10	42	52	On his last legs
Lapointe	Det	77	16	13	29	two-way player doesn't score a lot
Murray	Edm	78	21	18	39	Could get more time on scoring lines
Corson	Mtl	63	12	20	32	"injury problems and aging, but pp specialist"
Battaglia	Car	60	7	11	18	showed scoring potential when put on scoring line
Domenichelli	Cgy	23	5	5	10	Breakout season possibility
Pederson	NJ	76	11	12	23	two-way centre gets more ice-time this year
Mellanby	Fla	67	18	27	45	Getting older - less counted on for scoring
Doan	Pho	79	6	16	22	could get more ice time
"Miller, Kip"	Pit	77	19	23	42	Risky because needs to play with Jagr
Lang	Pit	72	21	23	44	career plagued by inconsistency
Niinimaa	Edm	81	4	24	28	Only scored after Mironov left
Ericksson	Chi	72	2	18	20	possible power play point time
Aucoin	Van	82	23	11	34	Lots of goals but no assists for PP pointman
Parrish	Fla	73	24	13	37	"Inconsistent, but can put puck in net"
Campbell	StL	55	4	21	25	risky but maybe with late late round desperation pick
Tsyplakov	LA	69	11	12	23	Risky business
Kjellberg	Nsh	71	11	20	31	Depens on situation
"Jonsson, Kenny"	NYI	63	8	18	26	injury prone
Brisebois	Mtl	54	3	9	12	risky because you never know what he's going to do
Johansson	Wsh	67	8	21	29	PP pointman
Zednik	Wsh	49	9	8	17	Time to show what he's got
Brunette	Atl	77	11	20	31	Could be left winger on first line
Andreychuk	F/A				0	unsigned at press time
Forbes	TB	80	12	8	20	Needs time but shows potential
Ward	Buf	78	20	24	44	Always does better than expected
Grier	Edm	82	20	24	44	solid two-way player can't be counted on to get points
Lindgren	NYI	60	10	15	25	"defensive centre but can score, too."
Knuble	NYR	82	15	20	35	quality ice time a concern
Muckhalt	Van	73	16	20	36	Faded badly as season went on
Donato	Ana	82	11	16	27	Better fit than the three teams was with last year
Ricci	SJ	82	13	26	39	defensive specialist not a great scorer
Kubina	TB	68	9	12	21	impressive rookie could get lots of PP time in point
Walker	Nsh	71	15	25	40	Feisty player could move down notch on scoring list
Brendl	NYR	0	0	0	0	Rookie is not a sure thing yet
Brown	Det	80	9	19	28	aging veteran could be phased out
Pellerin	StL	80	20	21	41	will have tough time duplicating
Perreault	Tor	76	17	25	42	Playing time in jeopardy
Tkachuk	Cgy	0	0	0	0	Will have a chance to be a regular
Yake	Atl	60	9	18	27	First or second line centre
Watt	NYI	75	8	17	25	Somebody has to score on this team
Marshall	Dal	82	13	18	31	"valuable player, but not projected as scorer"
Selivanov	Edm	72	14	19	33	"A waste of a good uniform, but you never know"
Brunet	Mtl	60	14	17	31	Injury prone but surprising scorer when healthy
Brown	Pit	58	13	11	24	somewhat of a pp specialist
Tucker	TB	82	21	22	43	Wasn't supposed to be team's best player
Simon	Wsh	23	3	7	10	One of more injury prone players

Name	Team	GP	G	A	Pts	Note
Stevens	NYR	81	23	20	43	moves down a notch or two on depth chart
Sim	Dal	7	1	0	1	feisty rookie will get a chance to show stuff
Bartecko	StL	32	5	11	16	Showed talent to break out
Slegr	Pit	63	3	20	23	injury prone but could get pp time
Boynton	Bos	0	0	0	0	Rookie will get power play time
Modin	Tor	67	16	15	31	One more chance
Gonchar	Wsh	53	21	10	31	PP pointman
Hlavak	NYR	0	0	0	0	Rookie is not a sure thing yet
Black	Wsh	75	16	14	30	Surprise performer for Caps last year
Rasmussen	Buf	42	3	7	10	Has to prove himself first
Barnaby	Pit	62	6	16	22	Not just another scrapper - can score
Krog	NYI	0	0	0	0	Good rookie candidate
Quint	Pho	60	5	8	13	could get pp time
McKay	NJ	70	17	20	37	Always seems to come through
Matteau	SJ	68	8	15	23	Should improve from last season
"Jonsson, Jorgen"	NYI	0	0	0	0	Kenny's brother
Kovalenko	Car	74	19	21	40	Mr. Inconsistency
Nabokov	NYI	4	0	2	2	Hasn't shown anything yet
Zubrus	Mtl	80	6	10	16	"Looks talented, but a stretch at best"
"King,D"	Tor	81	24	28	52	Fading out
Sylvester	Atl	1	0	0	0	Gets a shot after good minor stats
Czercawski	NYI	78	21	17	38	Could score - could disappear
Yachmenev	Nsh	55	7	10	17	"risky, but could score in right setup"
Weinrich	Mtl	80	7	15	22	Gets some time on power play
Timonen	Nsh	50	4	8	12	could get PP point time
Hedican	Fla	67	5	18	23	"speedy, but only offensive on occasion"
York	Ott	79	4	31	35	should have one pp point
Salo	Ott	61	7	12	19	Showed potential from pp point
May	Van	66	6	11	17	Not the scorer he was supposed to be
Kallio	Atl	0	0	0	0	Finn expected to make immediate contribution
Moreau	Edm	80	10	11	21	Hasn't shown any scoring potential yet
Green	NYI	27	1	3	4	Should at least get playing time
Maholtra	NYR	73	8	8	16	Won't find ice time any easier to come by
"Johnson,C"	LA	69	7	12	19	Has some upside
Lapointe	NYI	82	14	23	37	"If he's traded, his value goes up"
Turcotte	Nsh	40	45		45	Too many injury problems
Prospal	Ott	79	10	26	36	Risky
"Mironov,D"	Wsh				0	Risky with back problems
Houlder	SJ	76	9	23	32	PP point
Kilger	Edm	77	15	12	27	"A possibility, but unlikely"
"Johansson,A"	TB	69	21	16	37	Disappeared in 2nd half in Ottawa
Daigle	TB	63	9	8	17	Risky sleeper pick in round 99
Handzus	StL	66	4	12	16	Still learning game
Kravchuk	Ott	79	4	21	25	Was being counted on to score more
Werenka	Pit	81	6	18	24	Gets some PP time
Mara	TB	1	1	1	2	Rookie offensive defenseman hopeful
Heward	NYI	63	6	12	18	Could get power play time
Plante	Dal	51	6	14	20	Return to form not out of question yet
Marha	Chi	32	2	6	8	"looked good as 2nd line centre, but iffy"

We hoped you enjoyed reading this book.
We welcome your comments. Please contact us:

Warwick Publishing
162 John Street
Toronto, Ontario, Canada
M5V 2E5

Telephone: (416) 596-1555

FAX: (416) 596-1520

Website: www.warwickgp.com

Email: mbrooke@warwickgp.com